AF731377

Social Science Research in India

Published by
ACADEMIC FOUNDATION
in association with

INSTITUTE FOR SOCIAL AND ECONOMIC CHANGE
BANGALORE

Social Science Research in India

INSTITUTIONS AND STRUCTURE

Editors

M.V. Nadkarni
R.S. Deshpande

ACADEMIC FOUNDATION
NEW DELHI

www.academicfoundation.com

First published in 2011
by

ACADEMIC FOUNDATION
4772-73 / 23 Bharat Ram Road, (23 Ansari Road),
Darya Ganj, New Delhi - 110 002 (India).
Phones : 23245001 / 02 / 03 / 04.
Fax : +91-11-23245005.
E-mail : books@academicfoundation.com
www. academicfoundation.com

in association with

Institute for Social and Economic Change (ISEC), Bangalore (India).
www.isec.ac.in

© 2011. Copyright: Institute for Social and Economic Change, Bangalore

ALL RIGHTS RESERVED.
No part of this book shall be reproduced, stored in a retrieval system,
Or transmitted by any means, electronic, mechanical, photocopying,
recording, or otherwise, without the prior written permission of the
copyright holder(s) and/or the publishers.

Cataloging in Publication Data--DK
Courtesy: D.K. Agencies (P) Ltd. <docinfo@dkagencies.com>

Social science research in India : institutions and structure /
edited by M.V. Nadkarni, R.S. Deshpande.
p. cm.
Contributed articles.
ISBN 13: 9788171888443
ISBN 10: 8171888445

1. Social sciences--Research--India. 2. Social sciences–
Research--India--Societies, etc. I. Nadkarni, Mangesh
Venktesh, 1939- II. Deshpande, R. S.

DDC 300.723 22

Typeset by Italics India, New Delhi.
Printed and bound in India.

Contents

About the Editors/ Contributors

Editors:

M.V. Nadkarni, Hon. Visiting Professor at ISEC since 2002, was a Professor of Economics at the same Institute from 1976 to 1999 when he retired. He was Vice-Chancellor at Gulbarga University from 1999 to 2002 and ICSSR National Fellow from 2002 to 2004. He presided over the Annual Conference of the Indian Society of Agricultural Economics at IRMA in 1995. He has 17 published books to his credit including co-authored and edited books and over 100 papers in reputed academic journals. His research interests extend beyond Economics and cover others social sciences, philosophy and religion. His earlier book, *Hinduism: A Gandhian Perspective* is also translated in to Hindi.

R.S. Deshpande is presently Director of the Institute for Social and Economic Change (ISEC), Bangalore. Before this, he worked as Professor and Head of the Agricultural Development and Rural Transformation Centre of ISEC and as Registrar at Gokhale Institute of Politics and Economics, Pune. His publications include two volumes in the *State of the Indian Farmer: A Millennium Study, Watershed Management, Where Water Seeps, Glimpses of Indian Agriculture, Contract Farming and Tenancy Reforms*. He has published extensively and has worked as Consultant to World Bank, DFID, and Land Equity, Australia. He has served in many policy bodies of the Government of India and the Government of Karnataka.

Contributors:

T.C.A. Anant, presently Professor of Economics at Delhi School of Economics, New Delhi. He was also formerly Member-Secretary of Indian Council for Social Science Research (ICSSR) at New Delhi.

P.K. Bose, Hon. Professor, Centre for Studies in Social Sciences, Calcutta.

Partha Chatterjee, Professor, Centre for Studies in Social Sciences, Calcutta.

John Crowley, Senior Programme Specialist at UNESCO and Chief Editor, *International Social Science Journal*, Paris.

Satish Deshpande, Professor, Department of Sociology, Delhi School of Economics, New Delhi.

Ravi Kanbur, T.H. Lee Professor of World Affairs and Professor of Economics, Cornell University, New York, USA.

Michael E. Lamb, Professor, Department of Social and Developmental Psychology, University of Cambridge, United Kingdom, and Chairperson, The International Advisory Committee of the Economic and Social Research Council of the UK.

Sugata Marjit, Director, Centre for Studies in Social Sciences, Calcutta.

George Mathew, Director, Institute of Social Sciences, New Delhi.

Michael Walton, formerly, Visiting, V.K.R.V. Rao Professor, Institute for Social and Economic Change, Bangalore and Professor at Harvard Kennedy School, Cambridge, UK.

Anjan Mukherji, Professor, Centre for Economic Studies and Planning, Jawaharlal Nehru University, New Delhi.

Narayanan Nair, Director, Centre for Development Studies, Trivandrum.

T.K. Oommen, Retd. Professor, Department of Sociology, Jawaharlal Nehru University, New Delhi.

M.S.S. Pandian, Professor, Centre for Historical Studies, Jawaharlal Nehru University, New Delhi and Visiting Fellow, The Sarai

Programme, Centre for the Study of Developing Societies, New Delhi.

V.R. Panchamukhi, formerly, Chairman, Indian Council of Social Science Research, New Delhi.

T.S. Papola, Hon. Professor, Institute for Studies in Industrial Development (ISID), New Delhi and also President of Indian Society of Labour Economics.

S. Parasuraman, Director, Tata Institute of Social Sciences, Mumbai.

Mihir Rakshit, Director, Monetary Research Project, Investment, Information and Credit Rating Agency (ICRA), Kolkata and formerly, Professor, Delhi School of Economics, New Delhi.

V.M. Rao, Hon. Professor, Institute for Social and Economic Change, Bangalore.

U. Sankar, Hon. Professor, Madras School of Economics, Chennai.

Khalil Shah, Researcher, Institute for Social and Economic Change, Bangalore.

T.N. Srinivasan, currently Samuel C. Park, Jr. Professor of Economics at Economic Growth Center, Yale University, USA. He is also Senior Research Fellow at Stanford Center for International Development, Stanford University.

G. Thimmaiah, formerly Director, Institute of Social and Economic Change, Bangalore.

A. Vaidyanathan, formerly Professor of Economics and Director of Madras Institute of Development Studies, Chennai.

Lakshmi Venkatachalam (IAS), presently, Director-General of Shipping and Ex-officio, Additional Secretary to Government of India and formerly, Principal Secretary, Planning, Government of Karnataka.

Foreword

India, in the last two decades, has seen dramatic changes in its economy, society and politics. Its economy has seen extraordinary growth and has become a much bigger economy in relation to other developing countries, barring China. Contrary to the fears expressed in early 1990s, its corporate sector has not lost out to the multinationals but has gone on to register phenomenal growth. So much so, that a section of Indian bourgeosie is buying up some of the most modern enterprises in the heartland of capitalism, in Europe and North America. What this shows is that this section of the Indian bourgeoisie is, in Leninist terms, in an imperialist mode of expansion. What this also shows is that Indian capitalism is drawing in the surplus value produced by the working class in the advanced capitalist world.

We have to ask what it may mean for the character of the Indian state. In what ways is the nature of the Indian state changing? What now is the type of its "dependence" on the advanced capitalist state? This question is important because there is no socialist world any longer. The old Soviet Union, now Russia and so much more, is as much capitalist as Germany or France are. The Chinese Communist Party is taking China into becoming a powerful capitalist state. (Large numbers of Chinese are gambling in stock markets as the Americans do convince that getting rich is a higher virtue than many other human qualities.) How does India play up to this world? In what ways are its strategic and foreign policy options different than in the 1960s and 70s when our understanding on these issues crystallised? Research in the social sciences has not, as I see it, asked and pursued any of these questions. These are important areas of research because most of us are framing our approvals, criticisms and assessments in terms of the old assumptions, leading to debates which are largely out of tune with the new realities.

Millions of very poor living in destitution are staring in bewilderment and repressed anger at the burgeoning middle class moving into high conspicuous consumption. We have left unresolved basic social problems like child care (half the children are stunted with malnutrition), health care, livelihood, etc. In short, the state does not seem to be properly tuned in for providing for the unmet daily needs at a decent level for people to feel a sense of dignity and self-respect. Can our democracy flourish when people have civil and political rights but are forced to live in conditions of unfreedom? How do we insure social order without resort to coercion? Now becoming a condition instead of being an exception. The point is that the government has much more money with buoyant revenues and we therefore have a big resource base than ever before to handle with urgency many of these problems including of research into these areas. Democracy cannot become secure when faced with a volatile social situation. I would like to ask, keeping my long standing Left critique and its preferences apart, what are the innovative, allocative and social strategies that we can think of, that can mitigate these conditions, within the framework of the system.

Changes in society have been enormous and of wide-ranging implications. New social classes, like those toiling in new types of unorganised sector, and communities (of kinship and belief) have come to the fore with new demands radically changing the ground level equations in society and therefore the very nature of the political process. Most backward classes (MBCs), OBCs, Dalits, *adivasis*, women (with a girl child who survived the scalpel of the surgeon in the lap) and so on, are all up in new forms of struggle and modes of articulation of demands. Forceful social and political mobilisations, participatory demands and assertions for inclusion have become a common sight.

This is a clear case of empowerment. A shift of balance in our politics. A change in the political process which conditions the democratic outcomes. Struggles have been extensive which are viewed by the established elites as an unnecessary din in public sphere, a scare on civil society. This is an elite which has become a "privilegensia", in reaction to this assertion as can be seen in how the elites respond to demands for affirmative action. But the outcomes have not been adequately in alignment with the levels of empowerment. Higher levels of some of these oppressed sections in political representations are visible but that is not the case when we look at the decision-making especially at the level of economic policy. So we are faced with a situation where empowerment does not necessarily lead to economic well-being. What does it mean for the future of our democracy and social harmony? In fact we are also faced with a grave contradiction. While politics is empowering the people, the economic process of growth is simultaneously disempowering the vulnerable amongst them. This will have serious implication for the "nation-building" process. How exactly and in what precise ways is for the research in social sciences to disentangle. I think we have not paid adequate attention to this area of research and investigations.

I have tried to identify some new areas of research and knowledge which require immediate attention. These are also the areas where a new national consensus can be evolved, as one existed before the 1980s; the one around the Nehruvian consensus on the future shape of India and its Left critique which was not so much its rejection but a critique more about the inadequacy of its conceptualisation and implementation. The research and knowledge which I have hinted above has deep implications for developmental planning and policymaking as well as for theory. In one way it links up with both the state and government, both as critique and input. Prof. V.K.R.V. Rao had noted in his recommendations (these became the basis for the formation of ICSSR in 1968) that social knowledge is important to promote and regulate social change and to produce a dynamic and healthy society, that is, a facilitative factor in "nation-building". The question is: how well we have and can contribute towards this? And, following on this, what ought to be the way we re-focus our work to contribute toward this?

It is most appropriate that Institute for Social and Economic Change (ISEC), another institution created and nurtured in its early days by Prof. V.K.R.V. Rao has taken upon itself to undertake this enterprise. The book with us is a comprehensive appraisal of various conditions that go into social science research in India. It covers all the facets of the social sciences in India including its institutional foundations and financial requirements. I am convinced that it will help us to refocus our energies in taking the knowledge in social sciences a notch or two above from where we stand today. As it does so, this effort of ISEC will have done us a great service. I have always believed that the level of excellence in social science research as a merit good is dependent upon the state of organised knowledge in various disciplines. We all know quite well that the organised knowledge in social sciences is on the one hand quite uneven across different disciplines and on the other, somewhat poor in many a discipline. Any effort that helps us in overcoming these shortcomings is a welcome development. ISEC deserves compliments for producing a work which will become a necessary reading for all of us interested in improving the standards of research in social sciences.

— Javeed Alam
Chairperson,
ICSSR

Preface

This volume of 13 papers presented at the conference organised to commemorate the birth centenary of Dr. V.K.R.V. Rao, examines the contemporary context of social science research in India. While it discusses the Indian experience, its findings are relevant wherever social science research takes place and especially in Second and Third World countries.

The conference was an appropriate tribute to Dr. V.K.R.V. Rao who was a distinguished scholar in the field of social sciences, founder of institutions of social science research, which have survived because of the thought he gave to the structuring of these institutions. He founded the Indian Council of Social Science Research (ICSSR) to promote research in the social sciences. His desire was for the different social sciences to conduct research in a way that the insights of different disciplines became available. He created governance structures that insulated the institutions from external influences. He aimed for maximum autonomy for researchers and for them to determine the research programme for themselves and the institution as a whole.

The thrust of the conference was the institutional structure of social science research. Participants who included many scholars in economics, political science, sociology and other social sciences, looked at issues of accountability, interdisciplinary working, transparency and dissemination, dealing with sponsored projects, resources available and needed, autonomy and inter-institutional cooperation. They also proposed directions for the future that would take these issues into account. Despite the possibly controversial issues, there was unanimity on the conclusions of each topic.

We can agree that the quality of social science research has been declining for some years. The reasons are related to declining relative remunerations especially in the private corporate sector, and declining autonomy at work. Some of India's best social science researchers work in overseas universities and institutions. Remuneration is better in overseas and there is also greater freedom because of a lower imposed workload. Corpus funding is generous and enables researchers to pick their own areas for research.

In addition to the pull of overseas, domestic markets such as financial sector, market research, management consultancy and corporate sector engaged in formulating strategies and building alternative scenarios are also the attraction for many as these provide much better remuneration. Economists, sociologists, psychologists, management scholars and statisticians in particular are in demand in the private sector. Growing recruitment in the private sector deprives social science research of talented potential researchers. The other loss is that private sector work is not in the public domain.

Further, there is little incentive for young students to enter PhD programmes because the scholarship amount available to PhD scholars are very low. Some improvement is taking place, but at scholarships ranging from Rs. 12000 to Rs. 18000 per month, bright young people with postgraduate degrees are reluctant to spend five years or so to work for their PhDs. Scholarship values must go up and institutions (including universities) must make efforts to find funding for this purpose.

The situation is made worse because the salaries when these PhDs enter fulltime research employment in universities or social science institutions are so low. The implementation of the Chadha Committee Report will give substantial increments to new entrants as well as researchers at different levels. All institutions must use these higher emoluments in order to demand higher standards in engaging new recruits, and better quality and work outputs by existing researchers.

However, the Chadha Committee does not bring parity with overseas or domestic private sector emoluments. It only reduces the gap. It is to be expected that the gaps in relative remunerations will again widen in future years. It is necessary therefore that corpus funding is frequently reviewed, that government and other grants be added to from time to time and effort be made by institutions to garner additional funding through sponsored project research.

Today, there is no automatic mechanism with the government to adjust social science research funding to maintain a steady relationship between private sector remunerations and researchers. Indeed in recent years, government funding has been declining in real terms and has been relatively static even in nominal terms. Even if the recommendations of the Committee chaired by Dr. A. Vaidyanathan to review the ICSSR are implemented, there is no certainly that such adjustments will take place regularly in future. They have not happened for many years in the past. Unless research institutions and universities take proactive measures to raise funds on their own, the problems will not go away.

Alternative funding to ICSSR is therefore to be explored by every institution. Funding must be related to the merit of the institution, not merely because it exists. There are many in existence and even among ICSSR institutions, there are some that could function better. ICSSR and the research community should seriously explore the closure of some institutions and merging them with stronger ones.

The sources of other funds are through Central and state government research programmes (around Rs. 600 crore a year through their different ministries), private and public sector sponsored corporate research, international multilateral agencies (World Bank, ADB, etc.), bilateral agencies (USAID, DFID, CEDA, IDRC, NORAD, etc.) and domestic and foreign foundations (Tata, Khemka, Ford, Rockefeller, etc.). Domestic and foreign foundations provide corpus funding while all provide funds for sponsored research. As in many other countries, universities and research institutions must go after fund-raising in a concerted manner.

Most sponsored research focuses on data collection. In the case of governments, the utility and usage of research findings varies in extent. There is no coordination between government agencies in spending money on social science research. If their spending was to go through a body like ICSSR, perhaps the funds could be better utilised to minimise repetitive work, and to evaluate the quality of the different institutions and their work. Such coordination is required and government must consider it.

Private sector spending on social science research is growing. Their spending is much more purposive and almost invariably leads to business decisions. However, little of the research and its use is public. Researchers must negotiate with private sponsors so that the research output is in the public domain within a reasonable period. Other researchers, too, should be able to work on the data.

In this broad context, ICSSR has an annual budget of Rs. 50 crore or so to support 27 institutions, contributing around 27 per cent to their budgets. State governments contribute around 46 per cent. Research institutions therefore have to raise the balance 54 per cent from corpus income and sponsored projects from the sources mentioned above.

Sponsored project research is becoming increasingly important as a source of funding. The criticism of such research is that it removes autonomy from researchers, that the output is not available to other researchers, the findings are rarely published and researchers themselves keep moving between disparate projects without developing conceptual findings from the research. However, sponsored research is a necessary source of funding.

The distinction between projects and long-term research is illusory. All social science research is ultimately grounded on data from field observations, namely research projects. Theories have to originate from such observations of men and women in society. The distinction that is made between theory and applied work is hence self-defeating since all social science theories require observation. What is important are the quality of work, easy access to the observations by other researchers, and the fit of the work in the research programme of the individual researcher.

An incidental benefit is that sponsored research brings in the much needed efficiency in working since the sponsor who is paying for it would be more demanding about the work being completed in a given timeframe and the research being of good quality. The essential precondition that each institution must follow is to ensure that the sponsored work is within the programmatic mandates of the institution and of the researcher. Any and all kinds of work must not be accepted just because there is funding available for it.

Accountability of sponsors, research institutions and individual researchers is another area that needs to be spelt out and implemented. Sponsors must not interfere with the conclusions drawn from any research. They may question and disagree but the researcher's final conclusions must not be interfered with, though the sponsor may decide to act differently from the research findings. Central governments and to a lesser extent, state governments, are reluctant to allow research sponsored by them to be published and widely disseminated. This has also been the case at times with multilateral funding agencies like the World Bank. All research should be disseminated widely within at most, a year, of completion. Institutions and researchers must have a clearly defined policy for this purpose.

The advantage of privately funded research is that the private sponsor is far more demanding of timeliness and quality. This is also the case with multilateral financing agencies, but not as true for bilateral ones, and far less so for Central and state governments. The researcher and the institution must have a method to monitor and insist on work being completed in time and within cost budgets.

Accountability of the research institution is in providing a conducive environment and adequate technical and other facilities to researchers. It must arrange to monitor and give feedback to researchers of their progress on the time schedule for the work, cost budgets, quality and the performance evaluation of individual researchers. Institutions must also begin to differentiate between 'good' and 'bad' researchers on the basis of their adherence to time and cost budgets, publications record in good journals, efforts at dissemination, etc. The institutions must also support researchers in persuading sponsors not to interfere with research conclusions honestly arrived at, and to permit early dissemination. A scheme of financial and non-financial incentives must be introduced so that the 'good' researchers are distinguished from the 'bad'. The equality of rewards to researchers has been detrimental to the quality of work.

The third is accountability of the researcher. He/she is accountable for concluding the work within time and cost commitments and ensuring quality. There must be no bias on ideological or other grounds, in the conclusions. The researcher must aim to publish the work not merely in learned journals but also in places where the layman can see and understand it. Researchers must be taught to understand that their time costs money and the quality of their work will help their reputation of themselves and their institutions.

Dr. V.K.R.V. Rao was a strong believer that social science research must be interdisciplinary. There are many areas that would benefit from the interdisciplinary working of economists with sociologists, anthropologists and other social scientists. However, it has been difficult to do this in practice, even when there is a conscious effort to do so. It requires mutual trust between the different researchers and between their disciplines. Our academic courses do not aim to teach such inter-disciplinarity. Academia must aim to do so at an early stage by exposing students to other social sciences, albeit in very basic ways. Further, there are areas like health and nutrition, environment, water, poverty that could benefit from interactions and interdisciplinary working of social scientists with physical scientists. Every effort must be made to develop contacts and initiate such joint working.

Natural sciences have a national science policy. However, social sciences have political and policy implications. It is undesirable and possibly dangerous to the social sciences and scholarship in them, if there were such a national policy for the social sciences. It would introduce strong external and non-scholarly influences on social scientists.

Clearly, the separation of universities from social science research institutions that took place in the 1950s has spread limited talent thinly. It has resulted in teaching being deprived of latest research findings. But amalgamating independent research institutions with universities is unlikely since they are now deeply entrenched in their separate working. Every effort must be made to ensure the outreach of social science research institutions through their researchers, with universities, encouraging interested college and university faculty to work on research projects and the participation of researchers in teaching in the universities.

A final word on the institutional structure of social science research is about their autonomy. In my view, there is neither lack of autonomy nor any threat to autonomy in social science research. Any lack of autonomy is the fault of the researchers and their institutions than of sponsors, governments and other funding agencies.

There is no doubt that instituitional structures must be reformed as must be their funding. The internal restructuring is in the hands of the institutions and the researchers. It is imperative that it be undertaken forthwith.

— S.L. Rao
Chairman
ISEC

Acknowledgements

Prof. V.K.R.V. Rao has been one of the pioneers in institutionalising social science research in India. He could be credited with the mammoth efforts in building social sciences research discipline in the country. Prof. Rao not only established three premier research institutions in India but also helped to concretise the structure of social science research institutions by lending his helping hand to establish Indian Council of Social Science Research (ICSSR), agro-economic centres, population research centres and has advised a number of other social science research institutions. The year 2008 was the birth centenary year of Prof. V.K.R.V. Rao and the Institute for Social and Economic Change (ISEC) celebrated it in a fitting manner to the status of Prof. V.K.R.V. Rao by organising many events.

One of the major events was a seminar on "Social Science Research in India" organised at the Institute for Social and Economic Change on 7-8th July 2008 specifically focusing on institutions and the structures. Many well-known national and international social scientists participated in the seminar. It was the love and affection of the participants towards Prof. Rao that brought forth elaborate and in-depth presentations in the seminar.

It was decided to bring the proceedings in the form of a volume as the papers covered very important aspects confronting social sciences today. Keeping this in view, the presented papers were revised down the line and brought in the form of this volume now. It was felt essential to weave these contributions in a sequential manner to provide a good reading of institutional structure about social science research. Prof. M.V. Nadkarni, Honorary Visiting Professor of ISEC and former Vice-Chancellor, Gulbarga University, helped me to do that in a systematic manner. In the spirit of a true *guru*, he developed the entire framework that is presented here for the readers. Shri S.L. Rao, the then Chairman of Board of Governors, ISEC readily agreed to write the 'Preface'. I am grateful to both of them for the encouragement and help that they have rendered. Prof. Javeed Alam, Chairman of ICSSR agreed to write the 'Foreword'. I prevailed upon him almost regularly and he spared his time for this. As the readers may notice that in his 'Foreword', he covered very significant and important issues in social science research. I am indebted to him for his efforts.

At the time of the centenary celebrations, Prof. N. Jayaram was the Director of the Institute and he spared no efforts to encourage me in organising the seminar and provided all the needed support. I must mention gratefully his efforts and encouragement. At the Institute, Mr. Khalil Shah and Mr. M.K. Mohan Kumar have helped me in correcting and word processing the various drafts and to put together the material in the present form. I must acknowledge their untiring efforts. It was the support of the Indian Council of Social Science Research (ICSSR) which enabled us to undertake the seminar and bring out this seminar volume. I am grateful to Prof. Javeed Alam, Chairman, ICSSR, Prof. T.C.A. Anant, former Member-Secretary and Prof. Ranjit Sinha, Member-Secretary of ICSSR for their strong support.

I must express my gratitude towards the contributors who have revised and helped me to get the papers in time. It is true that, after making a presentation and with the lapse of time, one finds it difficult to revise a paper but this experience is not exceptional in the academic circle. Despite this difficulty, all of them have taken the possible efforts to revise and send me their contributions. I express my sincere apologies and gratitude to them.

Finally, I must mention that the faculty and staff members of ISEC were supportive in all these activities. But for their support, this would not have been completed. In a way, this entire work belongs to them and I stand only as a conduit between the readers and the material. Many of the ICSSR institutions supplied the photographs presented on the cover and inside the volume. I must express my thanks to them for sparing those photographs. I am grateful to Mr. Sanu Kapila of Academic

Foundation, New Delhi, who agreed to bring out this volume in the best possible manner. I am grateful to him and the staff of Academic Foundation for their strenuous efforts in bringing out this volume.

— R.S. Deshpande
Director
Institute for Social and Economic Change

1 Introduction

M.V. Nadkarni and R.S. Deshpande

Though the title of the seminar as well as of this book necessarily suggest an exclusive focus on India and its social science research (SSR) situation, however, the papers here can be of general interest too, especially for other developing countries.

In pre-independent India, social science research was in its nascent stage, and was by and large confined to the departments in the Universities of Bombay, Madras, Calcutta and Delhi. But this was not significant enough considering the needs of the country and also compared to what the university system accomplished abroad. Individual researchers on their own, sometimes even spending from their pocket and using their spare time, also undertook research on social issues. Stalwarts like Dadabhai Naoroji had worked autonomously on important themes like poverty and the drain on the resources of the country caused by imperialism. Such research by independent scholars, in response to a bug in their brain, done in a non-institutionalised setting, continues to play a significant role even now, but was not considered adequate enough to meet the country's research needs.

Dr. V.K.R.V. Rao reflected over the poor institutional framework to support SSR in India. Important initiatives had been taken to boost research in natural sciences soon after Independence, thanks to the Prime Minister Jawaharlal Nehru's passion for science and technology as the main hope for India's development. But social sciences remained in a state of relative neglect. There was so much increased need (if not 'demand' in a strictly economic sense) for SSR after India's independence, particularly due to launching of social and economic development under the auspices of the state, that such need had no chance of being met if left to only private individuals and universities. We had to wait at least till 1969 when the Indian Council of Social

Science Research (ICSSR) was established at the initiative of Dr. Rao, the then Minister for Education in the Government of India under Indira Gandhi's Prime Ministership, with Shri J.P. Naik as the first Member-Secretary of ICSSR. Dr. Rao had proposed the setting up of such a council in 1965 itself when he was a member of Planning Commission. At least in the first phase of ICCSR, its main role was to stimulate and support SSR in the country as a whole including the university system. In the subsequent phase, ICSSR, in addition to this, also took up the role of providing grants for maintenance and infrastructure of a number of SSR institutions in the country directly under its umbrella, which were not a part of the university system. Dr. Rao himself started three SSR institutions of national importance, two in Delhi—Delhi School of Economics (DSE), in as early as 1948 and the Institute of Economic Growth (IEG) in 1957, and one in Bangalore—the Institute for Social and Economic Change (ISEC) in 1972. DSE was a part of Delhi University, but IEG and ISEC were autonomous and came under ICSSR. Dr. Rao as the Education Minister in the Government of India gave a thrust and active support to several other institutions as well, which directly and indirectly helped SSR. For example, it was through his initiative and effort that a chain of agro-economic centres and population eesearch centres were established across the country. At least a few of these institutions took to the task of not only SSR but also of capacity building in an unprecedented way, by attracting and nurturing talent. Some of these SSR institutions took up the task of training research students under well thought-out PhD programmes and also of training administrators in the country at different levels including IAS officers, by giving inputs from SSR and equipping them in the task of policy formulation and implementation.

Apart from the institutional set-up under the universities and the ICSSR, a third wing also started developing rapidly which was engaged in SSR. In the 1980s and 1990s, the non-governmental organisations (NGOs), consultancy firms and private research institutions in the form of independent trusts or societies entered the research arena, initiating a new culture of research which was both commercialised and professional. Though hardly claiming any high academic standard, these institutions promised quickness combined with professional quality, which the first two institutional wings of SSR found it challenging to match. This brought in the question of relevance, competition, duplication of research as well as coordination and inter-communication between institutions engaged in SSR. It also raised the issue of assessment of the whole institutional set-up engaged in SSR, including ICSSR itself. Over the last four decades, ICSSR has already been reviewed four times, with the Fourth Review Committee headed by Prof. A. Vaidyanathan having submitted its report in 2007. This report also in turn raised several issues for debate.

The present volume is the outcome of a seminar organised at ISEC for three days from 6-8 July 2008, as part of the Dr. V.K.R.V. Rao Birth Centenary Celebrations at ISEC, coinciding with the birthday of Dr. Rao (8th July). It is intended as our humble tribute to this great visionary and institution builder par excellence, and also to discuss in the process several issues which have emerged in the last four decades. A concept note raising these issues was circulated well in advance and papers were invited from eminent social scientists. The seminar gave a good opportunity for critical discussion of the institutional dimensions of SSR, its strengths, weaknesses and its opportunities. As it happens in many seminars, a few presentations were made only orally and their written versions did not come in after the seminar also. On the basis of recorded tapes and rapporteurs reports, we have tried to make up for this deficiency in the 'Discussions' presented separately in this volume. On the other hand, we also sent transcript of the orally presented papers to the scholars and got them revised. These papers are included as annexure in this volume. In any case, this volume does not aim at being an exact record, but attempts to not only reproduce the papers submitted, but also capture the flavour of rich discussions at different sessions of the seminar.

A major issue in SSR, particularly in an institutionalised setting, is the tension between individual research interest stimulated by a bug in the researcher's own brain or fired by intense curiosity and the needs of policy research. With increased public funding, it is only expected that the needs of policy research would receive greater emphasis. Dr. Rao had experienced this tension in the SSR institutions which he had not only founded but also nourished and developed, and naturally had reflected well on this. He gave expression to his stand on this issue in an inaugural address at a seminar in 1980 at IEG, Delhi, as follows:

> ...I would again reiterate that while relevance is important in Social Science research, it should not be made an inhibiting factor nor should it merely conform to the wishes of the policy maker. The individual researcher has a right to determine the context of relevance in the research work that he undertakes...At the same time it is important for the researcher to ask himself the question of relevance from the point of view of both understanding and policy formulation when he chooses a topic for his research and also prepares his outline of the data to be collected and the questions to be answered. If he does this, I have no doubt that social science research will have a far more effective and continuing impact... (Rao, 2008: 116)

Thanks to Dr. Rao's eminence and standing in the public domain, he had no difficulty in resolving this tension, but as a committed academic, he upheld the right of individual researchers, without having to sacrifice the need for social relevance in research. Elsewhere, he also clarified that social relevance is not to be interpreted narrowly for short term alone. We have to ensure that research 'takes a longer view of life and society than the immediate short period' (Rao, 1974: 13).

In addition to this issue of social relevance and reconciling individual research interest with the need for policy research, other issues were also taken up at the July 2008 seminar at ISEC. They were:

- Evaluating vibrancy, autonomy and creativity of research not only at the individual level, but also the institutional level. Are the research institutions and university departments able to create a stimulating environment of research for free debate, self-evaluation, constructive criticism and responsiveness to social concerns? If not, why? The discussion, however, was mainly confined to experiences in SSR institutions, rather than university departments.
- Given the diversity of institutional structure of SSR now, how to minimise duplication of research and how to evolve functional and effective roles for different types of institutions, promote better communication, cooperation and even collaboration between institutions, and ensure proper accountability for each?

- To what extent is the goal of openness in the form of inter-disciplinarity or multidisciplinarity followed in practice?
- How far do SSR institutions and university departments manage to reconcile the need to raise finance through short-term 'project'-based research with the long-term research goals that are consistent with long-term vision or perspective of institutions? Is there any attempt to develop schools of thought or new theories or new paradigms? Why is theoretical creative writing in SSR in India sidetracked or ignored? Do researchers experience a tension between theoretical and 'practical' or 'empirical' research?
- What is the status of funding SSR? How is its adequacy and effectiveness evaluated, or to be evaluated? How can funding method be so improved as to reconcile academic autonomy with accountability?

The positive change in the attitude of government to SSR after India's independence was reflected well in the speech of Shri B.S. Yeddyurappa, the Chief Minister of Karnataka, who was the guest of honour at the inaugural session of the seminar. He stressed the importance of the government's commitment of support to not only centres of learning but also to centres of knowledge creation including SSR institutions. By promoting such centres in social sciences, the government would immensely benefit from the guidance received both in formulating and implementing policy for social and economic development of people. He was also generous enough to say that the state's expectations from ISEC have been admirably fulfilled, and lauded the rich interaction between the state government and ISEC right from its inception to the present day. Prof. S.K. Thorat, Chairman, University Grants Commission, who delivered the inaugural address, took the remarks of the Chief Minister a step forward by observing that there should be a similar constructive interaction in respect of research between university departments in social sciences with both SSR institutions under ICSSR and the respective state governments where universities are located. He called for an exchange of scholars for at least short periods between university departments and SSR institutions, so that scholars in SSRs have greater teaching opportunities and exposure to students, and faculty in universities have greater opportunities of research collaboration and further stimulus to their knowledge creation. This is an important way to overcome the existing gaps in both types of institutions—inadequate exposure to teaching experience in SSRs and inadequate stimulus to research in university departments. While universities have to step up knowledge creation, SSRs have to step up knowledge dissemination to students.

Prof. T.C.A. Anant, the Member-Secretary of ICSSR at the time of the seminar, has quite a few interesting insights to give both in his paper here, "Social Science in India: Some Institutional Issues", and his oral presentation. He first traces the genesis of ICSSR and the development of the present institutional set-up for SSR. He is right in emphasising that the role of ICSSR and institutions under it or of SSR in general including the university set-up cannot be construed as one of mainly providing policy guidance to governments. The Planning Commission at the national level and planning boards or bodies at the state level can and do perform that role. The more important role is to give support to research that leads to new knowledge, new analytical tools, and new paradigms which may or may not be of immediate relevance to policy. He takes the example of game theory. When it was first developed, it was considered as merely an intellectual toy, but now it has become very useful not only in economics, but also in political science, sociology and a whole host of disciplines. Anant refers to 'delayed return research', whose impact and use may not be immediately evident. If such research were to be discouraged, then it may abort the emergence of new knowledge and tools which may be crucially useful to policy sometime. But in encouraging such research, tied-up nature of financing to research institutions can be an inhibiting factor. Anant observes that in 2005-06, while ICSSR and state governments respectively provided only 27 and 19 per cent of resources to SSR institutions (together 46 per cent), the institutions had to raise own resources which were project-based up to 54 per cent. In economics, we know how the margin is the main driver, and it is no surprise if these institutions orient themselves entirely to project-based short-term research in order to meet their resource gap.

It would be interesting to take a look at the statistics appearing at the end of Anant's paper, drawn from the Fourth Review of ICSSR. In spite of the fact that there are many more universities than SSR institutes and many more social scientists in the former than in the latter, the latter seem to have overtaken the former in published work. Of the 542 articles published in selected social science journals in India in 2004-05, SSR institutes together contributed about 40 per cent (ICSSR institutes—11 per cent, other autonomous institutes—29 per cent), while the universities accounted for 33 per cent. However, when we come to the number of books published, independent scholars who hardly figured in the publication of articles, emerge as significant contributors. Of the 998 books published by selected social science publishers, independent scholars accounted for 15 per cent and Indian universities 28 per cent. The SSR institutes together accounted for 22 per cent (ICSSR institutes—7 per cent and other institutes—15 per cent). SSR institutes other than those under ICSSR outnumber the ICSSR institutes, both in articles and books published. This is expected. While there are only 27 research institutes under ICSSR, SSR institutes other than them are many times more. The output of research institutes is, however, more than what is indicated by publications, since many research reports are not published at all, being more or less of consultancy nature. ICSSR's research support is not confined to institutes under its wing, but is extended to universities as well as to autonomous research institutes not under it.

Anant's comments on the role of professional associations of social scientists in India are not very flattering. The major role of these associations is to organise annual conferences, where papers of indifferent quality are often presented, and eminent academicians except for a very few hardly attend them. Considering the many valuable services provided by such associations in countries like USA, the scenario in India appears dismal. There are of course a few exceptions like the Indian Society of Agricultural Economics (ISAE), which runs a refereed quarterly journal, and the papers published in its conference number are also refereed. Detailed comments are also sought from the referees to help improve the papers. However, professional associations in India are yet to improve their services to the level of similar associations in advanced countries, particularly in providing help in the job market.

With the wide diversity of institutions engaged in SSR, there is need for not only communication between them but also of cooperation and even collaboration. No institution is perfect and all-round, but the gaps and inadequacies can be overcome through mutual cooperation. It was felt that there is more evidence of understanding and collaboration between Indian and foreign institutions, rather than between Indian institutions among themselves. There is competition, especially for funds and projects, but no or little cooperation. Prof. Anjan Mukherji, in his paper, "The State of Cooperation among SSR Institutions", discusses this issue of cooperation, and also the issue of ensuring the quality of scholars/academicians as well as of research. He seems to indicate that while the right kind of cooperation is scant, the wrong kind of cooperation is significant!

He emphasises that there is a need for the right kind of co-operation which would make the whole institutional set-up more efficient, flexible, responsive and responsible, with positive impacts all around. He observes that just as there is dependence of recipient institutions on the donors, the donors too are dependent for their own credibility on the good performance of their recipients, which is not often realised. The result is that there is a lot of bureaucratic rigidity and unnecessary conditions which hinder the performance of recipients. He gives several telling examples to illustrate his point. Mutual understanding and cooperation between donors and recipients is very much needed to create the right climate for research and academic productivity. There is similarly a need for cooperation between research institutions, including between university departments and research institutes, in respect of library, data sharing, exchange of scholars and collaboration in research projects and programmes. As an example of wrong kind of cooperation, Mukherji mentions 'peer review', where 'peers' may be none other than close friends!

Mukherji also takes up the question of quality of research and also that of attracting talent in to the academic field. He feels that donors do not always take the right care in screening projects. He gives a bizarre example of a research project getting 2 lakh rupees in the 1970s (a very good amount those days), which wanted to fit production functions to newspaper industry with only newsprint as the input! There is also a lot of research output which is not properly refereed and exposed to academic scrutiny. As to attracting talent into academic fields, he sees no escape from giving attractive salaries. He reminds us of the old saying—"If you give peanuts, you will only get monkeys"!

In his insightful paper on "Accountability of Social Science Research—Some Challenging Dimensions", Prof. V.M. Rao comments about the increasing societal role of SSR, emerging trends in SSR and their impact. He takes the stand that on the excuse of individual right to academic freedom, neither a social scientist individually nor SSR institutions can ignore their responsibility and accountability to the society at large (if not to the state as such). Such accountability is far more important than the formal accountability to donors. He does not claim that he is presenting a charge sheet against SSR. On the other hand, he gives a balanced overview which should guide researchers.

SSR has witnessed dramatic changes in the technology available in the form of computerisation, development of sophisticated models and analytical frameworks, growing linkages with funding agencies, expanding share of policy-oriented research, extensive contacts and communication network, increasing trend in research collaboration, and even increasing presence of researchers in media, resulting in not only better media coverage but also in media's own research, and wider readership and reviews. Though these are positive and welcome changes, there are also areas of growing concern. In his oral presentation, Prof. Rao took the example of computerisation of land records. Though a sophisticated technology is available for storing data and retrieval, one is not certain about the credibility of the data fed into the computer! There is also a concern about overspecialisation and fragmentation of SSR into 'relatively small non-interacting groups each with its own perspective, specialised jargon and exclusive theoretical and methodological concerns'. This may be, as Rao observes, in response to growing complexity of our globalising world, but results nevertheless in a failure to get fuller and deeper insights which can come through a holistic approach.

Rao then takes a critical overview of the impact of these emerging trends on: (i) quality of research, (ii) adequacy of database, and (iii) linkages with stakeholders. He advocates a balance between two types of research—innovation and replication. Replication also has a role, pushing the extensive margins of knowledge. But a disproportionate increase in replication "is likely to yield harvests of clones making no additions to knowledge". On the other hand, "abundance of innovative papers which do not percolate to the ground level of replication would give us grand looking white elephants with no work to perform." Regarding particularly official data, the need to make them credible needs more attention. As to field data collected by SSR, 'no arrangements have been evolved to store them for future use'. Analysis of data can at times be misleading, particularly if quantitative techniques like coefficients are applied mechanically. For example, he points out, an increase in concentration ratio can occur if a large number of landless get small pieces of land each compared to the earlier holding of land only by large owners! Rao insightfully observes that if field materials are banked, it would be easy to get a glimpse of processes underlying measures generated in typical sample surveys done by economists.

About linkages with stakeholders and accountability, Rao insists that researchers take note of both 'intra-profession norms' (IPN) which guide the researcher towards academic excellence, and also 'extra-profession norms' (EPN) which depend on the view taken by stakeholders about the value of research outcome. If IPN are ignored, the academic credibility of the researcher is affected. But if EPN are ignored, it may result in a certain alienation of researchers from the main society and its concerns, loss of relevance, and hence demand for research.

With the process of increasing specialisation of knowledge, there is also an increasing need for communication between disciplines. Studies which bridge the gap between two or more disciplines have a rich potential for creating new knowledge. Prof. U. Sankar, in an enlightening paper on "Multidisciplinary Research: Challenges and Opportunities" takes up this issue. He first discusses the status of multidisciplinary research with examples of how a multidisciplinary approach could have been more satisfying, identifies barriers to multi-disciplinary research and then offers suggestions for overcoming them.

In discussing this issue, Sankar reveals his own rich multidisciplinary sweep of knowledge, without which such a paper could not have been written.

Sankar clarifies that multidisciplinary research is not just putting people from different disciplines together in a compartmentalised manner without interaction and synergy. Real multidisciplinary work is difficult and rare, though it may be facilitated by putting different disciplines together making interactions easier. He illustrates by giving examples of how integrating inputs from different disciplines has a rich potential for creating new knowledge. First is that of production function analysis in agricultural economics, which traditionally has left an increasing gap between agronomy and econometrics. This is because such an analysis has ignored the sequential nature of input decisions, and also the fact that variance of output increases with some inputs but decreases with some other inputs. Sankar says, "what is needed is development of a sequential decision-making production model with weather affecting different sets of inputs differently." He feels that with further developments in dynamic programming, computer software and data generated by stage of production, the gap between agronomy and econometrics can be narrowed. He indicates rich possibilities of research by involving remote sensing, GIS, agronomy and economics. The next example he gives is that of sustainable development concept, which has at least three dimensions—economic, social and environmental. However, our knowledge of the two-way linkages between economy and ecology are still poor. It is particularly necessary to analyse how the local or indigenous people are affected by both economic and ecological processes, and to evolve mitigation strategies in consultation with affected people. Social costs and benefits of alternative technologies/ projects have to be assessed in a holistic manner, along with their distributional implications, so that benefits are translated into desired social, economic and environmental outcomes.

Why is multidisciplinary research, particularly one involving both social and natural sciences rare? What are the barriers to it? Sankar mentions learning costs and lack of encouragement to scholars from learning across disciplines. Scientists and technologists do not take social scientists—or even social issues—seriously. Another problem is the policy of social science publishers, particularly of academic journals. They value sophistication of analysis and methodology, rather than innovativeness of either approach or findings which come from looking across disciplines. Social scientists, on their part, are mostly concerned with *ex post* evaluation and its hypothesis, rather than with new designs, new methods of pricing and new institutional solutions. Sankar suggests flexibility in curriculum so that students can, after having studied under one discipline, also study topics of their choice under another discipline. To encourage this, special fellowships may be awarded. Publishers in social sciences also have to learn new ways of evaluating manuscripts submitted, giving more weight to innovation rather than simply to sophistication of analysis.[1]

The role and nature of SSR can very much depend upon whether the institution concerned is in the public domain or private domain. Prof. M.V. Nadkarni clearly distinguishes between the two types of institutions and brings out the role of public domain SSR in to a sharp focus. He asserts that the distinction between the two should not be based on the source of funding, as it would not be meaningful academically. It should instead be based on the criterion of whether the outcome of research is open to all interested academicians and the public, either for scrutiny or use or for both, in the form of publication and other forms of dissemination. If so, it would legitimately be in the public domain. If on the other hand, the outcome of research is claimed for private use by the sponsor of research, and is not open to the public, then it is a private domain SSR. Merely because a research is funded by the government, it does not become a public domain SSR. Even research funded by private agencies or trusts can be in the public domain, if its outcome is open to the public.[2] This criterion is applicable not only to research but also to SSR institutions.

1. Prof. V.M. Rao, in his oral presentation of his paper mentioned the interesting example of Dr. Samuel Paul's 'Citizen Report Card'. It was an extremely simple device of evaluating citizens' level of satisfaction with various services provided by the government. Normally, it would have had a ghost of chance of being published in a prestigious traditionally academic journal. But it received wide publicity, because of its high innovativeness and immense value. It was replicated in different states, and was reported to have been referred even by the Prime Minister.

2. It is not correct to assume that private funding for research is always market-oriented or with narrow interest, and that government funding invariably encourages research with a broad and long-term vision.

The role of public domain SSR follows from the above criterion. It is to inform public opinion or even to form it, kindle democratic debate, add to the stock of knowledge—both public and academic, help social and economic development and guide it and of course capacity building in SSR, helping to reproduce competent researchers. This role can be played by SSR only if it leads to dissemination of research outcome to a wider audience. Of course, a prior academic or peer review before publication is a healthy procedure to ensure quality. But even here the author should have the right to defend herself/himself and even reject peer suggestions, offering convincing explanation for such rejection in the genuine exploration of truth. Secondly, the refereeing peers should be genuinely autonomous, having a high academic standing, but not glorified agents of sponsors of research projects who would want only research findings palatable to them to be published. Often, however, the researcher herself/himself can be an obstacle in taking the research findings to the public, if she/he is not capable of putting them in simple terms and drawing out policy implications at least in the concluding section of the research.

Nadkarni is equally concerned about the dangers of doctored research, which can vitiate the very role of public domain SSR. Doctored research takes place when the researcher, consciously or not, succumbs to temptations and threats of sponsors of research projects to present the findings in a way palatable to the sponsors. But how to distinguish between doctored research and a genuine one? A balanced presentation of findings, pointing out both successes and grave failures supported with all relevant facts and figures, and taking all dimensions and factors in to account, is more likely to be an instance of free and fearless research. But it is far better to be cautious about doctoring in the first instance itself. For this, and for the general health of SSR institutions, it is necessary to have some core funding, untied to any particular research projects, so that these institutions are not overdependent on tied grants. It is also necessary to create an atmosphere of academic freedom. If an academician shows the courage to resist arm-twisting by bureaucrats or politicians in charge of giving fund and has such standing in academic stature that nobody would dare to influence her or him, such academicians should be supported in any hour of tension with sponsors. Right to publish, making the research open to public scrutiny and criticism also ensures free, fair and honest research. Any institution which prods researchers to jump to another project no sooner than one is published or without giving time to publish, is doomed to mediocrity.

Nadkarni also feels that wherever possible, 'activist research' or 'transformative praxis' should be encouraged on the part of researchers, so that ground realities in the actual process of social change in to desired directions are better understood. A glorious example of such research is that of Prof. Muhammad Yunus in Bangladesh, for which he won the Nobel Prize.

Nadkarni suggests a regular periodical monitoring of all SSR institutions by peers in terms of at least three criteria, among others:

i) how much scope is there for creativity and own research agenda?;
ii) how far is interdisciplinary at multidisciplinary research is undertaken?;
iii) How far is genuine fieldwork undertaken in field research?

SSR institutions have to play a much more active role in capacity building. Only one or two of them have a master level programme, and only one or two more have M.Phil. More, however, have a PhD programme, but not all of them offer coursework as a part of it. These institutions, to showcase their usefulness, have to give more attention to education and research training. Nadkarni suggests that the emphasis in research training should not be only on quantitative techniques, but also in enabling the trainees to acquire a wider vision, a larger picture, and develop aptitude and skills for holistic and creative thinking (see Nadkarni, 2009).

In his thought-provoking paper "Promoting Research Culture and Atmosphere", the veteran economist from Yale University, Prof. T.N. Srinivasan, raises an important issue. He brings to bear his insights from the experience from USA to see how the situation in India, particularly the incentive structure, could be improved. He is not very happy at the way teaching and researches are institutionally isolated, with the former assigned to universities and the latter to 'free-standing' institutes autonomous from the university. He mentions the consequent sad fact that 'not a single Indian university is among the top hundred universities in the world'.

Why India fares poorly in research culture is built in to the recruitment process itself. In any research institution or university in USA, the faculty as a whole is involved in the assessment of candidates. Secondly, permanent tenure is given only after an initial term of six years in the case of associate professors and nine years in the case of professors and that too, only if the departmental committee recommends it and if selected tenured academicians in other universities also approve it. The latter are free to recommend alternative names. On the other hand, in India, there is almost automatic job security after a brief period of probation. This creates complacence and blunts competition. In USA, teachers are expected not only to be good in teaching, but also be active at the frontiers of knowledge in research, the benefit of which is expected to go to students. The salaries are not uniform across institutions in USA, further stimulating competition and upward academic drive and mobility. The rules for consultancy and leave benefits are transparent, as also benefits like contributions to health care. The desirability of some of the changes in USA, however, may be debatable. For example, Srinivasan quotes Rebecca Lowen about the post-war university being a "large collection of academic entrepreneurs—scientists and scholars perpetually promoting themselves and their research to potential patrons". The amount of research grants won by teachers in universities is an important criterion of their eminence and success.[3]

Taking the desirable aspects of US research culture and atmosphere, Srinivasan offers an agenda of reform. He wants a healthier balance in research orientation as between universities and 'free-standing' research institutions. This requires increased emphasis on research in the universities. It may be recalled that ICSSR's research and publication grants for projects are open to university teachers too, but

3. Teachers and researchers obtaining large research grants are very highly regarded in Indian universities and research institutions too. However, teachers in universities are at the same time expected not to sacrifice their commitment to teaching. Besides, in India, it is relatively much more difficult to get funding for 'delayed return' research projects and easier to get it for projects of immediate policy relevance. In USA, it is not so, and the sponsors have a wider vision of what is expected of research. An exclusive emphasis on the faculty raising large grants in India may have an adverse impact on fundamental or 'delayed return research'.

its resources are too meagre to restore a balance between teaching and research in universities. The UGC has more scope, but university funds for research projects too are quite meagre. Srinivasan seeks more incentives for teachers to obtain funding from private sponsors too. He feels, however, that "UGC and ICSSR, in their regulatory roles, are quintessentially institutions of the late unlamented license-permit-raj (LPR) era. Just as the design of LPR stifled competition, creativity and innovation, the same is true in my judgement of UGC and ICSSR, notwithstanding their role in the creation of centres of excellence...." However, the ICSSR at least has much more of a promotional role than a regulatory role. Besides, it would be disastrous to dismantle ICSSR and bring its institutes directly under the government. Nor is it possible to leave universities and research institutes to fend for themselves on the basis of 'self-financing' principle. Srinivasan seems to think that an important effect of UGC regulatory framework is the rigidity in the salary grades and structures and his reform agenda is to loosen them up.[4] Srinivasan also recommends introduction of "analogues of summer research support as well as sabbaticals and also...clear rules for consultancies, leave of absence with or without pay, etc." He suggests a 'systemic approach' for ensuring the autonomy of research institutions and avoiding neglect of research in areas which are not attractive to private sponsors. He wants more seriousness to devices such as annual 'Activities Report' from teachers and researchers, which should not only be comprehensive enough to help in ensuring accountability, but should serve as an input for salary fixation from year to year. Prof. Srinivasan's suggestions deserve serious consideration both by academicians and policy makers in academics.

---

4. It is not that there is no flexibility in salaries paid in Indian colleges but ironically, it is downward and has disastrous implications. When I was the Vice Chancellor of a university in Karnataka, a delegation of teachers of a women's college which was 'unaided' (not receiving salary grants from the government) came to meet me and complained that they received salaries which were lower than that of peons in the university! Except trying "moral persuasion" with the college management, the university could not do much to improve the situation and give them UGC scales of pay. UGC scales can play the role of providing for at least a 'minimum price' or 'guaranteed price', but they may not work in 'unaided' institutions.

Prof. T.S. Papola has offered several valuable insights in his paper "National Perspective on Social Science Development in India". Tracing the development of SSR in India, he takes note of the fast increase in a huge output, "throwing up a large volume of useful information, which in many cases was fruitfully utilised". He adds, this information "succeeded in exploding certain myths about Indian society. It also brought out evidence to question several theoretical propositions on the inter-relationships among socio-economic variables and, in many cases, provided direction for formulating alternative propositions". He also observes that the formation of ICSSR itself, with the promotion of social science research as its main objective, helped considerably in the process of acceleration of research output.

Papola rues that "all this advancement of knowledge has not, however, been adequately reflected in the teaching of social sciences". He points out reasons for it. First of all, teaching and research are organisationally isolated from each other. University teaching is modeled after western theories and texts, and the textbooks in social sciences are slow in picking up new research findings and relating them to theory. There is a general inertia in universities and colleges to change the course content and to write textbooks which contain new knowledge. In many university departments of social sciences, "research activity is virtually non-existent". On the other hand, the research institutes do not have regular teaching as their main activity, so that "researchers in these institutions do not get directly incorporated in class room instruction, except in a limited way and with a time lag after the research results get published". Another reason for this cleavage between teaching and research is that, "the research findings themselves are not always of such definitive value as to get included easily in the syllabi, textbooks and classroom instructions".

Is this vast research output at least used in policy formulation and implementation? Papola of course observes that there is "increasing realisation of the importance of and greater responsiveness to social science research by the government and official agencies during the recent decades". Papola, however, also says that it is unrealistic to expect all this SSR output being directly used by the government. Often, the research findings are presented in such a guarded and qualified fashion, that officials may be wondering what to do with them. An eminent political leader (Winston Churchill?) is reported to have said that he wanted a one-handed advisor, and not someone who offers advice in terms of 'on the one hand' and 'on the other'. Papola asserts, however, that a dichotomy between rigorous, analytically sound research and research useful for policy is a false one. Good research should also be a useful research. It is the duty of researchers to state the qualifications or limitations to their findings clearly, and it is for officials to weigh the pros and cons of a certain policy in the light of those qualifications and risks involved. If the researcher had not stated such qualifications, such a prior scrutiny of policies would not be possible for officials or ministers. Social and economic changes are taking place at a fast pace in several instances, and policy recommendations made in a static setting without making clear under what circumstances such policy is desirable, would not be very useful for implementation.

Has this vast SSR output helped in indigenising social and economic theories or creating Indian schools of thought? Papola feels, it has not, though it has certainly improved our understanding of the Indian economy, society and polity. But it has not helped in developing new and indigenous theoretical frameworks. Though Papola's observation has some truth, it is also not true that there have been no such attempts. Dadabhai Naoroji's work on the Drain Theory and J.C. Kumarappa's work on developing Gandhian economics are classic examples of developing indigenous theorisations. Marxists have significantly contributed to theorising the Indian political economy, particularly with reference to Indian agriculture. Krishna Bharadwaj's work (1974) *Production Conditions in Indian Agriculture*, which stimulated a big 'Mode of Production Debate'[5] were serious attempts at theorising. No less noteworthy is C.T. Kurien's work on developing a theory of the Indian economy (1992 and 1996). When we come to sociology, we have the famous work by M.N. Srinivas on Sanskritisation. Theoretical work by Indian social scientists may not be quantitatively as significant as that of western social scientists. But we have to appreciate that this took place in a research environment heavily oriented towards empirical works. Perhaps that is why the Indian work

5. For a review of this debate, see Nadkarni (1991).

on theorising has a close relation with empirical research, and not divorced from it.

In his oral presentation, though not in the written paper itself, Papola took up the issues of autonomy and accountability. He commended the role of ICSSR, which acted as a buffer between social scientists and SSR institutions on the one hand and government on the other. If this buffer were missing, there would have been little autonomy in SSR, as it would have been directly funded and controlled by the government. Papola, however, insists that social scientists themselves have to evolve procedures and practices of accountability—both to the academics themselves and to the society. Autonomy cannot be sustained for long without accountability and if we resent government or official intervention, we have to evolve our own credible system.

In his perceptive paper "Social Science Research Capacity in South Asia", Prof. Satish Deshpande laments the fact that SSR institutions and universities are not attractive anymore to the 'elite' candidates. This is not only because of low salaries there, but also because, as he puts it, "the broader context where socialism, planned development, nationalism, and also the general urge for progress carried meaning" in the decades preceding the economic reforms, has changed in favour of other ideologies of the market, the individual and globalisation. As such, academic positions are not glamourous anymore, compared to careers in management, banking, journalism and "even the newly professsionalised and lucrative 'NGO' world". Deshpande also points out that "the major crisis in South Asian social science research capacity is not so much in the production of research as in the production of researchers". Elite preference is to go to the West both as students and teachers. This trend as well as the trend towards 'contract research' based on global tenders, affects both research and research capacity—not necessarily in a desirable way! Researchers based in the West look for collaboration mainly in short-term policy-driven research. This has "created a menu of globally portable 'pre-fab' methodologies that claim universal applicability". Such a development is hardly conducive to creativity. Deshpande observes that the unequal academic relationship with the

West is to be found within the country too. In the more economically backward regions, accessibility to facilities of research or developing research capacity is lower. When even the elite academic institutions find it difficult to recruit talent, one can only imagine the plight of the less fortunate. While academic exchanges with the West get fairly good amount of funds and attention, this is hardly the case with exchanges within the country or between countries in South Asia. A greater emphasis on academic exchanges within the country or within South Asia would have toned down the sharpness of academic asymmetries between elite institutions and others.

The paper by Prof. M.S.S. Pandian "Social Sciences in South India: A Survey", insightfully maps the institutional resources available for capacity building and research in social sciences in south India, followed by two case studies of Madras Institute of Development Studies (MIDS) at Chennai and ISEC at Bangalore. To start with, Pandian takes note of a 'sense of crisis in social science institutions', which is fostered by their treatment by the state as of 'non-utility', resulting in downsizing of state funding. Unfortunately, as Pandian remarks, these institutions have 'failed to come up with an alternative logic of their very existence'. The alleged treatment of SSR institutions by the state as of 'non-utility' may seem exaggerated, if we take note of the close relation between the state and at least some of these institutions, and the continuous, even if inadequate, support provided to them. A high level of state patronage may have its own academic costs, which is why some of these institutions have kept the state at a reasonable distance at least in governance. However, a greater keenness of the state governments to give project-based funding instead of untied block grants, can pose serious academic problems. Much depends on the relationship and understanding between these institutions and state governments, generalisations being hazardous. Often the crisis is due to a crash in the demand for certain courses in the job market. The example, cited by Pandian, of "dependence of history in a number of universities to reinvent their function as one of training students to be tourist guides" is more an illustration of the effect of the situation of demand in the job market than of treatment of such departments by the state as of 'non-utility'. Ironically, in the example cited, the department did come up with an 'alternative logic of (its) very existence', but it proved to be academically much less exciting!

Pandian presents a comprehensive scanning of institutions covering the most important aspects—capacity building in research, state of libraries, archives and documentation centres, professional associations, local social science journals, inter-institutional interactions, infrastructure facilities for research, state of diversity in academic disciplines, and of course, funding problems. His account is impartial and balanced, both in his wider scanning and his two case studies, throwing several useful insights.

For example, his account of how bureaucratic handling of the state archives in Karnataka, making it an appendage of the state legislature, has damaged the cause of historical research, is revealing. Pandian points out that researchers prefer to take up topics of research on the erstwhile Madras Presidency, because of a more professional handling of the state archives there. He observes that the reason for the poor state of archives in Karnataka is to be found more in the lack of vision as to how to make it useful for researchers, than in the lack of funding.

Pandian's another insight is on what factor is conducive for diversity in academic disciplines. He notes that ISEC could succeed in achieving a remarkable diversity both in the faculty composition and research output and in the magnitude of collaborative work done, better than many other SSR institutions, mainly because of its fairly larger size. It is the largest of ICSSR institutions and its sheer size made it successful not only in achieving diversity, but also in running a viable PhD programme involving coursework and in conducting other training programmes as well.

Pandian also raises the issue of the dilemma faced by SSR institutions between turning out quality research acceptable in terms of high academic standards and attracting more funds by way of project-based policy-oriented research (with which to finance infrastructure facilities, computers and library needed for research). He indicates that while MIDS opted for the first choice, ISEC opted for the second. Pandian concedes, however, that policy research need not be less academic, and can in fact bridge the gap between academia and society.

He quotes an interview with Prof. M. Govinda Rao (then Director of ISEC when Pandian's study was in progress), to the effect that it is possible to produce high quality research even out of project-based policy-oriented research publishable in reputed academic journals, apart from the fact that projects make it easier to get access to data which are not otherwise available.

We may come now to the issues related to ICSSR itself, which has been a significant—if not a bulk—source of support both fund-wise and academically, not only to institutions under it for block grants but also to others (including university departments of social sciences and independent SSR institutions). One such issue is that of autonomy from bureaucratic and political control by the state. What about the autonomy of ICSSR itself, let alone individual SSR institutions? The functioning and performance of ICSSR has so far been reviewed four times—first in 1973, second time in 1976, third in 1986, and the fourth after a pretty long gap in 2007 under the chairmanship of Prof. A. Vaidyanathan. An overview of the latest is presented in Vaidyanathan's paper here. The Review Committee observes that "social research is increasingly commercialised and driven by the interests of the sponsors as distinct from public interest". The ICSSR has been unable to reverse this trend, due to its organisational weaknesses and also lack of adequate resources. It is created and wholly funded by the government. Though it is supposed to be autonomous and is free to make decisions, these decisions are subject to government approval. Ex-officio government representatives presently constitute far too high a proportion of the Council membership. Appointments of the chairperson, member secretary and non-official members of the Council are all decided by the government. Lack of transparency in the criteria and procedures for these appointments and failure to observe the spirit of the provisions of MoA have eroded the credibility of the Council as an autonomous and professional body! The Review Committee further observes that all this has a cumulative effect, and have "severely constrained the Council's capacity to plan and consistently pursue a coherent long term strategy and prioritise different activities."

The Committee's recommendations are aimed at de-bureaucratising and professionalising the Council, strengthening its financial independence and augmenting its resources. The Committee proposes reconstituting the Council as the Indian Academy of Social Sciences, whose governing body will comprise eminent scholars from different social sciences and a limited number of government representatives. The governing body will lay down the general policy, and an executive council will be responsible for its implementation. The Committee proposes that the executive council will be free to decide, without any requirement of government approval, all matters relating to strategy and research funding, prioritising different activities, procedures, for giving grants and monitoring and peer review of outputs, internal personnel policies and financial controls. Periodic peer review of the Academy's performance, which should be compulsory, has to be done by a committee of eminent social scientists.

If promoting knowledge-generating research is the main mandate of the Academy (or the Council), the Review Committee feels that its sources of funding have to be widened. It cannot be confined to an individual department (like HRD, as is the case now). Since the country as a whole has a stake in the healthy growth of social sciences and SSR, the Committee suggests that "a mere 0.1 per cent of public sector plan outlay be earmarked for social science research", thus involving the government as a whole in funding it. The Review Committee is sceptical about the private sector and international funding agencies being interested in funding such research, but feels that the Council may be left free to decide whether and on what terms it accepts offers of funds from such sources. As Guha has observed (2008: 34), with the surge in the growth of the Indian economy, philanthropists from the private sector with a broad and long-term vision should not be found wanting. There were such philanthropists even in the past like the Tatas. If we are afraid of strings attached from such sources, shouldn't we be equally cautious about exclusive dependence on the government functionaries and politicians?

Coming to individual research institutes, while the funding of those under the Council should be much more liberal, the Review Committee at the same time proposes that renewals of research grants to them should not be automatic. It should be based on a review of the performance both in terms of quality and meeting time schedules. It may be desirable to identify both the strong and weak institutes, and learn from their experience. For example, a committee could probe in to the secrets of strength or of good performance in some, as against why some are laggards. Over-bureaucratisation, rigidity, lack of democratic structures and transparent procedures, non-viable faculty size, lack of incentives and prospects for the faculty, a reluctance to encourage a second line leadership may be some of the problems affecting growth and performance of such institutes, apart of course from the problem of paucity of resources. We know enough about the sad state of SSR in India on the whole, but we do not still have a clear enough idea about how to change it for the better. How do we attract talent in to SSR? How do we motivate them to innovative research and knowledge-creation? Will a more flexible, performance-based salary structure instead of the present uniform 'scales of pay' help? Once a person is made a confirmed professor, the increments are automatic, and termination of service on the basis of indifference to work is next to impossible!

The next paper by Prof. Partha Chatterjee "The Near Future of Social Science Research in India", takes a critical look at the Fourth Review Committee Report on ICSSR and offers alternative plans which may be more feasible for a better-though, near-future for SSR. Chatterjee is doubtful if the Committee's proposal to make the Government of India, as a whole—with all its ministries, instead of the single Ministry of Human Resources Development—responsible for funding the reconstituted council, feasible at all, given our bureaucratic culture. This culture, Chatterjee is afraid, is unlikely to change following the Committee's recommendations! Other ministries will hardly be willing to contribute, except giving project-specific grants, unless they too have an institutional control over the council. He also asks if doing away with or belittling government representatives on the council is desirable. They are 8 now, as against 18 social scientists. He feels, it is actually helpful to have government nominees on the governing body of an organisation, as they help to keep the channel of funds flowing smoothly. Chatterjee, of course concedes that it is important to have autonomy, whatever be the source of funding. Unfortunately, as he observes, "erosion of autonomy in institutions of high education and research, has not been a one-way process of aggressive intervention by politicians and bureaucrats". Academicians have been equally guilty of inviting intervention of politically powerful figures to sort out their institutional problems or furthering their professional interests." In any case, he is afraid, that it is unlikely that the formal system of government nominations will end any time soon, at least till we are financially dependent on them. Chatterjee also points out that only about half a dozen or so among the 27 ICSSR institutions are genuinely viable. Though the Vaidyanathan Committee report documents this, it does not indicate what to do with the non-viable ones. Chatterjee does not agree with the Committee's suggestion to freeze the funding of all ICSSR institutes at their current levels and leave them to fill the gap with project-based funds. Such an arrangement will hardly help the institutes in developing any long-term research plans and the process of knowledge-creation. This has been a weakness already, and will only be further aggravated. Even 'building and nurturing a faculty based on long term institutional vision' will not be possible.

Chatterjee offers two alternative plans. One, rank the ICSSR institutes in terms of performance periodically, and base the funding on such ranking. Second, connect ICSSR and its institutes with the imminent expansion of Central universities. The research institutes would be very useful in designing some innovative postgraduate and doctoral-level course and programmes. Chatterjee foresees rapid changes in India in the next few years in the scenario of higher education and research, and we have to think of our opportunities as well as dangers.

The paper by Prof. Michael Lamb of the University of Cambridge, "A View from Abroad" is also a comment on the Fourth Review Committee Report. As the Chairman of the International Advisory Committee on the Economic and Social Research Council (ESRC) of the United Kingdom, he read the Report and found it to be an invaluable resource to understand ICSSR and develop programme relationships between the two councils. He finds the Report sensitive and constructive, as well as candid. Lamb feels that, "all good social scientific theories need to be grounded in the real world and to make empirically testable predictions, just as all good applied research should both be grounded in and help further develop the theoretical aspects of relevant disciplines." But he was alarmed at the review report's suggestion that the prevailing situation in India falls far short of this ideal. Though "politicisation and commercialisation of scientific research is by no means unique either to India or to the social sciences", the situation seems to be more alarming in India, according to the Review Committee Report. This has damaging implications for the credibility of Indian social scientists, which is not good for India. At least for this reason, the Review Committee Report merits careful attention, adds Lamb.

He heartily endorses the Committee's call for major increase in funding, so that social scientists are not vulnerable to pressures of patrons to tailor their questions and answers to suit the patrons' interests. Increased funding on a transparent basis has the potential to rejuvenate social science disciplines in India, he feels. Social scientists, led by ICSSR, need to make the case that a vibrant social science community will save the country and its citizens more broadly, not only the narrow interests of social scientists themselves. For this, there is a need to judiciously advertise instances of high quality research informing decision-making. The council also has to demonstrate its willingness to differentially reward high quality social research and withhold support and funding from mediocrity and failure.

There are, however, other considerations too in funding social research institutes across the width and breadth of the country particularly. An important consideration is capacity building in social science research in different regions including the economically backward, so that research capacity is distributed more evenly, instead of being concentrated only in a few metropolitan centres. A second such consideration is to focus on the problems of a wide diversity of regions, through researchers from the regions themselves as far as desirable, as they are expected to know their regions from their lived experiences. They only need an opportunity for good training and expression provided by such institutes. Institutes located in *mofussil* areas have their own problems. Such institutes are generally of non-viable size, they find it difficult to attract faculty who on the whole prefer to live in large cities with well-developed infrastructure and their faculty are too shy to assert themselves and be heard. What is worse, a *mofussil* background is a negative factor with publishers who generally prefer authors from known and established institutions in metropolitan areas. With such disadvantages, such institutes deserve a special consideration. It is wrong to presume that their research output is all substandard or useless.

Given our obsession with the use of highly sophisticated quantitative and mathematical tools of research as the mark of high quality research, rather than social relevance in the long run, there is a risk at times of judging even good research as mediocre if it uses simple common sense tools understandable to all. Nobody will disagree with the need to encourage high quality social research and discourage mediocrity, but it is necessary to also realise that it is a complex issue with no straightforward and unambiguous criteria of judging, especially in borderline cases. As Anjan Mukherjee insightfully remarks in his paper here, "very seldom is there disagreement over which research is bad and which is not; disagreement generally occurs over marginal contributions. The difficulty is that a substantial volume of research is in this marginal category." A further difficulty is that this 'marginal category' research cannot be swept away as waste in terms of policy of social relevance. Often it may have very useful insights though they may be presented in a raw form or unattractive package! Seniors have to take some time off from pushing their own research agenda and spend some time with the younger researchers to guide them in improving their data analysis and presentation, and can also undertake an overview of such contributions on a particular issue separating grain from the chaff and bring together the findings in a coherent manner. Such an act on the part of seniors will yield the double benefit of capacity building and also of transforming what could have been a waste in to a useful research outcome. To suspend support to all such research in the name of discouraging mediocrity is like discouraging the production of paddy as it comes with some husk!

The seminar, and consequently this volume, has succeeded in analysing complex issues in social science research in a frank manner, bringing out rich insights. It is hoped that they will contribute in serving the purpose of improving the social research situation in the country, at least through sharpened awareness of our shortcomings made possible by the seminar.

References

Bharadwaj, Krishna (1974). *Production Conditions in Indian Agriculture—A Study Based on Farm Management Surveys*. London: Cambridge University Press.

Guha, Ramachandra (2008). "Autonomy and ideology", *Economic and Political Weekly* 42(5): 33-35, February 2.

Kurien, C.T. (1992). *The Economy: An Interpretative Introduction*. New Delhi: Sage.

———. (1996). *Rethinking Economics—Reflections Based on a Study of the Indian Economy*. New Delhi: Sage.

Nadkarni, M.V. (1991). "The mode of production debate: A review article", *Indian Economic Review* 26(1): 99-104.

———. (2009). "Limits of analytical method: A perspective from Bhagavadgita for holistic social science research", *Think India Quarterly* 12(2): 32-45, April-June.

Rao, V.K.R.V. (1974). *Growth with Justice in Asian Agriculture: An Exercise in Policy Formulation*. Geneva: UN Research Institute for Social Development.

———. (2008). "The problem of relevance in social science research", reproduced in *The Indian Economic Journal* 56(2): 110-117, July-September (Special issue on Dr. V.K.R.V. Rao), (Inaugural Address at a Seminar in IEG, Delhi, in April 1980).

2 Social Science in India

Some Institutional Issues[1]

T.C.A. Anant

Introduction

Social science research as a private endeavour has ancient origins. But public, state supported, social science research is of more recent origins. In part, it is related to the fact that development as a goal of policy is a relatively recent phenomenon in political history. While social scientists had engaged with issues and concepts of development even earlier, it was not explicitly stated as an objective of governments. It is in the UN charter, for the first time we find the signatories pledging themselves to "promote social progress and better standards of life". In India, in a similar vein we see the Constitution seeking to secure social and economic justice for all its citizens, and explicitly stating in Article 38 "State to secure a social order for the promotion of welfare of the people. (1) The State shall strive to promote the welfare of the people by securing and protecting as effectively as it may a social order in which justice, social, economic and political, shall inform all the institutions of the national life." But this emphasis posed special challenges for the Government of India, as with other emerging new states in the post-colonial world, of converting these goals into specific actions of policy.

In 1947, the government of the newly independent republic faced exactly this problem. They sought to fill this gap through the establishment of the Planning Commission. But the process of

1. The views expressed in the paper are personal and do not reflect the decisions or position of the Council. This paper draws extensively on the data and material gathered by the Fourth ICSSR Review Committee (FIRC) report. I have also benefited from discussions and comments from Prof. Andre Beteille, Prof. Javeed Alam, Dr. Arun Bali and Dr. Ranjit Sinha who have seen earlier versions of this note. However, all faults and lacuna are on my account.

formulating plans needed information and knowledge about specific social problems. In 1953, the Planning Commission established the Research Programmes Committee to work out and administer suitable schemes of research and investigation into social, economic and administrative problems relating to national development. Thus, in its first three years the Committee chose four areas related to: (1) savings, investment, employment and small-scale industries, (2) regional development and urbanisation, (3) land reforms, cooperation and farm management, and (4) social welfare problems and public administration.

The Planning Commission, and more specifically its Research Programmes Committee, marked the first attempts (Goodall, 1957) to incorporate social research into policy formulation in India. In an analysis of this programme it was pointed out, "Majority of these projects...are being directed by a ranking professor of a university department, most frequently economics, but also anthropology and law, among others. These men are busy, overloaded with government assignments, and many of them, are now for the first time engaged in empirical studies." In addition, the late fifties and sixties also saw a rapid growth in the higher education system, in part as a result of the recommendations of the education commissions, putting even greater stress on the research infrastructure. It was in this background that there were concerns about the institutional framework in which the research was carried out. There was a felt need to examine this structure with a view to give it a clearer focus and make it more effective. Thus in August 1965, the Planning Commission set up a committee for social science research (CSSR) under the chairmanship of Prof. V.K.R.V. Rao (Planning Commission, 1968).

The CSSR pointed out that the importance of social science research goes beyond the immediate needs of policy. They thus sought to expand the framework of public support for social science research beyond the objectives of the Research Programmes Committee (RPC). The committee pointed out that "understanding of the social phenomena and human behavior, knowledge about the social process and its determinants, are essential for designing policies to promote social change and to produce a dynamic society capable of absorbing and utilising the scientific and technological developments, for the welfare of human beings." They also noted that existing mechanisms of funding through UGC or the project research of government would not be adequate to create the capacity or the body of work needed for a robust national social science. Thus, they felt there is need for public funding for social science research and recommended the creation of an independent autonomous body for the promotion of social science research.

There was a second factor underlying the setting up of the ICSSR to promote an autonomous national research agenda. In the fifties, India's development strategy combining markets and the state was seen as a counter to the emerging "threat of communism".[2] Thus, a number of US agencies and foundations began working in India. However, the sixties saw a distinct cooling in this relationship. Further the developments in Vietnam and the disclosure that a number of US universities and foundations were funded by or in collaboration with the CIA[3] raised fears about hidden agendas and the possible loss of control over national research and thus policy. Though not officially articulated, these concerns get reflected in numerous places. Thus from the beginning, it was felt that the ICSSR would help promote a "national" research agenda. In this paper, we explore some institutional dimensions in social science research from the perspective of ICSSR and its policies.

The ICSSR

The ICSSR was set up pursuant to Government Resolution No. F.9-50/68.plg dated 12 December 1968. The Council was to function with a

2. The Ford Foundation's assessment of its role in India described in *Forty Years: A Learning Curve: The Ford Foundation in India 1952-1992* (Eugene S. Staples, Ford 1992), "the Gaither report in January 1950 shows clearly that the Foundation's trustees were deeply concerned about the Communist takeover in China and the broadening of the still new conflict between Soviet-led communism and the Western democracies that was already being called the 'cold war'. Hoffman believed that world peace 'might well be determined by what happened in India'. Chester Bowles, soon to become the American Ambassador to New Delhi, had reported to Hoffman his own enthusiastic views about India's plans for development and the Indian Government's receptivity to new ideas and technology."

3. The Asia Foundation, it was revealed, had received CIA funds. It was asked to leave India in 1972, (Source see for instance, Datta-Ray, 2005).

variety of objectives. But principally these involved the sponsoring of research programmes and research projects, coordinating research activities in the field of social sciences, acting as an intermediary between government and the research community and finally to give development and maintenance grants to research institutes in social science that do not constitute or are affiliates of statutory universities in India.[4] The work of the ICSSR has been documented and reviewed in reports of four independent review committees. The most recent (fourth) review has just been completed and is in the public domain for detailed discussions.

The Council in 1971 declared that "The primary objective of the Indian Council of Social Science Research is to promote research in social sciences and to facilitate its utilisation. To this end it will strive to identify and develop research talent, provide support to research projects and programs of quality, build up the essential infrastructure including clearing house facilities and promote the development of professional organizations of social scientists." In this connection, they identified the role of the council in four distinct ways:

Responsive Role: Research in social science being a creative endeavour, requires freedom and initiative on the part of the individual scholar. The Council therefore should respond with understanding and sympathy to the initiatives of social scientists in the promotion of research.

Promotional Role: There were many elements to this which included: to identify and develop young talent; promoting excellence in research by supporting scholars and centres of proven worth; to broaden the research base by providing support in far-flung areas; take the initiative in encouraging and developing collaborative research; to conduct surveys of research; to identify research gaps and promote programmes in such priority areas; and to identify and promote development of critical areas of social science research. However, it was

4. This was added as an objective at the end of the Fourth Plan, but was quite significantly, for the point of its future functioning, never reflected in modifications of its articles of association. Consequences of this lack of institutional concern are clearly outlined in the various ICSSR review reports.

noted that in doing this it will ensure that funds are available in other areas as well.

A large part of the effort of ICSSR has been in implementing these two roles. To meet its responsive obligations, it has created schemes for giving grants to scholars for fellowships, projects, holding and attending seminars and such other purposes. The promotional mandate was partly admixed with this in giving some weight to youth, location, discipline etc., in the process of selection. In addition, the council has sought to promote research in certain identified areas such as health, elections, gender as part of its promotional mandate. But there is a considerable lack of understanding in the Council about these two roles and their distinct procedural requirements.[5] As we note later in the paper, it also started funding research institutions in what can be described as in pursuit of the promotional objective.[6]

Coordination and Networking Role: That the Council should maintain close relationships with other agencies involved in funding social science research. It should seek to play a clearing-house function. In promotion of this goal, the Council created small schemes to fund journals and associations of social scientists. It established a documentation centre to facilitate networking. But these remained rather limited. And finally there is also an advisory role; the MoA (Memorandum of Association) of Council mandates that it will advise the government on matters referred to it.[7] This is an enabling role for the Council, its use depends on other wings of the government recognising the Council and asking for its advice. There have been some

5. The best example can be seen in the internal confusion on funding for training in research methodology. This is clearly by its definition and objective a promotional activity but was, for lack of clarity on its fundamental purpose effectively, converted over the years to a responsive activity.

6. Though one must note a frank historical assessment of the actual process followed in funding some of the research institutes and sponsored programmes, they can only be described as responsive as they originated not out of any internal initiative of the Council but rather in response to suggestions and requests from individuals or group of individuals.

7. Significantly what the Council does not have is an advocacy role. This would allow the councils to engage with the government on its use of social science. However, as social policy research has strong ideological elements to it, an advocacy role would raise complex issues of maintaining autonomy in a democratic setting.

significant outcomes of this, most recently was the research programme initiated at the request of the Ministry of Minority Affairs. But its effectiveness depends to a large measure on the awareness of the Council and its objectives amongst the different agencies of government, which even after 40 years is low.

The actual working of the Council over the past 40 years has seen an unbalanced and unstable mix of these roles. This imbalance has had various consequences: first, what was an add-on programme, namely institutional funding, has grown to dominate the Council's activities; funding for research institutes has grown from around 33 per cent in early eighties to close to 60 per cent of the Council budget in recent years. The non-institutional funding has been reduced to primarily responsive mode funding with the most promotional elements being limited to preferences for age, location etc., in selection of responsive mode grants. This compositional change has had a major impact on the quality and direction of the Council's effort. The latter two categories of coordination and advice have attracted less attention. The eventual elimination of coordination elements from the Council's list of activities has hampered the growth of a dynamic social science community. The last category of advice, is as we noted almost non-existent, and whatever activities take place under it are more due to happenstance than any serious sense of purpose in government. We examine some of the implications of this imbalance in our discussion.[8]

Research Institutes

It is important to note that the 1971 description of the Council's role and activities does not include what has become the major role of the Council namely funding research institutions. Along with its recommendation for setting up an Indian Council of Social Science Research, the CSSR had suggested that one of the main functions of the Council would be, "To give maintenance grants to research institutions in social sciences that do not constitute either affiliated or constituent institutions of statutory universities in India."

8. The Fourth Review Committee does a similar assessment; an excellent summary of their recommendations can be seen in the overview paper presented by Prof. Vaidyanathan in the February 2, 2008 issue of the EPW.

However, while accepting the report, the Government of India decided to keep the programme of supporting research institutions as a separate scheme. The scheme of grant-in-aid to research institutions in the field of social sciences, which are not eligible for assistance from the University Grants Commission (UGC), was introduced in 1969. In 1971, rules were framed for assisting research institutions in the field of social sciences, which were not eligible for grants from the UGC. In the Fourth Five Year Plan, it was operated directly by the Ministry of Education and Social Welfare (now Ministry of Human Resource Development). The Ministry of Education and Social Welfare at the behest of the Planning Commission also started entering into dialogues with state governments for establishing new research institutes.

The objective was to supplement the university system and help rectify some of the major gaps in social science research in India. More specifically, the institutes were intended to undertake in-depth research in social sciences, especially of an inter-disciplinary nature, focusing major socioeconomic issues both at the national and regional level; to facilitate collaboration and interaction among academics working in different universities and institutes; to enhance the capability of young, prospective researchers through well-designed training programmes; and bring out the policy implications of the research findings. This led to the setting up of institutes in Calcutta and Allahabad. In addition, some pre-existing centrally funded institutes[9] were also brought under the scheme. At the end of the Fourth Five Year Plan, close to nine institutes were receiving support and a few others were being examined. The Ministry of Education then proposed that this scheme be transferred to the ICSSR in the Fifth Year Plan period.

To examine this proposal, the ICSSR set up a committee under the chairmanship of Prof. M.S. Gore.[10] They make some observations that

9. Notable amongst these were Institute for Economic Growth (IEG), Delhi; Centre for the Study of Developing Societies (CSDS), Delhi; Centre for Development Studies (CDS), Trivandrum; AN Sinha Institute of Social Studies, Patna; amongst others. ANSISS as far as I can make out was initiated by the state government but also brought under the scheme.

10. This report is a fascinating document. The Council was faced with a classic Hobson's choice of an offer it could neither accept wholeheartedly or reject.

are remarkably prescient but as with all such observations little heeded.[11] They therefore agreed to take up the programme but hedged it with a number of qualifications. Unfortunately, most of these were lost sight of over the years.

This programme in a short period of 20 years grew from 4 institutions receiving ad hoc grants before 1971 to 27 institutes receiving support by 1993. These research institutes have a special place in overall social science structure both because of their character of being supported by state and Central governments as well as because of the interdisciplinary character of their research. Further unlike the institutes funded exclusively by state governments or ministries, they enjoy a remarkable measure of functional autonomy. So far as the institutes' academic activities are concerned, they are free to choose their own research agenda and training programme, subject only to a five-yearly review of their performance by an expert committee. Permanent faculty of the institutes numbered close to 500 in 2005, averaging about 18 per institute. But there is considerable variation across the institutes, with some having only 4 to 10 social scientists, while others employing far in excess of the average. There is also a significant difference among the institutes in respect of the scope and nature of their academic programmes. Only a few institutes run relatively comprehensive training programmes on a regular basis, though some others occasionally conduct short-term courses in specific areas. One area of concern is that only a few institutes undertake studies on all major branches of social science, while many are engaged in research in narrow areas or on specific issues of purely local interest.

The ICSSR institutes have made a positive contribution toward social science research in India. Of particular significance have been a

---

11. "The development of an institutional base for research in social sciences, as in other fields, should be mainly the responsibility of the university system...The ICSSR is also seeking to promote research within the university system and the bulk of its funds go to university departments and affiliated colleges for promotion of research. This is the right policy and should continue. We are conscious of the fact that it is easy to set up research institutions in social science. There is therefore a great danger of multiplication of institutions if recurring and non recurring grants become easily available from the center and this will defeat the very purpose of the scheme and scarce resources will be frittered away in maintaining a large number of small non viable institutions of doubtful quality."

large number of socioeconomic studies at the regional level, which have highlighted the wide diversity of economic, social and political conditions in different parts of the country and also within different regions. Thanks to the studies conducted by the regional institutes, social scientists are now better aware of the multiplicity of forces at work in promoting or impeding socioeconomic development at the grass-root level and of important issues and questions requiring further research. Performance of the ICSSR institutes in recent years, judged by the magnitude of their research output, also appears good. Apart from the research projects and PhD theses completed, the institutes have also to their credit a large number of monographs, working/occasional papers, seminar/conference presentations and published books and articles.

In spite of all these attributes, there are still some major problems. ICSSR provides regular maintenance and development grants to the institutes. For research institutes set up by the ICSSR outside Delhi, the state governments are supposed to match the grants provided by the Council. But in reality the picture is more complex. The FIRC gathered data to show that in 2005-06, ICSSR provided approximately 27 per cent of the resources to these institutes and state governments approximately 19 per cent, which is less than 50 per cent of their budgets. Even if we allowed for some income from their corpus funds, the total of all such autonomous support is still around 53 per cent. A significant amount of their funding thus comes from research projects and other activities. The pursuit of externally funded projects, and their requirements, then becomes an objective that overwhelms the vaunted autonomy and multidisciplinary character of these research institutes. These institutions were viewed as multidisciplinary entities focusing (mostly) on development studies. As we have noted, the funding anomalies created a bias towards those skills and specialisations that would be better suited for the requirements of external funding agencies. This problem arises because right from the beginning while it was stated that the eligible institutions would be entitled to 'recurring' non-plan support, the basis of such support was never clearly defined. Compounding the problem is that the institutes themselves are of two types: 'private' i.e., those originating as private initiatives but becoming eligible for public support and those that originate in explicit state (either Centre or state) decisions to create research institutions. While the latter can be called 'public sector' they are at best a form of 'joint sector', borrowing terminology from the industrial sector. Developing a suitable long-term policy for them requires solutions to problems not dissimilar to those in the case of conventional public sector companies. The actual structure of this scheme for funding research institutions involves shared responsibilities between the Council and the government (both state and Central). This structure of shared responsibilities created anomalies which have contributed to these institutions not delivering to their full potential. A related problem is that as the scheme was never formally incorporated into the legal-organisational structure of the Council; the anomalies did not have a mechanism under which they could be addressed.[12] A second problem arose in the facts that as these were, explicitly by original mandate, not universities, they needed to get affiliation with universities to design and run PhD programmes. This implied that instead of developing new *sui generis* doctoral research programmes of their own,[13] they emulated and incorporated the existing weaknesses of the universities, structure of disciplinary programmes.[14] Part of the problem was due to a complete lack of understanding of the role doctoral programmes play in a healthy social science structure.[15]

12. A classic example is the problems which arose and continue to date in relation to the Gandhian Institute of Studies, Varanasi.

13. Further as they were located in different states, and often were better funded for research expenses, they encounter familiar problems of turf protection and envy.

14. In fact the problem was complex. What would happen in a centre with multidisciplinary faculty seeking to register students in conventional specialisations as economics, sociology etc.? The university departments would, possibly correctly, argue that such centres were inadequately structured to ensure the disciplinary training and inputs for these degrees. Thus, they would often insist on co-supervision from departmental faculty, who ironically, would often have much poorer research experience.

15. There are examples in the Council's debates which seems to think that doctoral programmes will somehow detract from the focus on research. This problem is not unique to social sciences; the same problem comes up in the Council for Scientific and Industrial Research (CSIR) system which was a model for the ICSSR. One may see the articles by Gautam Desiraju "Science Education and Research in India", EPW 43(24), June 14-20, 2008, and a rejoinder by the emininent CSIR Scientist Prof. Pushpa Bhargava "On the organisation of Science Research in India", EPW 43(31), July 26-August 01, 2008.

In addition, the research environment has changed substantially over the past 40 years since the formation of the ICSSR. In 1968, the CSSR identified 47 institutions outside of universities and government departments who were engaged in social science research. This position has changed dramatically with the growth of a large number of research institutions, both in the public and private sectors. Thus, most government ministries have their own research/training establishments and in addition they give grants-in-aid to a number of autonomous bodies. The Report of the Fourth ICSSR Review Committee using data gathered by NASSDOC indicated over 800 such institutes. This does not include a substantial number of, what are essentially post-box NGOs operating in different metropolises of the country, as ancillaries to our universities and large research institutes. These research institutes range across a wide spectrum of areas. This development has given social science research in India a depth and variety that is exceptional in the developing world. The problem is what role should they play in a public funded research system, and equally what does this mean for the health of the structure of social research. These are questions which have, to date, not been effectively discussed in the social science community.

Other Research Programmes of the Council

The importance of the research institutes in ICSSR's overall research programme is seen in the data presented in the Annexures. Expenditure on research institutes is by far the largest component of ICSSR expenditure. Between VIIth and Xth Plan, their share in total ICSSR outlay averaged nearly 46 per cent, showed a rising trend, and had reached more than 50 per cent in 2005-06. Indeed, out of the total ICSSR expenditure directly related to research, the share of expenditure on institutes went up from 73 to 81 per cent between VIIth and Xth Plan, while that on research projects and research fellowships declined from 9.1 and 13.2 per cent to 5.3 and 8.9 per cent respectively over the same period.

There are some other characteristics that emerge from ICSSR's funding of research projects and fellowships. The FIRC reported that ICSSR's post completion assessment of research projects had found that close to 2/3rd of them are rated as mediocre and/or substandard usually by the same expert who had originally evaluated them. Further, there is no effort to track the reasons for poor quality and systematically address them. Secondly, as this is a responsive mode activity the larger institutional benefits from these programmes would depend on the effective dissemination of research results. This has not happened to the extent desired on account of both weak mechanisms for dissemination and poor incentive schemes to reward academic publications.

As these are responsive mode activities, they are essentially focused on individual scholars. This implies that there is little scope for *exante* coordination from these grant schemes. The possibility of *expost* coordination or linkages across projects and fellows is hampered by the weak secretarial structure at the Council. To illustrate the problem, ICSSR has sanctioned close to 3000 research projects over the last 38 years of its existence. This translates to an average of 75 projects a year. Given that the average project runs for between two and three years, it means that Council has at any time close to 200 active research projects functioning. Thus, effectively all that the secretariat has been able to do is provide a very limited financial and procedural oversight. Academic oversight with coordination for mid-term evaluations, workshops etc., would require internal academic staffing at levels which have never been available to the Council. Thus in effect with such responsive mode schemes, the quality of the output is largely dependent on the degree of academic supervision and involvement in the recipient's host institution. This has been weak due to numerous weaknesses in the governance of our universities.[16] Here a second factor has come into play; weaknesses in the internal administration of universities has meant that there has been a further outsourcing of these such projects to a new category of post-box NGOs.[17] Thus, depriving the universities

16. One must also mention here the fact that our public universities are almost exclusively driven by a concern for numbers graduated rather than quality of training.

17. Essentially grants are received by private research societies, who are mere accommodation addresses in proving a legal cover for receiving and accounting for funds. They have no faculty, no infrastructure and other assets one associates with a research institute. The execution is undertaken by faculty from the said university. A large number of such NGOs exist in the various residential colonies that abut our universities.

from these resources and moving the possibility of academic feedback through internal mechanisms of dialogue in the departments.[18]

Finally, it is worth noting that social science research is also sponsored by a number of government departments and ministries. This they do both through captive research institutions and through funding research grants. Unfortunately as there is little recognition of, or development of, the clearing-house function of ICSSR, this has led to a further growth in NGOs and institutes to harvest these resources. There is a vast diversity in this group. They include some very good independent research institutions, some post-box NGOs involving moonlighting by competent university faculty and some of which are pure scams. ICSSR's preoccupation with its own scheme of institutional funding and its limited secretarial resources and the virtual absence of any coordination or advisory function implied that, a vital resource is not optimally used.

The promotional role of the Council as already noted, also similarly, gets neglected over time. Most of its promotion work was done through setting up of the research institutes, noted earlier and a few research programmes.[19] Further most of these came to an end by the 80s. This is both because of a paucity of resources, in part due to inadequate appreciation of the funding requirement of the institutes and in part due to the overall budgetary position of the time. But there was another important reason; the promotional role requires qualified social science professionals. The rigidities in the internal organisational structure in the Council and the unwillingness of the government to address it had meant that over time, the Council's human resources were incapable of coping with these challenges. All this then adds to the overall weakness in the institutional framework.

18. The breakdown of internal dialogue in academic departments is a separate and major issue in its own right. The limited research resources of universities combined with this process of freelancing of faculty research has meant that departmental dialogue, at least in social sciences, has become limited to administrative matters of examination and teaching schedules.

19. Some of these have been very successful and influential, For instance: ICSSR played a pioneering role in gender studies, health, election studies. In fact, most of the users of these results are surprised when informed that the work originates in ICSSR grants.

Social Science Associations

India at independence was endowed with a rich network of social science associations. Thus we see that in economics, political science, history, philosophy, psychology and anthropology, there were associations from the early 20th century. A number of others, notably in sociology, were set up in the immediate post-independence era. The last decade has seen golden and platinum jubilees of a number of them. These associations have remained active, holding annual conferences and producing journals. In addition to the major disciplinary associations, there are, both interdisciplinary groups as in gender studies and in sub-specialties such as, labour economics, econometrics, cultural psychology etc.

In spite of this rich array, one finds considerable despondency about the state of these bodies; these range from statements about their poor academic quality, the poor quality of the papers presented at the sessions and the general lack of interest in their proceedings by well-known academics.

At the level of ICSSR, there are token schemes to assist them by giving small grants in running their journals and secretariats; the Council also gives partial assistance to them for their conferences. But in spite of all this, there is no process of interaction between them and the Council, nor is this been taken up in any major way in the councils.

The state of social sciences in India has attracted much attention and discussion over the years. Both Economic and Political Weekly (EPW) and SEMINAR have had many articles on this issue; in all this discussion it is intriguing that the state and role of professional associations has not attracted scholarly attention.

The relatively low status and profile of these bodies is worth looking into. In countries where associations are strong they play a variety of roles and emerge as key factors in the institutional apparatus of social science research. To illustrate, we may consider one of the older professional associations 'The American Economic Association' which in addition to hosting major conferences and leading journals, also provides variety of services and resource to its members, most notable of those is a active job market for young and senior economists.

Casual observations on these issues from various social scientists indicate that reasons for the poor state of affairs in the disciplines may be found in our experience with these associations. The Council of Social Sciences (COSS) in Pakistan has recently published a study on social science associations in Pakistan. Some of their problems are suggestive: these include dominance of a few departments/regions; dominance of a few eminent individuals; the poor emphasis and training for research. In Pakistan, the decay took the form of poor participation and virtual disappearance of major associations. In India, the associations continue, they hold meeting, receive grants but are fundamentally marginal to the disciplines they represent.

Emerging Challenges and Issues

If we were to take a quantitative picture of social science research at the aggregate levels, one may get a misleading sense of depth and diversity in comparison to other developing countries. This aggregate picture hides a number of weaknesses and diversities. The research output and concentration of both ICSSR institutes and of the vast number of other state sponsored and independent institutions are not uniform in either their disciplinary coverage or in their regional focus. The active participation or involvement of state governments in this process is also subject to significant regional variations. The passage of the 72nd and 73rd amendments has meant that there is a need for research inputs at a further decentralised level of districts and *gram panchayats*. Unfortunately, the higher education infrastructure at these levels is woefully inadequate.[20] There is a some recognition of the need to expand public investments in education and social programmes but this so far exclusively focused on brick and mortar rather then effective capacity, a lacunae that is likely to further accentuate these gaps.

The policy of developing research infrastructure independent of the university system along with the weaknesses in internal administration of the universities and the burden of catering to the requirements of generating a 'university qualified' workforce has created structural

20. Some illustration may be seen in the report of UGC expert committee on educationally backward districts, *http://www.ugc.ac.in/notices/dpr374model colleges.html*

weaknesses in the capacity of the universities to contribute to the research generation process. The separation, between research institutes and the university, as we had noted earlier, induces a critical gap in the higher education system. The training of young scholars through post-graduate and doctoral programmes, by active researchers, provides for future talent and the mechanism for the system to continuously renew and enlarge itself. The separation implied that a significant group of active researchers were effectively not involved in the training process and this problem is now further accentuated by the fact that increased opportunities in corporate and international job markets leading to the few who do get properly trained, opt out.

The structural weaknesses in the formal institutional framework of social research has been partly met and partly challenged by the emergence of the large number of NGOs and civil society groups engaged in social activism and research. A recent example of their synergy and cooperation has been in the evaluation of the NREGA programme. The evaluation of the programme has drawn both researchers in existing institutions and universities working in collaboration with key activist groups. But the growth of such NGOs also raises a number of questions of how best to work with them. Further compounding the problem is that such NGOs come from a diverse group of backgrounds with at times somewhat opaque principles and objectives. The issue of accountability, which is extensively researched and discussed in the context of formal institutions, is still a complex problem for such amorphous networks and NGOs. As we had noted earlier, this remains a major challenge for the social science community to research and analyse.

Finally, social science research has traditionally been pulled between two competing drivers. These are: (a) a curiosity about the functioning of society in its diverse social, cultural, political and economic dimensions; and (b) the practical needs of policy makers and managers in government, civil society and the private sector for reliable information and professional analysis. These different engines manifest themselves in different combinations in different disciplines. Thus in academia there has been a tension between the cries for 'relevance' on one hand and the freedom and ability of an individual scholar to pursue his curiosity on the other. This debate is not unique to India and finds echo in the various social science professions all over the world. The challenge in India is to maintain space for what Prof. Beteille has termed as "delayed return" research in an environment where 'relevance' attracts more funds, greater recognition and acclaim. The limitations on public funding and the emphasis on own generation of funds has meant that research establishments have to focus on the requirements of funding agencies.

An imbalance between these different components tends to weaken the disciplines constituting social sciences. Research which is not immediately focused or derived from issues of current policy concern often is the basis for future policy. The importance of what is sometimes termed as 'irrelevant' or 'abstract' research in developing the future growth of the disciplines should not be understated. One such example can be seen from the field of economics. Game theory for a long time was seen as mathematical curiosity. Today, it finds a wide variety of uses from designing auction mechanisms to understanding political processes and governance systems. An imbalance in a profession that is excessively focused on the needs of current policy is that it will be weak and unable to provide for the requirements of the future. Providing for a balanced social science research community is as major a challenge today as it was 40 years ago when the committee on social science research presented its report.

Conclusion

The involvement of social research in policy formulation, implementation and evaluation has had a long history in India. This involvement has led to the growth of a large academic community. These developments however like the overall growth achievements of the past 60 years still hide a number of significant structural challenges. There is still an enormous need to develop capacity and respect for independent research. This calls for an engagement and dialogue with the state in its diverse federal and institutional structures on the one hand and academia and civil society on the other.

References

Datta-Ray, Sunanda K. (2005). "Spying days that were", *Tribune* October 1, *http://www.tribuneindia.com/2005/20051001/edit.htm*)

Goodall, M.R. (1957). "Planning in India: Research and administration", *Public Administration Review* 17(2).

Planning Commission (1968). *Report of the Committee on Social Science Research*. Government of India.

Annexure Table A-2.1

Expenditure on Research-related Activities in the Budget of the Central Government, 2004-05

*(in Rs. Crore)**

Ministry	Budget Head	Data Collection and Processing	Research: Others	Research: Government	Total
Agriculture	Agricultural Census	7.7			7.7
	Cost of cultivation surveys	15.4			15.4
	Others			16.3	16.3
DARE	Economics, Statistics & Management	14			14
Commerce	Indian Institute of Foreign Trade		1.7		1.7
Industry	Economic Advisor	3.1			3.1
Finance	National Institute of Financial Management		1.4		1.4
	National Institute of Public Finance and Policy			1.7	1.7
Home	Census & Statistics	126			126
Human Resource Development	National Council for Educational Research and Training		54		54
	Indian Council of Social Science Research			41.5	41.5
	Indian Council of Historical Research			7.8	7.8
	Indian Institute of Advanced Studies			6.7	6.7
	Indian Council for Philosophical Research			4.8	4.8
	National Institute for Educational Planning and Research, and others		5.2		5.2
	National Institute of Public Cooperation and Child Development		10.2		10.2
Communications	Indian Institute of Mass Communications		5.5		5.5
Labour	National Labour Institute		4.6		4.6
Law	National Juridical Academy		0.8		0.8
Planning	Human Development Reports			2.6	2.6
	Institute of Applied Manpower Research & other research	9			9
Programme Implementation	Indian Statistical Institute			47.5	47.5
	National Sample Survey	86.9			86.9
	Economic Advice & Statistics	16.3			16.3
Urban Development	Others			14.6	14.6
Water	Research & Development		10.8		10.8
Environment and Forests	Forest Survey of India	10.7			10.7
	GB Pant Institute		7		7
	Management Capacity Building			16.7	16.7
	Environment Impact Assessment			2.8	2.8
Culture	Anthropological Survey of India		12.4		12.4
	Asiatic Society, Kolkata		5.2		5.2
	Nehru Memorial Museum and Library	7.3			7.3
	National Archives	9.9			9.9
Total of above		306.3	118.8	163.0	588.1

Note: *Taken from demand for grants data published on the MoF website. The figures in the last column relate in several cases to expenditure on research on technical as well as socioeconomic research.

Source: Fourth ICSSR Review Committee, 2007.

Annexure Table A-2.2

Disciplines and Institutional Affiliations of Authors of Books Published by Selected Publishers

Discipline	*ICSSR Institutes*	*Indian Universities*	*Other Research Institutes*	*NRIs and Foreigners*	*Independent Scholars*	*International Agencies*	*All*
Economics	29	77	53	94	38	17	308
Sociology	19	96	41	101	43	4	304
Political science	14	59	35	82	44		234
History	6	26	16	39	17	1	105
Geography		1	24	4	10	8	47
All	68	259	169	320	192	30	998

Note: The publishers covered are: SAGE, OUP, Manohar, Permanent Black, Social Science Press, Orient Longman, Rawat and Concept.

Source: Fourth ICSSR Review Committee, 2007.

Annexure Table A-2.3

Institutional Affiliations of Authors of Articles Published in Selected Social Science Journals in India, 2004-05

Institution	*Number of Authors*
ICSSR supported research institutes	58
Other autonomous research institutes	156
Foreign scholar/NRIs/foreign universities	131
International organisations	7
Universities/colleges	179
Government departments	9
Independent researchers	2
Total	542

Note: Based on articles published in the following journals: *Contributions to Indian Sociology*; *Demography India*; *Indian Economic and Social History Review*; *Indian Journal of Agricultural economics*; *Indian Journal of Labour Economics*; *Journal of Quantitative Economics*; and *Sociological Bulletin*.

Source: Fourth ICSSR Review Committee, 2007.

Annexure Table A-2.4

Sources of Funds for ICSSR Institutes during 1995-96 and 2004-05

	1995-96		*2004-05*	
	Rs. (lakh)	*Percentage*	*Rs. (lakh)*	*Percentage*
1	*2*	*3*	*4*	*5*
ICSSR	347.6	19.2	1426.1	28.3
State govts.	423.8	23.4	977.9	19.4
Govt. units	141.5	7.8	387.7	7.7
Corpus				
Own	63.4	3.5	174.7	3.5
Other	66.3	3.7	198.6	3.9
Ford	0	0	10.1	0.2
Projects	699.5	38.6	1287.8	25.5
Other	68.6	3.8	581	11.5
Total	1810.7	100	5043.8	100

Note: Relates to 21 institutes and covers resources used for both current and capital expenditure.

Source: Fourth ICSSR Review Committee, 2007.

Annexure Table A-2.5

Expenditure Pattern of ICSSR during Different Plan Periods (Rs. Million)

Sl.No.	Expenditure	Vth plan		VIth plan		VIIth plan		VIIIth plan		IXth plan		Xth plan estimate	
		Value	%	Value	%	Value	%	Value	%	Value	%	Value	%
1	Expenditure on research	49.5	63.62	90.1	68.2	199.9	63.5	253.1	63.8	580.6	60.5	1089.8	54.6
	a. Research grants	16.3 (32.93)	21.0	19.8 (22.0)	15.0	19.1 (9.6)	6.1	16.2 (6.4)	4.1	22.8 (3.9)	2.4	69.5 (6.4)	3.5
	b. Research institutes	25.2 (50.91)	32.4	54.9 (60.9)	41.6	153 (76.5)	48.6	210 (83.0)	52.9	512.1 (88.2)	53.4	904.1 (83.0)	45.3
	c. Fellowships	8.0 (16.16)	10.3	15.4 (17.1)	11.7	27.8 (13.9)	8.8	26.9 (10.6)	6.8	45.7 (7.9)	4.8	116.2 (10.7)	5.8
2	International collaborations	—	0	5.5	4.2	6.6	2.1	8.4	2.1	31.2	3.3	67.2	3.4
3	Regional centres	5.1	6.6	10.5	7.9	15	4.8	21.6	5.4	43.4	4.5	142.3	7.1
4	Other programmes	0	0		3.4		1.1	4.1	1.0	41.6	4.3	150.3	7.5
5	Support services	0		0		0		0		0		0	
	a. Documentation	4.4	5.7		7.3	5.5	3.6	1.1	0	17	1.8	41	2.1
	b. Data archives	0.7	0.9	1.5	1.1	0.4	0.1	0.3	0.1	4	0.4	9.5	0.5
	c. Training	1.1	1.4	0.5	0.4	1.6	0.5	3	0.8	4.3	0.4	9.4	0.5
	d. Publication subsidy		0		0	5.1	1.6	3.3	0.8	4.9	0.5	18.2	0.9
	e. Study grants		0		0	0.2	0.1	0.2	0.1	0.3	0	1.9	0.1
6	Administrative expenditure	17	21.9	16.7	12.6	79	25.1	102.7	25.9	231.8	24.2	468.1	23.4
7	Current exp. (1 to 6)	77.8	100	132.1	100	314.8	100	396.7	100	959.1	100	1997.7	100
8	Capital: building, equipment	1.8		1.5		40		46.4		71.6		48.3	
9	Grand total (7+8)	79.6		133.6		354.8		443.1		1030.7		2046	

Note: 1) Figures for Vth and VIth plan from Report of the 3rd Review Committee, 1986, p.62. Not comparable with figures for subsequent periods which are as given by the ICSSR secretariat. International collaborations include IDPAD; other programmes include NER centre and 150 years of independence war.
2) Figures in parentheses denote percentages of total research expenditure.

Source: Fourth ICSSR Review Committee, 2007.

3 The State of Cooperation among SSR Institutions

Anjan Mukherji

Introduction

Social science research in India is carried out in universities and research institutes under the general support of the University Grants Commission (UGC) or the Indian Council of Social Science Research (ICSSR) or the Indian Council of Historical Research (ICHR) and similar bodies. Apart from these bodies, there are institutions like the Reserve Bank of India or the State Bank of India or various public sector banks or sometimes even private sector institutions which also fund and support social science research. I shall consider any grant to an educational institution as being support for academic activity and funding received by social science departments in universities and research institutes, in particular, as support for social science research. Thus, the regular grants from UGC to Central universities, used to pay salaries to staff as well as special grants for particular research programmes are all in support of research and academic activity; similarly any grant from the ICSSR to the research institutes even if they are for paying staff salaries, may be considered to be supporting social science research. I shall therefore consider grants from agencies such as UGC or the ICSSR or other agencies, private or public, which are provided to academic institutions, universities and research institutes.

Given this diversity of agencies supporting research, there is naturally a diverse set of research areas supported. This of course is nothing unique: more or less the same set-up exists elsewhere as well. However, what is different in India from say, the United States, is the process through which this support is provided and the manner in which the recipients make use of these funds and the levels of accountability expected from the recipients. The entire process whereby recipients are selected seems to be rather random and often programmes get supported which should not have been chosen.[1]

At the outset let me make clear one thing: social science research is not homogeneous and the kind of support provided varies from area to area. I shall speak mainly about the area of economics since the little experience that I have is from this area. In other areas, I have had only some second-hand experience from colleagues in different disciplines and hopefully things are not too different across disciplines.

Dependence among Donors and Recipients

We are supposed to discuss inter-institutional cooperation and dependence among SSR institutions; we shall call institutions such as UGC, ICSSR or other bodies funding SSR to be donors and the institutions such as universities and institutes to be recipients. This perhaps is not an exact nomenclature because sometimes funding is received primarily by individuals and in such cases we shall refer to them as recipient individuals and their institutions as recipient institutions. To study cooperation or the lack of it, amongst the various donors, recipients, non-recipients and other players, we must proceed by looking at the situation on the ground, the ground reality so to speak, if only to see what exists. We do so by looking at various situations which I have encountered and draw the inferences from such experience; to keep these examples and anecdotes separate from the main line of argument, these have been relegated to the footnotes.

The cooperation and dependence between donors and recipients is clear: the funding from the UGC to Central universities, for example, provides the main source of support and the universities would cease to function without this support; for state universities, state governments provide them with their main support. But dependence is thought to be clearly unidirectional: recipients depend on donors; the donors do not seem to realise that there is another line of dependence *viz.*, that of the donors on recipients because the very credibility of the donor institutions

1. I was informed about a bizarre example in the late 70s, early 80s. A researcher wanted to fit a production function to the newspaper industry and chose newsprint as the only input, yet this completely inane activity received handsome support.

depend on the performance of the recipients; the donors, in turn, are recipients as well when they need to argue before some other authority for their annual allocations. The little cooperation between donors and recipients ceases when we consider cooperation between donors as well as cooperation among recipients. Notice that for a successful, meaningful and vibrant SSR programme, all of these aspects are crucial.

It should be noted that this dependence can lead to an erosion of the autonomy of an educational institution particularly when the head of the institution becomes a servile follower of the funding agencies. There are many examples of heads of institutions, who with an eye on their next appointment, always blindly follow the merest whims and fancies of donor agencies. If these whims and fancies are detrimental to academic excellence, the effects would also be disastrous. The institution also suffers from being led badly.

The area of economics is generally well-funded: donor institutions have been generally sympathetic to the needs of recipient individuals; but the donor institutions have not been usually sympathetic to the problems faced by the institutions being supported. What should be remembered, particularly in the case of sponsored research, is that the research programme may not be of great interest to any one except the donor.[2] And consequently the supported research programmes get slanted in directions which may not be of any great importance. Consider the lack of funds to study the contamination of water by arsenic, prevalent in parts of Bengal and Bangladesh, in contrast to the fat funds available to study the problems associated with HIV/AIDS, when the persons affected by the former outnumber those affected by the latter.[3] On a much more restricted plane, consider too, the lack of support for research in economic theory; there is any amount of money available to analyse issues relating to, say, globalisation or governance;

2. We have heard that some times not even this may be true.

3. Government of India calculations based on the National Family Health Survey's third wave in 2005-06 suggests that approximately 2.47 million people in India are affected by HIV in the 15-49 age-group (NFHS-3 Final report). Contrast this with the incidence of arsenic poisoning in India and Bangladesh that affected more than 4000 villages and contaminates the drinking water of 330 million people (see Kumar, 2003).

but if you wish to study the possibilities of cyclical growth paths,[4] not only is no money forthcoming, you may even be treated as being abnormal. There is an additional problem. Most of the time, the recipient institutions are not particularly supportive or helpful to the needs of the recipient individuals. The 'dog in the manger' attitude of individuals who are not recipients is of course quite another hurdle.

Consider for example, the spectacular reaction to the Delhi School of Economics or the Ratan Tata Library receiving special support which many of you will recall. May be the fact that DSE received a bonus at a time when all Central universities had their budget slashed, made people unhappy but the fact that the maintenance of a library in economics (the RTL stocks books in other social sciences as well) benefits all, is missed out as a result and the spirit of cooperation among recipients and non-recipients, is non-existent, to say the least.

As far as my experience goes, there is generally a lack of cooperation even among recipients and donors. Support is received under heads and these amounts cannot be shifted to other items; unspent accounts have to be surrendered even when the sanctioned money is not adequate for the purpose it has been sanctioned for. Institutional support to recipients is sometimes lacking: this signifies a lack of cooperation between recipients and recipient institutions and one must conclude then that generally, institutional support has been less than desirable since no one was interested in finding a way of helping out.[5]

4. This is not a really abstract search for truth, but clearly something a lot more mundane, with applicability to the real world. Of course, I do not see why today's abstract work cannot become tomorrow's down-to-earth stuff and thus even such work deserves support.

5. There is also another aspect that we should keep track of: the administration's lack of support for special funds of any kind. In the School of Social Sciences, JNU there were five departments receiving support from UGC under the Department of Special Assistance Scheme. The funds so received had to be accounted for separately: the finance branch of JNU routinely reported that this work was too much and that they will do it once all the other 'more pressing' work was completed. Naturally this delayed matters and I recall that as Dean of the School, I had suggested the appointment of one person to be paid for by all the DSA programmes jointly, who would look after the work. It did not take me very long to convince colleagues who were in charge of the DSA programmes about the efficacy of this suggestion. Unfortunately, this did not find favour with the finance branch and when I suggested that an officer of the finance branch be designated to carry out the work and be given an honorarium for this purpose, the finance officer said that this will not be allowed.

The support received from private donors is often troublesome for recipient institutions since these often have requirements which recipient institutions are bothered by. Such funds also require recipients to behave a lot more professionally than they are accustomed to; such expectations create problems and are hence resented by recipients.[6] Consider the creation of special chairs in universities. Apart from the UGC, ICSSR and similar concerns, a common form of support is the creation of special chairs. I do not know how these are treated usually but in a particular University, these are treated as 'projects' and the administrative support to these chairs is provided by the so-called project cell. Consequently, holders of these chairs were treated separately: their salary was disbursed if at all, at the whims of the project cell. A few years ago, the holder of the chair instituted by a Bank, had to make several trips each month to collect his salary; he ultimately gave up and returned to the appointment in Hong Kong that he had given up to accept the 'prestigious' chair. The university did not seem to mind. More recently, I am given to understand, a chair was instituted in a University with the donation of Rs. 1 crore. As a part of the signed agreement, the concerned university was required to submit audited utilisation certificates each year showing interest earned on the corpus and expenditures incurred. Yet in spite of the agreement, from the very beginning, the university declined to adhere to the requirements, providing only an audited combined statement for all chairs in the university: it was too much work for them to provide a break-up, they argued. Or was this lack of transparency meant to cover up some things, one is not sure. While I have been using specific examples to illustrate the lackadaisical approach of university administration or the bureaucracy or academia, I believe the situation is not confined to a few isolated cases; they are all pervasive.

Research institutes may actually be better in handling some of these matters. It should be pointed out that such hassles eat into the precious research time and additionally provide a great disincentive for setting up new research programmes. The inability of recipient institutions to provide such support indicates a clerk like mentality at

6. Generally, private donors wish to donate money in memory of some relative or to commemorate some event. These may take the form of a fellowship or a chair.

most levels of decision-making in recipient institutions; while these may be good for many things, they cannot be good for nurturing social science research or indeed any kind of research or more generally for any kind of meaningful academic activity. To set up programmes of cooperation therefore which might require the spending of funds becomes singularly unattractive. A considerable amount of change in the mindset of administrators in all academic institutions is called for before we can undertake any new steps.

Quality of Research: A Constraint on Cooperation?

This deteriorating situation is of course due to our own shortcoming: the recent report by the committee reviewing the working of the ICSSR commented on this aspect. The concept note prepared for this seminar put it mildly: "Professor Vaidyanathan Committee has reached short of saying that most of the SSR in the country are not up to the mark." Even this is a very damning statement.

How does one judge the quality of SSR? One may suppose the best indicator would be to note whether the research gets published in peer reviewed journals but then this indicator will depend upon the quality of the peer who review and which journals. Many years ago, in the 1970s, I recall telling a colleague in the school (not an economist) about (what I thought was) the unfair rejection letter I had just got from a journal, only to be told that they do not have any such problems: their journals publish whatever is sent to them. There are those even among economists, who have either a captive journal or a press or publishing house run by a relative or a close friend, and they publish in such places claiming that these are peer reviewed. Then there are also those who publish their research in C or D grade 'foreign' journals and the exceedingly few who publish in A or B grade journals. I have even heard of scholars making a virtue out of the fact that they lack publications in standard journals by saying that they did not "hanker for foreign publications". The matter becomes complicated because I also know of many who regularly publish in B or C or D and even in A class journals, but strangely enough do not even know the basics of the subject concerned and thus, their contributions are worthless. So just looking at the journal name is not sufficient to judge the quality of research. A colleague, while agreeing, would still like to stick to the class of journals as an indicator since that way you are less likely to make an error of judgment. But there are good research papers which appear in the most unlikely of places which are not peer reviewed in the sense that we understand them. So there is no mechanical way of judging the quality of SSR; the research contributions need to be carefully considered before forming an opinion. Although there is the problem of subjectivity in this approach, it is somewhat surprising that very seldom is there a disagreement over which research is bad and which is not; disagreement generally occurs over marginal contributions. The difficulty is that a substantial volume of research is in this marginal category.

Thus, judging the quality of social science research, in a meaningful and objective manner, will necessarily have to be time consuming and labourious. Shortcuts are therefore usually taken (you consider the work of people known to you as being good) and hence, erroneous conclusions are arrived at: the errors which enable shoddy work to be labeled as competent are the most costly. But even though there is hardly any debate about the quality of some scholar's output, action is seldom taken by the funding agencies on the basis of this 'common knowledge'. It does not appear that funding agencies and donors are worried about the quality of research: they have not done anything to show that they care. In a more general context, quality is never something which has been kept track of. And it appears to be the case that 'peer review', which is something people seem to agree on, consists of review by friends and followers. This is conducive for cooperation only among friends and followers.

Many more universities and institutions are being planned: but no one mentions the fact that we do not require more universities, we require more superior institutions; replicating third rate institutions will not help anyone. And consequently instead of cooperation we shall get more non-cooperation.

National Institutes and University Departments: A Dichotomy

Is the above equally applicable to scholars in research institutes and university departments? The answer is yes unfortunately, but there are of course exceptions on both sides. This raises a somewhat different question: why are there so many research institutes set up by the state? In other countries, the example of a state setting up standalone research institute is rare; there are countless private research institutes (these are coming up now in India) but usually when the state sets up a research institute, which is generally the case in other countries, it is done within the framework of a state university.

Why did this not happen in India? I can only guess why this has been so. I believe this was due to the fact that our policy makers decided that universities were not doing an adequate job and to make up for this deficiency, institutes had to be set up.[7] Thinking back, this may have been the reason why ISI was formed in the first place: Prof. Mahalanobis must have felt that creating an adjunct to the Department of Mathematics (statistics perhaps was not a separate subject or department then) in Calcutta University would not provide him the freedom that he sought. Similarly Prof. V.K.R.V. Rao must have set up IEG outside the ambit of Delhi University and ISEC separate from Bangalore University for the same reason. The existence of such institutes was a signal for two ideas: first that universities are incompetent to carry out research and second that research can only be undertaken by scholars who do not teach. Both of these implications have had disastrous effects.

If this feeling between institutes and universities is indeed so, one can then explain the lack of cooperation between the institutes and the

7. I was first alerted to this state of affairs, several years ago; the International Economic Association (as far as I remember) and its then President, Jacques Dreze, was interested in setting up a Centre of Development Economics and Prof. Dreze had come to India to discuss matters with various people. I do not know exactly who all he met but he did meet me and asked me for my opinion and views. I felt at that stage that the proposed centre should come up within some University: since research scholars would then have the chance of interacting with academics of various disciplines. If I recall correctly, Prof. Dreze was partial towards Indian Statistical Institute and while I agreed that this would be the best possible location among institutes, locating the centre in a university would be even better. At that point Prof. Dreze told me that this was what he had thought but people had advised him that a new centre should be set up completely separate from existing institutions. Further that all existing institutions were useless and that there was no hope of breathing any life into any of them. I did disagree with him of course but realised that many influential people had strongly advised him in the matter.

university departments: how can one cooperate when there is this feeling between them? Thus, to discuss questions of cooperation we need to first address this issue: why have institutes as standalone entities? Why should students in university departments be denied access to the research produced in institutes and why should academics in university departments be denied access to the so called better facilities for research? I have even heard a very senior central minister argue that research is not supposed to be carried out in universities: universities are supposed to teach. Research is only meant to be conducted in institutes. The discussion was with respect to science departments; I dare say the same would be applicable to social science. The basic point that research clarifies issues and therefore helps one to become a better teacher is not understood. Consequently, the basic synergies between research and teaching are enjoyed in only a few places.

The conflict between research and teaching has always been there: how much time should one apportion for each activity? And what about one's own strengths and weaknesses: one may be an excellent teacher but not a very good researcher, what then? And from the point of view of the concerned institution, should one value teaching more than research?[8]

In Delhi University, till recently, undergraduate teachers when they came up for reemployment upon attaining 62, were supposed to show

8. I recall a situation, when I was visiting a well-known department of economics, where this comparison had to be made: the question of tenure of a young assistant professor came up for consideration. The concerned department was trying to build up its image as a competent research-oriented department and the then chairperson, a very competent researcher, found the candidate's research credentials weak. But the candidate was a wonderful teacher having won awards for his teaching. There was no reason to doubt the candidate's credentials as a teacher: every one said that he indeed was good. I, as a visitor, did not take part in any of the deliberations and the applicant felt that as an outsider, I would be able to provide him with some solace since he knew the department was not going to recommend his case. My sympathies were with this applicant since I feel good teaching must be valued. The department did not recommend him for tenure; but the concerned Dean overturned the decision and gave him tenure. I was feeling rather happy since this is what I would have done. But I later learnt that the applicant, had he not been given tenure would leave and so would his wife, who apparently was an excellent secretary and guess what, she was secretary to the Dean. The end result was the following: the applicant left having got a job elsewhere, the chairperson resigned in a huff and went on long leave and of course, the Dean lost his secretary and moreover, the department itself was in a complete mess: it had probably lost its best researcher as well as the best teacher.

evidence of research (all of a sudden) and the evidence that I had to examine while I was chairman of the governing body of a DU college, really stretched one's imagination. Fortunately this charade ended when the retirement age was extended to 65 years and extension beyond that entailed other things.

The research institutes were set up ostentatiously because researchers would not have teaching duties and hence would have some flexibility in their schedules; almost all of them, these days however, have reverted to some teaching and/or supervision, carrying out tasks from which they had been given respite. Some of them have almost converted themselves to universities by acquiring the 'deemed university' status.

As indicated earlier, I think there are many reasons for institutes to be closely associated with university departments; since in spite of the setting up of institutes, only some of them are doing good research and some universities are also engaged in at least equally good quality research and teaching. But given the rigidities in the universities and the kind of flexibility that institutes offer, cooperation between the two sets can only be nurtured if such a relationship is to the mutual advantage of both. Researchers from institutes may get to teach and supervise students; teachers from university departments have access to facilities for research which perhaps they do not have in their own institution. There are externalities from such association and for the returns from such relationships to be enjoyed, the relationship should be forged in a manner which allows institutes to keep their flexible set-up. Clearly, these things cannot be achieved by waving a wand: they would require sustained collaboration on a basis of mutual trust and respect and with a proper appreciation of the constraints that each is operating under. The difference between institutes and university departments has narrowed over the years and consequently, now is the time to think of a more meaningful and closer relationship between these two entities. A first step towards this direction would be for UGC and ICSSR to set up visiting professorships specially designed for professors from one institution to visit the other and spend a minimum of an academic year. I must also add that to make this work, the leave granted to enable academics to go to another institution under this scheme should be considered as duty leave; this should put the seal of bureaucratic approval on such visits since otherwise, an academic would be hard pressed to explain why such visits were useful.

The Establishment of the Necessary Conditions for Effective Cooperation

I think it is fair to say that the situation is not desirable and we should talk about what needs to be done. There are three sets of issues which are important for social science research to prosper under effective cooperation:

1. the quality of persons who are choosing the academic profession,
2. the organisation of departments in universities and research institutes, and
3. the quality of administrators who help run these institutions.

Let me take up the last first; I have always maintained that we deserve better administrators; usually this aspect is not appreciated. In most cases, a senior academic is chosen to run the place without taking into consideration whether he or she has any administrative skills. If the incumbent is administratively skillful then there is no reason to complain but very often this is not so; then the petty clerks take over and function entirely to satisfy their own aims whatever they might be; they soon convince the head that this is what should be done. This usually ends up with the kind of strange but true scenarios that I have mentioned earlier. These hinder academic activity. Ideally, a good administrator will try to find out how to get desirable things done or suggest alternatives which are more readily feasible. It should be realised that good administrative skills are rare: as rare as good analytical minds so essential for research and so the rewards or wages for administrators should be commensurate with his or her importance to the smooth functioning of the institution. Clearly academic decisions should be kept outside of the purview of such administrators.

I have already devoted some time to the second point and do not wish to spend any more time on it except to point out that should it be desired that universities and institutes cooperate, then some steps need to be taken at this juncture when differences between them have narrowed.

Next, no matter what one attempts in other spheres, these are not likely to bear any fruits, unless there is a steady stream of good academics available for appointment in universities and institutes. Right now this is not so: the main reason is the nature of remunerations in the academic profession. Across the board, UGC scales rule whether in universities or in institutes; dearness allowance at Central government rates make a hefty difference between educational institutes at the state level and those governed by the Central government rules. But these scales are not good enough.[9]

After a Master's degree in economics today, students are offered annual salaries in the region of Rs. 10 lakh; some may actually get a bit more; those who complete an MBA from IIMs, I understand, get a lot more. Last year, the top salary earned by an IIMB student was Rs. 43 lakh; this does not include foreign salaries. At the top of the scale, a professor earns just under Rs. 6 lakh. Why should some one choose to slog for a PhD for four to five years and then earn less than Rs. 3 lakh? The net result has been that students do not choose an academic way of life; quality of students in the M.Phil/PhD classes continues to drop drastically and consequently people contributing to research activity are not as bright as they were once. Incidentally these salary differences are generally well known but the bodies like UGC and MHRD have let it persist and widen.

What has happened in the circumstances is wholly rational: fresh graduating students neglect academics as a career option; and, most existing academics have taken to sponsored research like duck to water,

9. When I took up my first job in 1967, it was as a research assistant in the Indian Institute of Management, Calcutta (IIMC) with a basic salary of Rs. 325; DA and other allowances made total emoluments about Rs. 700: a princely sum those days and this was a university lecturer's salary with allowances at the Central rates. In 1968, the top salary got by a student from IIMC was Rs. 1000 per month; that was almost 43 per cent more, but it never felt that I had chosen something vastly inferior financially. In fact the Director of IIMC knew of my background and enquired whether I would be interested in a similar well-paying job and I could cockily say that 300 odd rupees was not adequate compensation for wearing a tie the whole day.

to make amends, so that their aggregate earnings (salary plus consultancy fees) are not wholly out of line with what they could have earned elsewhere. If in the process, social science research suffers: so what? If salaries are increased what is to stop academics to keep their consultancies as well? More, we teach, is always better. Increase in salaries therefore must be accompanied with increased accountability as well: regular periodic reviews with feedback. I would even advocate that tenures should be contractual for five years at a time, provided retirement benefits are not foregone. It should be the case that those who take up the academic profession are not penalised; in turn, they must be held responsible for whatever duties they are expected to carry out.[10]

A Chinese academic asked me the other day why the salaries of academics were so low in India; the question was in relation to the discussion that we were having about the new universities being set up in China. The central mistake of our policy makers has been not to realise the importance of adequate salaries which could keep attracting talent. It should be kept in mind that what attracts talents today is not the same as the wages which attracted talents in past. Even in the *Arthashastra*, one of the conditions for wage fixation was precisely that, and we seem to have lost sight of it. Do we wish to make amends? If not, then the old saying should alert us: if you pay peanuts, you will get monkeys. And no matter what we try to do, our efforts in restoring the quality and status of social science or any kind of research would not be

10. Some years ago, some economists then working in different institutions (universities and research institutes) in Delhi decided to come together to try and set up a Centre for Studies in Economics and Related Disciplines; a meeting was called at the India International Centre and one of India's senior and most respected economists agreed to Chair; when the person making the presentation described the budget, and revealed that he had budgeted Rs. 50000 as the per month salary, the Chair was furious and ticked off people. If memory serves me right, at that time the basic monthly salary of a full professor was perhaps Rs. 15000 and the Chairman took offense that some upstarts were trying to demand atrocious salaries for themselves. As far as I recall, many among those present at the meeting ultimately left the country; maybe they would have left anyway but maybe they would have stayed if they had been given some flexibility in terms of scales and working conditions. I do not know why the Chairman was so upset: he clearly felt that academics do not deserve such salaries and should in fact lead a life of denial and hardship.

effective nor would induced cooperation between such institutions amount to anything beyond the blind leading the blind.

References

Kumar (2003). "Millions more at risk of arsenic poisoning than previously thought", *British Medical Journal*, 326-466 (1st March).

4 Accountability of Social Science Research

Some Challenging Dimensions

V.M. Rao

Introduction

The ICSSR institutions have now completed three decades of their work and evolution. They have elaborate provisions for monitoring and evaluation to help them in moving on the path of progress. ICSSR's visiting committees review their work and functioning every five years to analyse their strengths and weaknesses and to recommend the support they need over the next five years. The institutions themselves have the system of annual reports, periodic assessment of faculty and evaluation by external experts as a part of schemes for promotion. Funding agencies impose a variety of procedures for initial selection of projects for sponsoring, their concurrent evaluation and assessment of the extent to which the final output meets the requirements of the sponsors. On the whole, it can be taken that institutionalisation of procedures to ensure accountability of social science research has made substantial progress since the inception of ICSSR institutions.

The purpose of this paper is to suggest that the task of making social science research (SSR) accountable needs a fresh look as SSR gains in strength, sophistication and confronts new challenges such as understanding the globalising world. My comments are based on my observations in Institute for Social and Economic Change (ISEC) and few other institutions with which I am familiar. They are also based on the limited number of development issues on which I have worked. I must admit that it is presumptuous for me to claim that this note is about SSR as a whole. I only hope that the points I make are of some help in focusing on the theme of accountability of SSR. In my view, the present procedures to secure accountability of SSR focus on the administration and financial soundness of institutions, evaluation of academic activities of faculty and progress of sponsored projects according to the performance norms stipulated in the MoU. The distinguishing feature of these procedures is that their concern is primarily with the operational aspects of SSR. If there are financial irregularities, improprieties in recruitment, meagre research output or long delays in completion of projects, these are bound to get noticed and looked into according to the procedures laid down for this purpose. On the other hand, consider the role that SSR is expected to play in the development of society by building up a body of valuable knowledge about the structure and dynamics of different subsystems in the society, by providing feedback to and interacting with other social sciences to establish linkages and develop interdisciplinary perspectives, to provide inputs for policymaking and above all, to make citizens more aware and informed about the state of the society, tradeoffs involved in development and the progress towards long-term goals. Are the present procedures adequate to ensure accountability of SSR regarding its performance in relation to this broader development role? This note is concerned with the accountability of SSR from this wider perspective.

Emerging Trends in SSR

There have been some trends during the last three decades which suggest that SSR has made substantial gains in its capacity to play the broader role mentioned above. Taking ISEC as the illustration, I notice dramatic change in research style and technology as reflected in computerisation, extensive use of sophisticated quantitative models and analytical frameworks, growing linkages with funding agencies, universities and researchers within India and abroad, expanding share of policy-oriented research, continuing contact and collaboration with policy makers and implementers, and increasing presence of researchers in media with widespread readership/viewers. These are indeed favourable trends. However, there are also trends, if not adverse, which are at least ambiguous about their implications for SSR. There has been a remarkable growth in the number of SSR institutions and researchers and their regional spread. This, by itself, is a welcome trend but there are indications that the new institutions and the new entrants may not be adequately equipped as contributors to SSR. Inadequate funds, poor facilities and faculty not large and balanced enough in terms of discipline-wise composition appear to be serious handicaps. While those trained in regional languages are increasing in number, little is being done to help them to adjust to mainstream SSR which remains tied to English. The other worrisome trend is the specialisation within disciplines occurring at an accelerated pace. Economics now looks like a discipline fragmented into a number of relatively small non-interacting groups each with its own narrow perspective, specialised jargon and exclusive theoretical and methodological concerns. This again may be essential to keep pace with the growing complexity of the globalising world, but fragmentation can also diminish the capacity of a discipline to put together the fragments to get fuller and deeper insights.

Impact of the Emerging Trends on SSR

These are formidable problems. The limited purpose of this note is to point out their impacts on SSR and emphasise the need to discuss how they may be included in the institutionalised arrangements to make SSR accountable. This may be regarded as extension of these arrangements to cover the accountability of SSR in relation to its societal role. We consider the impacts under three heads:

i) Quality of research.
ii) Adequacy of database.
iii) Linkages with stakeholders.

i) Quality of Research

It is the experience of academic journals that a substantial part of papers received for publication gets eliminated in preliminary screening itself where the papers are scanned to select those which seem promising enough to process further. The processing will yield a further crop of rejected papers. It is plausible that the space for publication available in academic journals is not expanding with the output of research papers. However, the two categories of rejected papers fail to get selected not because of constraint of space but because of poor quality. Surely, an arrangement to analyse the trends in rejected papers—numbers, regional spread and distribution by researcher categories—would give helpful clues to control the problem of rejected papers indicative of wasteful researches and help those who are weak and in need of guidance. It is likely that as a combined result of unplanned growth in research institutions and number of researchers and the trend towards specialisation and sophistication in research, this problem becomes even more serious in future than now.

Among the papers getting published and contributing to the expanding research literature, it is useful to distinguish between two types of papers: i) replications, and ii) innovative. The replication category extends the known models and methodologies to new areas, periods and larger data collections to push further the extensive margin of knowledge. Innovative papers, on the other hand, scrutinise the models and methodologies themselves to make them more appropriate and relevant to the changing real world situations. These may be regarded as deepening the intensive margin of knowledge. I would like to suggest that for the healthy growth of a discipline, a measure of balance is necessary between these two categories. Disproportionate increase in replications is likely to yield harvests of clones, making no addition to knowledge. On the other hand, abundance of innovative papers which do not percolate to the level of replication would give us grand-looking white elephants with no work to perform. An interesting possibility to keep in mind is that the replicators and innovators are distinct groups living in their own worlds without discovering each other. Thus, we can have abundance of both clones and white elephants! My point is that it is important to keep a watch on the changing balance between replicators and innovators in SSR.

Wasteful research and lack of balance in research are serious enough problems in SSR to merit a close watch. It could be difficult to eliminate these problems. But not having any arrangement at all to keep a watch on them is, in my view, an inexcusable gap in the accountability of SSR in relation to its societal role.

ii) Adequacy of Databases

SSR has a strong empirical orientation. A crucial requirement of SSR is a reliable and continually updated database capable of supporting probing investigations and analyses. The two major sources of data for SSR are: (i) official statistics on population, agriculture, villages, individuals, development schemes etc., (ii) field material collected by researchers for studies undertaken by them. Regarding official statistics, the shocking point about them is that the government itself is unhappy with them. I give two examples. Recently, a central minister described the land statistics as garbage. The word is unparliamentary but researchers would wholeheartedly agree with the assessment! Second, measurement of poverty by the Planning Commission and identification of the poor in five-yearly BPL surveys done by the states give such widely differing numbers as to defy explanation! The interesting point to note is that SSR has done little to improve the official statistics. Is it really true that SSR has no role to play in improving official statistics?

Regarding the field materials collected by SSR, a major weakness is that no arrangements have been evolved to store them for future use. Field materials consist not merely of data but also include profiles, cases, pictures, field notes etc. If the materials collected over the last three decades of ICSSR supported SSR were banked, we would have created a rich source of information and insights remaining out of the net of official statistics. A consequence is that often SSR relies on coefficient estimates delinked from the processes underlying them. Let me give a cooked-up example. We are often tempted to interpret increase in a measure of concentration of landownership as undesirable and a decrease as a good change. However, increase in the measure can occur if a large number of landless get small pieces of land each as compared to the earlier holding of land only by large owners! The measure could decrease if these new owners lose land and we go back to the earlier state of ownership of land by only large owners. If field materials are banked, it would be easy to get glimpses of processes underlying measures generated in typical sample surveys done by economists.

iii) Linkages with Stakeholders

For balanced development, a profession needs to pay attention to two sets of norms. Intra-profession norms (IPN) guide a researcher towards excellence in work leading to recognition, prizes and awards. I believe that it is natural for individual researchers to be motivated by IPN and pursue his activities in the direction indicated by IPN. But the profession as a whole should also take note of extra-profession norms (EPN) which depend on the views of clients/consumers/stakeholders regarding the value of products/services provided by the profession. EPN reflects the extent to which a profession is playing its societal role. It seems to me that IPN and EPN are not unrelated, but I believe that IPN tends to make individual researchers inward-looking. This, along with specialisation, has the effect of alienating SSR researchers from the main society and its complex problems. The result is a certain unwillingness to measure their performance by EPN. I recall an article by Prof. Kaushik Basu in *Economic and Political Weekly* on the occasion of award of Nobel Prize to Prof. Amartya Sen revealing that he got the prize for his theoretical writings which few can understand and not for his ideas on human development for which he is widely known. It is a mark of the deep concern which Prof. Sen feels for the disadvantaged in the society that he pursues with a missionary zeal his policy-oriented researches on human development. I am not sure that SSR as a whole has paid enough attention to EPN. SSR should do much more than what it is doing now to find out what the stakeholders—policy makers and implementers, those in other sciences and common citizens trying to make sense of diverse changes occurring in society—feel about the role that SSR plays in meeting their needs. The responses could be very embarrassing, but they would certainly help SSR in improving its performance by the EPN yardstick.

It is not the purpose of this note to present a chargesheet against SSR. My attempt is only to illustrate the growing importance of the societal role of SSR. India is entering a phase where the temperature would rise in both the economic and political realms. There would be severe strain on our modest capacity to govern, manage conflicts and create a workable coalition for development by bringing together groups with diverse and opposing interests. Issues in social sciences will be at the top in the research and policy agenda. If SSR remains preoccupied with IPN and fails to help the society at this crucial juncture, it will lose its credibility. Higher education is already being viewed as a pampered elitist sector. SSR belongs to higher echelons in this sector. Its campuses and personnel display obvious signs of being well-off, even affluent. It is only to be expected that the performance of SSR will be watched by many—besides auditors and ICSSR committees—including media not all of whom are favourably disposed towards it. SSR should take lead in organising auditing of its performance by EPN yardstick. If it fails, it will remain vulnerable to attacks not necessarily confined to fair and objective assessments.

5 Multidisciplinary Research

Challenges and Opportunities

U. Sankar

Introduction

The Report of the Fourth Review Committee of the ICSSR notes the dearth of good quality collaborative research and interdisciplinary studies in India. It also states that "ICSSR had at one stage envisaged close collaboration and interaction with the Indian Council of Agricultural Research and the Indian Council of Medical Research to promote multidisciplinary research in a broader perspective. But this was not seriously pursued and petered out fairly early. Efforts to promote interaction among institutes, and between institutes and the university system at the regional level, have also not been conspicuously successful" (ICSSR, 2007: 30).

The need for and importance of associating researchers from different fields were recognised, but the institutional structure of such projects was such that the tasks of different research groups were often compartmentalised and finally the research outputs were put together. What is missing is lack of synergy among experts in developing new concepts, paradigms and new ways of generating and interpreting data.

This paper illustrates the scope for exploiting synergies among experts in different disciplines and thereby developing new concepts, paradigms and tools for fruitful policy applications. It then illustrates the status and issues with a few examples: specification of production relations in agriculture and use of new sources of data, operationalising sustainable development and a few issues in science and technology policy. Finally it identifies a few barriers to fruitful and policy-relevant multidisciplinary research and suggests some institutional options for overcoming such barriers.

Scope for Synergising Multidisciplinary Research

Production Relations in Agriculture

Agronomists possess rich knowledge about soil management and production of field crops. Economists are interested in the production relations, input demands, supply responses and technological change. When an economist uses a neoclassical production function, often a Cobb-Douglas production function with an additive or multiplicative random error term to capture weather effect, the gap between agronomy and econometrics increases in atleast two ways. First, the formulation ignores the sequential nature of input decisions. Decisions on applications of chemical fertilisers and pesticides, labour use in weeding etc., depend on the states of nature during the production period. Second, in this formulation variance of output increases with the level of each input, while agronomists are aware that variance of output increases with some inputs and decreases with some other inputs. There are other specification problems. In the Cobb-Douglas form, if any one input is zero, output is also zero. To overcome this problem, researchers prefer exponential form for the input but this implies that marginal product is increasing at an increasing rate.

What is needed is development of a sequential decision-making production model with weather affecting different sets of inputs differently. Antle (1983) made an attempt to formulate a sequential decision-making model, but did not make the distinction between inputs. With further developments in dynamic programming, computer software and data generated by stage of production, the gap between agronomy and econometrics can be narrowed.

RS and GIS Data

We have new source of data on crop area and yield based on remote sensing (RS) and geographic information system (GIS) techniques. The Indian Society of Agricultural Economics (ISAE) organised a national seminar on "Remote Sensing and Agricultural Statistics" in 1998. Most papers deal with experiences in the use of RS data for crop forecasts and comparison of the accuracy of the data with the conventional data sources. See *Indian Journal of Agricultural Economics* (2000). Now, the project Forecasting Agricultural output using Space, Agrometeorological and Land-based observations (FASAL) is in progress and natural resources census has begun.

There are opportunities for fruitful collaborative research involving remote sensing, GIS, agronomy, statistics and economics. For selected application, see Sankar and Rao (2007). The RS-GIS data generation process is different from conventional time-series, cross-section or panel data. The data are huge in terms of synoptic, spectral and temporal coverage. We need techniques for innovative applications of the data for natural resource management and also for integrating the data with the data generated from conventional sources.

RS data covering the same geographic area periodically, available in digital form, provides an opportunity to understand how information changes with new observations; how our prior probabilities change with the new data to arrive at posterior probabilities; and assess the economic value of better and early information for policy analysis. The economic and social value of early information on crop production for the market participants, the market regulators and the functioning of future markets require careful modeling. Developments in economics of information, expected utility approach and Bayesian learning models can serve as building blocks for developing robust theoretical and empirical models relevant for policy-oriented research. For earlier attempts, see Hayami and Petterson (1972), Bradford and Kelegian (1974) and Hirshleifier and Riley (1992).

Sustainable Development

The concept of sustainable development has become a buzzword. The UN agencies, the WTO, most multilateral environmental agreements and most governments endorse the concept. Despite some ambiguity about operationalising this concept, there is a consensus in policy circles that this concept has three dimensions: economic, social and environmental. Serious policy-oriented research requires collaboration among ecologists and other scientists, social scientists, technologists, legal experts and policy makers.

Our knowledge about the dynamics of ecological processes, the threshold limits/carrying capacities/assimilative capacities, and the two way linkages between economy and ecology is poor. The reasons are complexity of ecosystems, location-specific characteristics of ecosystems, incomplete documentation of flora and fauna and non-availability of data for a long period to assess trends/changes in the stock and flows of natural capital.

Social scientists have to tackle problems such as how to correct market failures, institutional failures and policy failures by designing new institutions—community-based, markets, cooperatives—for sharing costs and benefits for achieving sustainable development. The involvement of locals/indigenous people becomes necessary because they possess traditional/indigenous knowledge and decades of experience in managing their resources. Their association is necessary not only for ensuring their support in natural resource management but also in evolving mitigation and adaptation strategies. Such collaborative research in other countries has resulted in development of sustainability indicators and techniques for sustainability assessment of policy changes.

Science and Technology Policy

There is growing awareness of the need for associating social scientists with other scientists on decisions regarding development/adaptation/and diffusion of new technologies. In areas such as climate change, genetically modified crops, nuclear energy and sustainable management of ecosystems, "typically facts are uncertain, values in dispute, stakes high and decisions urgent" (Pereira and Funtowicz, 2009).

India's Science and Technology Policy recognises the centrality of science and technology in raising the quality of life, creating wealth for all, making India globally competitive, utilising natural resources in a sustainable manner, protecting the environment, and ensuring our national security (Government of India, 2003). Social scientists can play useful role in the following ways: (a) assessing social costs and benefits of alternative technologies in a holistic manner e.g., energy from fossil fuels *versus* renewable energy sources; viewing solid waste management in an integrated manner considering health benefits and use of wastes;

(b) considering distributional issues in terms of access to new technologies and their social impact; and (c) suggesting ways and means of addressing 'the last mile problems' so that the benefits of technologies are translated into social, economic and environmental outcomes.

Barriers to Multidisciplinary Research and Suggestions for Overcoming the Barriers

There are many barriers to multidisciplinary research. First, multidisciplinary research requires knowledge in more than one field. It can yield fruitful results only when researches from different disciplines recognise the need for and importance of other disciplines and are willing to work together by resolving communication barriers in developing new paradigms and techniques, new ways of generating and analysing data and convincing funding agencies and users about the benefits of such collaborative research to society. For any subject specialist, participation in a collaborative research involves learning costs and foregone benefits (in terms of publication in one's own area, promotion, peer recognition etc.). Many journals seem to care more for rigour and sophistication in articles (even though the improvements may be marginal and their social relevance questionable) than for articles containing insights, innovative approaches, use of better database and opening avenues for further research.

Second, social sciences get low priority in public and private funding. It is true that some research outputs of social scientists may have lower commercial values compared with those of scientists and engineers but their social values need not be lower. Third, most social science research, particularly in economics, is confined to *ex post* project evaluation, assessing effectiveness of existing institutions, and testing of hypothesis. Research on design of new legal regimes, creation of new institutional and incentive structures for resource management under different property regimes, design of policy instruments satisfying economic, social and environmental objectives is scarce.

We often hear the complaint that the law/policy is good but its implementation is bad. It is possible that implementation and enforcement issues were not fully considered at the time of passing of the law or announcing the policy. It is also true that in many instances, law/policymaking is left to legal experts/administrators with little or no inputs from the concerned subject specialists and affected parties. When the relevant science is uncertain and information is asymmetric between policy makers and affected people, involvement of experts and stakeholders in policy formulation will help in identifying behavioural reactions of the affected people and thereby ensuring smooth implementation of policies.

What are the options for removing barriers to policy-oriented multidisciplinary research? The first option is to induce existing institutions to undertake collaborative research on topics of national importance. A coordinating institution with veterans in identified subject areas may be entrusted with planning and implementation of the projects. Opportunities should be given to young scholars. The second option is to create a few national centres for multidisciplinary research in certain thematic areas with overarching/cross-cutting issues funded by Planning Commission or some other Central agency. The third option is to appoint subject experts from related fields in existing institutions primarily for multidisciplinary research on long-term basis with equal opportunities and incentives.

To stimulate multidisciplinary research, we need other measures such as: (a) flexibility in curriculum choice at graduate and postgraduate levels; (b) fellowships for scholars who have done significant research in one discipline to shift to another discipline or/and interact with experts in other disciplines; and (c) publication policy of journals encouraging multidisciplinary research resulting in new paradigms, new concepts, new insights, new methods of generating data, and new avenues for further research.

References

Antle, J.M. (1983). "Sequential decision making in production models", *American Journal of Agricultural Economics* 65(2).

Bradford, D.V. and H. Kelegian (1974). "The value of information for crop forecasting with bayesian speculators: Theory and empirical results", *NASA NASW* No.2558. Princeton: Eco.Inc.

Government of India (2003). *Science and Technology Policy*. New Delhi.

Hayami, Y. and W. Petterson (1972). "Social returns to public information services", *American Economic Review* 35: 519-30.

Hirshleifer, J. and J.G. Riley (1992). *The Analytics of Uncertainty and Information*. Cambridge University Press.

Indian Council of Social Science Research (2007). "Restructuring the Indian Council of Social Science Research", *Report of the Fourth Review Committee*, March.

Indian Journal of Agricultural Economics (2000). Proceedings of the National Seminar on *Remote Sensing and Agricultural Statistics: Rationale, Scope and Aims, Supplement* 55(2).

Pereira, A.G. and S. Funtowicz (eds.) (2009). *Science for Policy*. Oxford University Press.

Sankar, U. and D.P. Rao (2007). "Indian Remote Sensing Programme" in Sankar U., *The Economics of India's Space Programme*. Oxford University Press.

6 Role and Functioning of Public Domain Social Science Research

M.V. Nadkarni*

What is Public Domain?

It is useful to clearly distinguish between public domain social science research (SSR) and private domain SSR and avoid superficial criteria to do it. The distinction should be meaningful both academically and for policy purpose. It should not be based merely on the source of funding, but rather on the criterion of whether the outcome of research is available or open to all interested academicians and the public; either for scrutiny or use, or both, in the form of publication in journals, books, newspapers or other periodicals accessible to the public. If so, it should legitimately be considered as public domain SSR. If, on the other hand, the outcome of research is claimed for private use by the sponsor of research and not permitted to be open to the public, then it is private domain SSR.

A government department may sponsor research for its own guidance and use, and its publication may not be permitted for quite sometime or not at all. Merely because such research is funded by the government, it does not make it a public domain SSR. On the other hand, a private or non-government organisation may sponsor research for a public cause and for public debate, permitting the publication of the outcome of research making it accessible for public scrutiny or use. Merely because it is funded by a private source, such research cannot be taken as private domain SSR.

---

* The author is grateful for the comments made by participants, especially for remarks made by the session chairman, Dr. Y.K. Alagh.

This criterion should apply to SSR institutions (SSRIs) too. Merely because an SSR institution is funded by private sources, it does not become a private domain SSRI. Similarly, merely because an SSRI is funded by government, it does not become for that reason alone, a public domain SSRI. A government funded management or technical institution may do a lot of consultancy work for private use, but it cannot be considered as public domain SSR.

The Role of Public Domain SSR

Once the meaning of public domain SSR is thus clarified, the rule of such SSR follows logically from it. But the role cannot be fixed in terms of a single objective. It is essentially manifold. The multiple roles of public domain SSR may be set out as follows:

a) help the formation of public opinion, or inform it, kindle democratic debate, add to the stock of knowledge in the process;
b) help social and economic development to occur, and guide it;
c) capacity building in SSR and help reproducing competent researchers in social sciences.

SSR can play a constructive role in forming public opinion on any issue of social or public significance by clearly stating facts, views and arguments on both sides of the problem/issue. While the researcher may have her/his own stand on the issue, which s/he may state clearly or explicitly, it is also her/his duty to critically weigh and assess all dimensions of the problem being probed in to. In Gandhian terms, the foremost objective is to seek the truth, and state it without fear or favour. This role of adding to the stock of knowledge which occurs in the process, is liberative in impact. The ancient Indian seers declared—*saa vidyaa yaa vimuktaye* (that one is knowledge which liberates). The ancient seers thought of liberation from worldly woes and ignorance at an individual or personal level. But in the modern conditions, liberation has to be thought of in terms of liberation from the worldly woes of oppression, poverty, hunger, disease, and deprivation and ignorance at the social level for large masses of people.

This role can be played by SSR only if it leads to dissemination of research outcome to a wider audience. If research does not lead to publication, it is tantamount to abortion. If research output is not delivered to the public, it has to be deemed to be aborted research. It does not mean that all research should be immediately made accessible to the wider public without any prior scrutiny by peers in the field. But addressing findings first to experts is only to vet and scrutinise the research outcome. Even in this process, two things have to be clearly borne in mind. First, that the author should be given enough scope to defend herself/himself and the freedom to accept or reject peer criticism in a spirit of genuine exploration of truth. Second, the refereeing peers should be genuinely autonomous in academic or public standing, but not glorified agents of official sponsors of research projects who may be interested in making the research outcome palatable to them. In no case, peer review should have the objective of merely blocking research outcome or its public accessibility, however, embarrassing research findings may be.

Often, the researchers themselves are the main obstacles in giving access to the public to their own research. Many social scientists employing mathematical or econometric models are unable to state what all their research paper/book adds up to for a policy maker or a social activist, even in the concluding section. The unstated presumption is that the more incomprehensible a research writing, the higher is its quality. A person who knows a problem thoroughly should have the capacity to state it in simple terms to the wider public. Even a physical scientist like Albert Einstein could do that, using illustrations and parables. Such ability, may be rare, but needs to be cultivated.

Prof. V.K.R.V. Rao thought that public domain SSR should not only study social and economic change, but help it to occur in desired directions, by guiding it, monitoring it and even helping mid-course correction of implementation of government programmes and policies. Though he did not deny a direct role for researchers as change agents, he thought that in a democracy, governments and non-government social organisations are in a better position to play the role of change agents. The more important role of researchers consists in informing on this process of change and guiding change agents, rather than take on the role of change agents directly. But Prof. Rao would not have been opposed to an academician taking a well-intentioned and effective activist direct role. He could see, however, that public policies and programmes in a democracy are formulated through a political and collective process, rather than through an individual in an isolated fashion. In his scheme of things for research, therefore, government and other public organisations played an important part as stakeholders, who naturally turn out to be significant sponsors and consumers of research. Prof. Rao, therefore, laid great emphasis on rich interaction between social science researchers and government, but he also stressed that the interaction had to be as between two equals, and not in the spirit of a patron-client relationship. If researchers saw any lacuna in either policy formulation or implementation, it is their duty to point out the same and speak the truth. It should be done neither with a submissive spirit of making research palatable to the government, nor with the spirit of projecting oneself as an anti-establishment romantic rebel. Balance and objectivity were key principles to Prof. Rao in social science research.

Even while conceding an important role to the government in starting and supporting SSRIs in sponsoring research projects of public interest in them, and in promoting interaction between government and SSRIs, Prof. Rao was even more zealous in safeguarding academic freedom and the right to publish on the part of researchers. He knew that politicians out of narrow and short-term political interests may try to dominate SSRIs and even influence the outcome of research. So even while he did not hesitate to have financial support from the government, he kept politicians away from the governance of the SSRIs, which he started and nurtured. The President of the ISEC, for example, is not the Chief Minister of the state, or Education Minister, but the relatively non-political Governor. He saw no harm, however, in having a few ex-officio members on the Board of Governors, but ensured that they would be in a minority and would not dominate the proceedings of the board. While it was necessary to make the government feel that they are stakeholders, he ensured, not only through the power of his personality, but also through the constitution of SSRIs that such stake would not be overwhelmingly high, for the sake of academic freedom and thus for credibility and respectability of research.

The fear of doctored research can, however, be quite real, even if avoidable. Young academicians are eager to demonstrate their competence by taking research projects, successfully completing them, and thereby taking more research projects. For several SSRIs, raising money through research projects is very necessary for survival and thus, they openly encourage research sponsored from outside. Among these outside sources, the government organisations are the most important, as they have almost a constant need to get their programmes and policies evaluated and sometimes even concurrently monitored by knowledgeable researchers. But politicians and bureaucrats have also an innate desire to have success stories of their efforts composed and sung, rather than accounts of failure. There can thus be a conscious or unconscious temptation on the part of bureaucrats sponsoring research projects to influence the research outcome, which needs to be curbed. They may not hesitate to blame the researchers for lack of commitment, competence and knowledge, if results of research show embarrassing facts and findings. They may even threaten to stop funding future projects. The potential threat to stop projects, even when unstated can be very real. The young researchers are, therefore, generally too ready to please the bureaucrats rather than get into trouble for themselves or their institutions. Sometimes researchers may try to compensate for lack of competence and in-depth research, by covering it up with contrived findings palatable to the government/sponsors. Not that such hypocrisy is common, but it is something about which both the sponsors and researchers should be wary.

The problem is how to distinguish a doctored or insincere research from an independent research fearlessly conducted and how to avoid insincere research. A balanced presentation of research findings, pointing out both successes and grave failures, supported by all relevant facts and figures, is more likely to be an instance of free and fearless research. But it is far better to take steps to prevent doctoring in the first instance. For this, and for the general academic health of SSRIs, it is necessary to have some core funding, untied to any particular research projects, so that SSRIs are not dependent for their very survival on short term and tied project grants. It is important for SSRIs to do some research at least with their own resources drawn from regular untied grants. Prof. V.K.R.V. Rao was so careful in this regard that he wanted a balance between the Central and state governments as sources of funds, even if a significant part of research is of greater interest to the state in which a SSRI is located than to the country as a whole. More than sources of funding, however, it is important to create and maintain an atmosphere of academic freedom in SSRIs, a point to which I come again in the next section. If an academician or researcher shows the courage to resist arm-twisting by bureaucrats or any attempt to doctor the research outcome, the heads of SSRIs should protect their academic freedom rather than threaten their survival, and safeguard their right to speak the truth. Prof. Rao ensured this in all the institutions he started. However, he did not want academicians to be smug and unopen to criticism, though he acknowledged and heartily supported researchers' need to defend their research provided that such defense is based on logic and facts. He wanted a genuine interaction between bureaucrats as implementers of government programmes and policies and academicians as evaluators. If evaluation had to be credible, it has to be not only fearless, but also fair.

One more requirement for ensuring free, fair and honest research, is to always insist on the right to publish, and make the result accessible for wider academic and public scrutiny. The willingness to publish and the act of publication mean that the research concerned is thereby open to public scrutiny and criticism, an awareness of which is necessary for healthy research. A SSRI which impatiently prods researchers to jump to another project no sooner than one is finished (or even before), without giving time or encouragement to them to publish their work, should be regarded as a second rate institution and no respectable academicians will stay long in them. Any explanation that this is necessary to get funds to survive cannot deny the mediocrity of such an institution. Nor can an explanation in terms of priority to help the government in policy exonerate it from mediocrity. Prof. Rao saw no conflict between guiding the government and its agencies in policy formulation and implementation on the one hand, and addressing the research to wider public on the other. In fact, he felt they would strengthen each other.

Even if we assume that the risks of bureaucratic doctoring or bureaucratic resistance to the right to publish are easily avoidable, there is still greater risk in too much reliance on research projects sponsored by the government organisations alone, which consist in the tendency to ignore longer vision or perspective. Bureaucrats often have no patience for theory, literature review, and insist on directly relevant actionable research outcome. They have also no patience for the 'on the one hand' and 'on the other hand' tendency of researchers. This is not to deny that there are academically-oriented sophisticated bureaucrats with a wider vision. The point, however, is that even if bureaucrats may not directly discourage publication of sponsored research, any impatience with academic trappings, if transmitted to researchers, can very effectively block any potential for publication, given particularly the hurry to move to another project no sooner than one is finished. For the purpose of publication, however important a finding may be, it has to be set in terms of a larger perspective. The important point is that such perspective has to be there from the beginning and not added at the end for publication.

The supposed conflict between theoretical and empirical research is a false dichotomy. Even a purely theoretical piece of research has to have some empirically acceptable postulates. It is not necessary that every economic research be based on field surveys, but its empirical dimension should be realistic enough or should be able to explain real world phenomenon. Economic theory may use a lot of abstractions, but it is nevertheless aimed at understanding economic reality in all its complexities. On the other hand, it is equally necessary for any empirical research to have a sense of wider perspective, vision or theoretical framework in terms of which empirical reality is attempted to be understood. It is said that while a research without such perspective is blind, a theoretical research without any practical implications is lame, at least so in social sciences. Sometimes, however, research is so conducted and presented that it may be both blind and lame! It is helpful if the researcher makes explicit both the theoretical background, or vision or perspective, and the practical implications of her/his research.

From this point of view, a presentation of literature review is essential in every piece of research, even if briefly. Some researchers, however, treat it as only formal requirement and that too in formal research dissertations at the Master's and PhD level. That it is equally necessary in other research too, is sometimes ignored. Even when a literature review is done, it tends to be mechanical, merely listing what this person said here and that person said there. A good literature review, even if brief and not exhaustive, should help in sharpening the academic or policy debate on the issue at hand and help the researcher in answering why s/he has opted for the objectives and methodology adopted. It should help in seeing the research at hand in a relevant perspective.

Should SSRIs take up the role of being change agents themselves, instead of merely studying change and offering suggestions for mid-course correction to policy makers and implementers? In an off-beat article, Felix Wilfred makes a case for social scientists going beyond just academic field work, and for taking up 'transformative praxis' ("The struggles of liberation theology for a new paradigm", *Review of Development and Change*, January-June 1999). Though 'action research' both as a concept and practice has come into vogue already in social sciences, it is yet to be popular with major SSRIs. Social scientists could take up the role of change agents and study whether a particular problem is correctly identified, if its solution is correctly diagnosed in different circumstances, and what obstacles arise in implementing the solution. 'Detached' field work through occasional field visits may not provide the same insights as 'action research' in which the researcher is actively involved. We have the sad situation of social workers with rich insights and experience, but without having time or inclination to sit down and write down in an academic way their lessons learnt, coupled with even a sadder situation of social scientists equipped with all the time and inclination necessary but without these field insights. Sociologists like M.N. Srinivas made a good success of themselves offering rich field insights, without being change agents themselves. Among economists, such field insights are rare. They depend mainly on data collected by others, though collected in a systematic and very scientific way guided by experts. While this approach has its own advantages, it is worth experimenting with 'action research' even if in a limited way on the part of economists too.

A glorious example of success of 'transformative praxis' is what Prof. Muhammad Yunus did for Bangladesh in micro-credit for the poor, for which he won the Nobel Prize in 2006. His experiment became a model for India too. Many books and papers have come out on the theme. But the major lessons about the benefit of transformative praxis by social scientists should not go ignored. We have many SSRIs now active in research on environmental issues. Could not anyone in SSRIs take up an action research project, say for example, on practicing environmentalism at home? A research team can take up an urban ward, actively educate and motivate housewives about saving water, cooking gas and electricity and about waste disposal through practical steps, and study the results. Lessons learnt can then be disseminated. A major problem in enthusing researchers with such projects is that such research is assumed to have no potential to find a way in prestigious international journals. But all social scientists do not after all contribute articles regularly to international journals. Why not do something useful, which if successful, may still achieve national and international acclaim ultimately, as Prof. Yunus could do? This certainly accords well with Prof. V.K.R.V. Rao's idea of an Institute for Social and Economic Change.

The last, but not the least, of the three important roles of SSRIs is capacity building or ensuring enough reproduction of research skills and competence among succeeding generations. Quantitatively at least, the universities are in a better position to play this role, whereas SSRIs are constrained when they are not 'deemed-to-be-universities' and need to work out an arrangement of affiliation with Universities in the area for guiding research leading to M.Phil and PhD degrees. In general, academic administration in universities is pathetically slow and overburdened, and does not enthusiastically welcome the extra work created by research students guided by SSRIs. Waiting for two years to get the result after submission of a PhD thesis is considered normal, particularly in the case of research students guided in SSRIs. Even under such circumstances, institutions like ISEC have done well in producing a large number of PhD students, who are spread throughout the country and occupying good positions. Institutions like Centre for Development Studies (CDS) in Thiruvananthapuram have focused more on M.Phil than on PhD. CDS has done outstandingly well in this regard; their M.Phils awarded by JNU are rated highly, because of the excellent training given in CDS.

The relative advantage of M.Phil over PhD is that it can cover more students, having shorter duration. But M.Phil requires commitment to more hours of active teaching through lectures, for which SSRIs are not prepared, given the shortage of good teachers and their large commitment to sponsored research. They feel it is better to take students who have done their M.Phil already. In any case, it is unfair to insist on a formal requirement of M.Phil for admission to a PhD course, for which the minimum requirement is a Master's degree only (MA/M Com/M.Sc). The main limitation of a direct PhD programme in many SSRIs and even universities is that either there is no preparatory coursework or it is too short to be adequate. A proper PhD programme should contain coursework for a minimum of one year, in which not only training in quantitative techniques in particular and research methodology in general is provided, but also insights from related social science disciplines, philosophy and logic are provided. When teaching is combined with research, the faculty become both better teachers and better researchers. PhD students should also be made to understand that they are not going to be narrow specialists on the particular topic to be taken up for dissertation, tending to know too much about too little, but are being trained to be competent researchers in social sciences as such, with the dissertation only providing a training tool and experience in becoming so. While the usual emphasis on quantitative techniques and mathematical and statistical tools should be welcome, the coursework should not end there, but provide a wider vision, a wider perspective in terms of which researchers develop a capacity to take a total view of things, even while being analytical.

The Functioning of SSR

The functioning of SSR both in SSRIs and universities has to be periodically monitored, and the assessment conveyed to the faculty at least to make them aware where they stand. SSRIs are better positioned in this regard than the general universities, since SSRIs publish annually at least reports on the research output, publications and other academic activities of the faculty. The faculty can thus compare themselves not only with others, but also with their own earlier record to see if they are progressing. There is thus a better motivation for academic activity and excellence in SSRIs than in universities, where such annual reports are not obtained from the faculty or simply filed and ignored, instead of being made available to the public. My observation of universities in general is that except for a leading few, in most of them, the academic environment in social science departments is too dismal for any complacency. The faculty have hardly any motivation for excellence either in teaching or research. There is on the other hand smugness, and a feeling that their priority for teaching leaves little time for research. Do they excel at least in teaching? They depend on notes made once upon a time, which are hardly updated from time to time. Visits to the library are rare and consulting journals for latest developments in the field rarer still. A significant number of teachers do not take classes regularly, and when they do take, it is not for the full duration of lecture hours, hardly encouraging classroom discussion. There are of course exceptions, and the reputation of social science departments depends on the work and image of the minority of one or two teachers, the rest being parasitic beneficiaries of the reputation of this minority. The general atmosphere is one of petty jealousies and squabbles, often based on caste, and not one of academic debates and discussions.

The matters are made worse for universities due to inadequacy of financial resources for research projects by the faculty. The available resources are spread too widely and thinly across as many applicants for grants as possible, with the result that practically no project is left with adequate resources. This hits hard, particularly projects requiring the employment of even short-term field investigators for field surveys. Yes, the faculty can try to raise funds from outside, for which there is not enough enthusiasm and talent. Also research sponsors prefer to assign projects to SSRIs which are better positioned in this regard than university departments. Government departments at the state level should nevertheless give specific grants to social scientists in universities who come up with research proposals, at least to encourage capacity building and research motivation. Wherever possible, projects involving collaboration between social scientists in universities and SSRIs also should be sponsored. But there is not much likelihood of matters to improve unless both positive and negative incentives are created and enforced for the faculty. Granting of annual increments should not be automatic, but should depend on the performance of the faculty, with a provision to withhold increments where it is bad and give more than one increment where it is good.

In the case of university teachers, an assessment of performance based on research alone can be problematic, as they may plead that pre-occupation with teaching does not make it possible to spare much time for research. Though such pleading does not deserve any more serious consideration than a petty excuse (because really speaking, teaching and research do go together), there is nevertheless a case for a separate assessment of teaching, both in universities and SSRIs. This can be done through an annual teacher-evaluation by students on three simple and objective criteria: (i) whether the teacher takes classes regularly, (ii) whether the teacher engages for the full period assigned, and (iii) whether classroom discussion is encouraged.

To assess research functioning, both in SSRIs and universities, it should be mandatory to bring out an annual report for each SSRI and for faculty of social sciences in each university. The report should include for each researcher, publications during the preceding year, mentioning the name of the journal/publisher for each article/book, invited lectures given outside, research grants obtained, research projects in progress, papers submitted in seminars and conferences, the number of dissertations successfully guided, and such other details. The report should also give the names of the faculty who have not submitted their reports. In addition, non-submission should also be treated as an act of serious indiscipline, and dealt with accordingly.

It is equally necessary to make a peer review of 'every-day-life' in the faculty of social sciences in universities and SSRIs at least once in two years, under which one or two eminent social scientists visit each such institution, spend at least a week informally talking to a cross-section of faculty and students, gather information, and submit a report to the vice chancellor/director of SSRI, with a copy marked to the minister of education in the state government/chairperson of SSRI. The peer assessment should cover at least three dimensions of functioning:

i) How much scope is there for creativity and own research agenda?
ii) How far interdisciplinary or multidisciplinary research is undertaken?
iii) How far is genuine fieldwork undertaken in field research?

The environment in such research/academic institutions should be such as to provide stimulus and enthusiasm to take initiative, to throw up new research ideas and agenda, for free academic discussion, and for academic excellence in general. How many seminars take place? Do faculty members visit library, consult new arrivals, and show evidence of intense study?

Secondly, it is not enough to provide scope for several social science disciplines, though even in this, some SSRIs are found wanting due to preoccupation with economics. It is more important to see how far there is interaction between disciplines, and if research projects show some evidence of interest in more than one discipline. SSRIs are in a better position in this regard than universities, which are too neatly compartmentalised into isolation cells even when all social science departments are placed in one building. Even where there is evidence of interdisciplinary or multidisciplinary approaches in research, it is necessary to check if such research rises above mediocrity and comes up with new insights.

Social science research often involves fieldwork. It is necessary to check if the principal investigator personally visits the field, acquires a feel of the field, or instead, depends only on the field investigators. Further, do investigators go beyond routine structured questionnaires, or are they encouraged to jot down their field observations, field insights and interesting field incidents? Is action-research or 'transformative praxis' at least permitted, if not encouraged?

Public domain SSR has a crucially important role to play in the contemporary world in which social/economic problems and governance issues are more pressing than technical issues. Yet, there is somehow much less attention on encouraging them to excellence than in the case of natural sciences and technology, though social sciences need a fraction of funds guzzled by natural sciences and technology. A healthy democracy particularly needs a healthy state of development of social sciences.

7 Promoting Research Culture and Atmosphere

T.N. Srinivasan

Introduction

The seminar on institutional structure of social science research is timely. The seven themes of the seminar cover the whole waterfront of social science research, emerging research areas and interests, and above all the recent expansion of privately-funded research opportunities. One of the themes covers the age-old issue of the allocation of resources between fundamental research, whose potential value not only cannot be foreseen, let alone forecast, but also whatever it is, would be in the distant future and applied research. Another theme is on the autonomy of research institutions with choice of research areas and appointments from undue influence by private and government funders. Although it is not mentioned explicitly in any one of the seven themes, though it is implicit in more than one, the complementarity and competition between university-based (both in academic departments as well as research centres) research and research done at free-standing research institutions needs some discussion. In establishing the Council of Scientific and Industrial Research (CSIR) and the various national laboratories under its auspices and later with the establishment of the Indian Council for Social Science Research (ICSSR) and research institutions under its sponsorship, India chose to focus on research at the free-standing institutions and emphasise teaching, rather than research, at universities. India is not, of course, the only country to make this choice, but the choice has had its consequences, in particular on the incentives for research and more generally the relative significance of research for recruitment and promotion decisions in universities. It is a sad fact that not a single Indian university is among the top hundred universities of the world. This reflects the culture of research, not only in social sciences as raised in one of the themes of the seminar, but also for all field of scholarly research in India.

Prof. Jayaram invited me to share my thoughts on one or more of the themes of the seminars. Let me say at the outset that, not having been a resident researcher in India for nearly three decades, I have not followed institutional developments in social science research in India closely, nor have I had an opportunity to read the four reviews of ICSSR including the most recent one by a committee chaired by Prof. A. Vaidyanathan. I apologise in advance if, in what follows, I have misunderstood, misinterpreted or worse still, distorted the reality of social science research in India. I assure you that any distortion that there is, is unintentional.

I found the issues raised in the seven themes of the seminar are not peculiar to India but have their analogous or counterparts elsewhere, including in the United States (US). I will, therefore, confine my remarks on some of the more common issues such as promoting a culture of research, balancing of incentives (pecuniary and non-pecuniary), of individual researchers and their institutions of employment, between undertaking fundamental and applied research, between private (including corporate) and public funding and their possibly differential impact on the autonomy of the institution with respect to allocation of resources, choice of research topics and appointments, and whether service to society including assistance to Central, state and local governments should be a part of the mission of universities and research institutions in addition to knowledge creation broadly conceived.

My remarks draw on my experience in working for a global research university, namely Yale University and in my earlier career at another renowned research institution, the Indian Statistical Institute (ISI). I am fully aware that the institutional context of India in which almost all universities and most research institutes are publicly funded is vastly different from that of the US where private universities and those funded by state governments compete. Also in the US, universities and their research centres are dominant in research in most disciplines, with free-standing institutes (private and public) playing a secondary role, although in specific fields of research the roles could be reversed. However, the federal government, through the National Science Foundation (NSF), the National Institutes of Health and other agencies, and the state governments support and fund a significant part of the research undertaken in private universities and research institutes. The role of the so-called 'land grant' universities established in the late nineteenth century by the state governments in agricultural research is well-recognised. With significant public funding of research, the fact that private universities are dominant in producing research loses some of the significance it might otherwise have. Also, the research culture and procedures of recruitment and promotion of the faculty or researchers in private and public universities (and to a large extent in free-standing institutes) are very similar. For this reason and for the reason that private universities are being established in India, I believe that some of the more desirable aspects of the organisation of research in the US are relevant for India.

Research Culture

Jawaharlal Nehru long ago, in his address to the Indian Science Congress in 1937, eloquently and pithily articulated the virtues of the scientific approach, which is the foundation of any research, and its relevance to all our problems including that of the overreaching objective of our development (at least since Dadabhai Naoroji's classic work of 1873 on poverty in India), namely, eradication of mass poverty:

> The applications of science are inevitable and unavoidable for all countries and peoples today. But something more than its application is necessary. It is the scientific approach, the adventurous and yet critical temper of science, the search for truth and new knowledge, the refusal to accept anything without testing and trial, the capacity to change conclusions in the face of new evidence, the reliance on observed fact and not on preconceived theory, the hard discipline of the mind—all this is necessary, not merely for the application of science but for life itself and the solution of its many problems...The scientific approach and temper are, or should be, a way of life, a process of thinking, a method of acting and associating with our fellow men.

> Politics led me to economics, and this led me inevitably to science and the scientific approach to all our problems and to life itself. It was science alone that could solve these problems of hunger and poverty, of insanitation and illiteracy, of superstition and deadening custom, of vast resources running to waste, of a rich country inhabited by starving people.

It is no surprise therefore that the establishment, not only of most post-Independence institutions of research and higher education, but also the Planning Commission charged with the task of planning for national development, presumably in a 'scientific' manner, was at his initiative.

Nehru was advocating a scientific approach to all aspects of human interaction and behaviour, not just the pursuit of knowledge in natural and social sciences as well as humanities. Clearly, it has to be the foundation of all research and teaching and the defining characteristic of research culture. This means that all other aspects of research culture have to be judged by the extent they conform to and promote a scientific approach.

There are several aspects to building and cultivating a research culture. The first and foremost is the process by which researchers and faculty are recruited, promoted and rewarded. In any highly ranked research institution, including universities in the US, the process of recruitment is rigorous though not the same across disciplines. For example, for the entry-level assistant professorship positions in economics, the interviews of candidates by each recruiting institution take place at the annual meetings of the Allied Social Science Association,[1] the interviewees are chosen by the junior recruiting committee of the relevant economics department after reading the *curriculum vitae* and the job market papers of candidates. A subset of interviewees is invited to present their papers and visit the campus. The full faculty of the department formally votes on which of them are to be given a job offer, based on their presentations and other discussions during the campus visit. The active involvement of full

---

1. The participation of applicants to most economics departments induces many academic (including some non-US ones) and non-academic employers to participate as well as to take advantage of the "job" market at the meetings. Recently a few Indian research institutes, though not universities, have begun to recruit at these meetings.

faculty in the choice of their colleagues is very important for building collegiality and research atmosphere in a department.[2] The number and fields of offer are usually determined by departmental needs and positions authorised by the university authorities.

In most universities the entry-level positions are on a "tenure track", meaning that a tenured (i.e., permanent) position would be open for the recruitee if she or he satisfactorily completes an initial term, usually six years (or nine years) depending on whether the tenured position is at the level of associate professor (full professor) and meets tenure criteria. A tenure review can take place even prior to the completion of the initial term, particularly if the candidate receives a tenure offer from outside. Although the procedures for tenure review do vary across disciplines and universities, they all have some common features that include a review by a departmental committee. The committee reviews the research, teaching and service to the department of the candidate for promotion to tenure and advises the department on the tenure decision. If it recommends tenure, a letter is sent to selected tenured researchers in the candidate's field in other universities inviting them to compare the candidate's accomplishments with a few others listed in the letter and to suggest other names, if they thought appropriate. After receiving responses and considering them, the tenured faculty of the department vote whether to offer tenure.[3] If the vote is for tenure, it goes before higher level committee (committees) of the university to ensure that proper procedures according to university rules have been followed by the department including importantly, the review of research. Although this last step is usually a formality, occasionally an even higher level committee can reject the committee's recommendation, for example, if it considers the recommendation to be premature.

2. The time spent by faculty in reading files of job market candidates, interviewing them, attending their presentations, and participating in the discussion and vote on job offers at the department faculty meeting is substantial and most faculty consider it important and worthwhile for building the standing of their department.

3. It is sometimes suggested that the participation of tenured faculty in the vote on their possible future colleagues could lead to a perpetuation of mediocrity since they might fear competition from anyone who is better in research than themselves. This fear in practice appears ill-founded.

A very important aspect of the recruitment process at these levels is that the US academic job market is very competitive and the competition in principle is global. The importance of competition cannot be overstated, whether it is in the supply of goods and services or for recruitment of researchers. If a potential recruitee does not happen to be a citizen or permanent resident of the US, the recruiting university helps her/him to obtain the appropriate immigration status. In global research universities such as Yale, a tenure-level appointee is expected to be one of the best in her/his field in the whole world. The competition for outstanding candidates operates at another level also, given the culture of mobility of academics across institutions. An assistant professor at one university, whose research in the form of published and unpublished work is recognised to be outstanding, can expect to receive tenure offer from other universities, thus putting pressure on her/his home university to tenure her/him early. An already tenured professor could also attract competitive offers from other universities. By the same token, denial of tenure at one university need not mean that such a person would be denied in all other institutions. Depending on that person's research and the reason for denial of tenure, such a person could receive a tenure offer elsewhere.

Among the terms of competition are, first and foremost, salary, time allowed for outside consultancies, frequency and other terms of sabbatical and other paid leaves of absence, research support during summer and given the fact that spouses of faculty also work, the opportunities for employment for spouses. These terms not only vary across institutions, but salaries and summer support for example could vary across disciplines and departments within a university. Even within a department, the earnings of faculty at the same rank and experience could vary significantly, in part influenced by outside competition for them and in part their consultancies.[4]

At Yale, outside consulting time is set by the rule that activities, including consulting and other gainful employment, that are consistent

4. It is not unusual for a highly regarded young researcher to recruit whom many universities compete for, is offered a much higher salary than some of the senior professors in a department. The variation in faculty salaries is accepted as not only normal but also essential for recruiting and retaining outstanding researchers in a competitive environment.

with the primary obligation of a faculty member to further the university's essential purposes, are acceptable and even encouraged provided they do not average more than one day per seven-day week in any academic semester or in any summer month in which the faculty member is being paid a full-time salary. Transparent rules of consultancy, paid leaves of absence, process of appointment and promotion, benefits of employment including contribution to health care and retirement plans are clearly laid out in the faculty handbook. Also, there are checks to ensure the integrity of the various procedures including there being applied in non-discriminative and unbiased ways, and also for dealing with grievances of faculty and staff. The point is that not only the potential attraction of outside consultancies to faculty and the demand for employing faculty with established reputations as consultant in their fields are recognised, acceptances of such consultancies is encouraged subject to transparent rules. It is encouraged in the expectation that faculty working as consultants would be open to fresh perspectives and ideals including importantly ideas that, if successfully implemented, would have commercial as well as social value. Moreover, the spillover from them to the research and teaching at the university is expected to be positive and significant. Thus, consultancies are not viewed uniformly as harmful—a perspective that is evident in some of the themes of the conference.

The second aspect of sustaining, if not in building a research culture, is the research atmosphere in the relevant department or research centre in a university. The atmosphere has several dimensions, starting from the balance between teaching and research expected of faculty and the weights assigned to their performance in each in the promotion and retention of faculty. Among US universities, there is a lot of variation in teaching loads and the weight assigned to teaching performance. At some universities, though no longer at leading research universities such as Yale, a faculty member with a research grant could, so to speak, buy off his or her required teaching time. However, in most universities, especially those which have graduate schools, the importance of research to teaching, particularly graduate teaching, is recognised. The basic idea is that bringing graduate students to the current frontier of knowledge in their fields and preparing them for research careers, their teachers should be actively engaged in frontiers of research. A good PhD programme is impossible to build in a department whose faculty is not engaged in such research.

Equally important to graduate training is an active programme of workshops and seminars in various sub-disciplines of each field. In the workshops, ongoing research is presented by faculty, graduate students and visiting speakers for comments. At seminars, the composition of speakers is tilted towards outside speakers and presentations are of completed research. Most of the scheduled workshops and seminars are publicised within universities, often with a copy of the presentation online, so that attendees could come well-prepared. Since the workshops and seminars of other departments are also available to researchers in each department, interdisciplinary research is fostered. In fact, at Yale such talks are regularly scheduled, for example, in law and economics at the law school and political economy at political science.[5] Other occasional interdisciplinary research talks are held at the School of Forestry and Environmental Studies, School of Public Health Medicine and the School of Public Health. Besides participating in in-house workshops, seminars and conferences, faculty participate in seminars and conferences elsewhere, including professional meetings. Above all, a process of peer review operates at many levels—including evaluating articles for publication, in evaluation of proposed research proposals for research grants and in evaluation of research of candidates for promotion. It plays a vital role in sustaining research culture.

Substantial financial support for faculty comes from research grants from foundations, federal and state governments and from the private corporate sector, rather than from the universities themselves. The CV of faculty routinely lists the grant support their research has received

5. Prof. P.C. Mahalanobis, the founder of the Indian Statistical Institute (ISI) believed that statistics is a "key technology" and a foundation for testing theories and hypotheses in natural and social sciences. At the same time, statisticians working in isolation from scientists in other fields including social sciences would be handicapped in their research without the stimulation of such scientists and their ideas for problems that need research attention by statisticians. For this reason, he established research units within ISI in various applied and pure fields such as economics, mathematics, physics, biology, linguistics, sociology and others. However, this strategy ran into the problem that scientists in those units which were small felt isolated from fellow scientists in their own disciplines.

besides awards and honors. To the consternation of some, the grant support received, rather than the merit of the research supported by the grant, often plays some role in the evaluation and promotion of quality. The shift towards outside funding and its associated, but unavoidable impact, not just on research priorities, but also on the very nature of the universities themselves such as departmental autonomy has been debated extensively in the United States.

In some instances, research centres outside of the departmental structure were established in part to take advantage of available outside funding and also to outmanoeuvre departments. To a significant extent, the shift in the US became pronounced during the Second World War and even more so during the Cold War. In her fascinating book published in 1997, *Creating the Cold War University: The Transformation of Stanford University*, Rebecca Lowen points out that:

> Before World War II, America's universities were peripheral to the nation's political economy. They were committed to promoting the scientific method, to allowing academic scientists and scholars to discover and study "truths," and to developing the character of business who were, for the most part, the sons of the nation's business and professional elites. While some universities included service to society as part of their mission, none of them conceived this service as direct assistance to federal government. *Autonomy from the federal government was in fact central to the definition of the university as well as of the science and scholarship conducted within it. Similarly, the concept of autonomy, from private industry, and more broadly, the world of commerce, distinguished the university from the mere technical institute. Universities in their own imaginary ivory towers.* (page 2, emphasis added).

Universities underwent vast internal changes consistent with the move of leading universities from the periphery to the centre of the national political economy after World War II. It is worth quoting Lowen again:

> Large laboratories staffed with myriad researchers having no teaching duties and working in groups with expensive, government-funded scientific equipment became common features of leading research universities...As the organisation and funding of science changed, so did the kinds of knowledge produced and taught. Universities made room for new fields of study...which have obvious relevance to the nation's geopolitical consensus. *Traditional social science disciplines also shifted their emphasis, stressing*

> *quantitative approaches over narrative ones and individual behaviour and cultural studies over sociological ones.*
>
> Most commented upon then and now [i.e., around 1997 when Lowen's book was published], were changes in the education of students and in the role of university preferences...*professional advancement in the post-war university depended wholly on research and publication [the cliché "publish or perish" was not entirely a caricature], which in turn depended on the development of patronage. Thus, undergraduate teaching received short shrift as professors, not surprisingly, showed more interest in and loyalty to their patrons outside the university than to their own institutions and students. If university before World War II was a community of scholars and scientists, the post-war university was...a large collection of academic entrepreneurs—scientists and scholars perpetually promoting themselves and their research to potential patrons* (page 3, emphasis added).

It is evident that Lowen's description of the profound changes in American universities after World War II and their effects on research and teaching echo many of the issues to be discussed at this seminar.

The changes that came about in American universities after the Second World War were not universally welcomed. Clark Kerr, Chancellor of the University of California in Berkeley, one of the leading state research universities, in his Godkin lectures in 1963 noted them. Kerr, while regretting the loss of a sense of community and the emphasis on undergraduate education that had characterised the pre-Second World War University, nonetheless appreciated the transformation of the university into a "multiversity" with a strong emphasis on research. Others were not so welcoming of the changes. I suggest reading Lowen's book for a detailed account of the developments since then and for its impact on Stanford. Briefly stated, the change in the incentives towards research that is attractive to outside funders and its influence on hiring and promotion of researchers, adverse effects on undergraduate teaching, the erosion of autonomy of the university and also that of departments within the university have not completely disappeared. What has happened, however, is the development of various mechanisms to cope with and to mitigate the adverse effects while augmenting the beneficial effects.

Conclusion

The Indian university and research culture and institutional features are very different from the ones prevailing in the US. To the best of my knowledge, first of all, there are few private universities and most research institutes are either public or largely publicly funded. Governing bodies of most institutions do not include representatives of their faculty. Second, teaching and research positions at all levels are permanent, so that after a short period of probation, job security is assured. Third, peer review of research and research performance do not play a dominant role in promotion decisions, although at leading research institutes this is changing. Fourth, the group conducting interviews for appointment and/or promotion is appointed by administrators and include outside experts. The senior faculty of the concerned department or the institute have no formal role in the appointment/promotion process. Fifth, the recruitment is in principle open to all who meet the eligibility criteria and in this sense, there is competition. It is fair to say, however, that competition is somewhat limited. Sixth, although there is some mobility of researchers among universities and institutes, for various reasons the mobility once again is limited and reduces potential competition to internal candidates. As far as I know, there are not many research projects in which faculty from different universities collaborate. However, some universities have begun collaboration with foreign universities through memoranda of understanding, though the collaboration is mostly in exchange of students and faculty than in joint research projects. Seventh, the number of research conferences and symposia, some of which are international in their participation, have been increasing rapidly. Eighth and last but certainly not the least, there is no analogue of the UGC in the US and the role of the Social Research Council in the US does not have the regulatory dimension of ICSSR on the research institutes it funds. However, it is fair to say that they play only a limited role in the training of graduate students and junior researchers. Although in many ways the US system is different from the ones in Europe and the UK, let alone India, it is clear that transplanting the US research culture and university system to India would be unfeasible, even if it is desirable given the much greater differences between the two. This does not mean, however, that some of the desirable aspects of the US research culture and atmosphere cannot be implemented in an appropriate form in the Indian context. Let me conclude with suggesting a few.

The first item in my agenda of reform would be bringing about a significant shift in research done towards universities and away from free-standing institutes. In my view, this is essential for revitalising our universities. At the same time, it will bring about a healthier balance in research between them and the free-standing institutes without doing away with the latter. For this shift to occur, a necessary condition is the reform of UGC, ICSSR and other such institutions. In what many would deem an unfair characterisation, I suggest that the UGC and ICSSR, in their regulatory roles, are quintessentially institutions of the late unlamented Licence Permit Raj (LPR) era. Just as the design of LPR stifled competition, creativity and innovation, the same is true in my judgment of UGC and ICCSR, notwithstanding their role in the creation of centres of excellence, etc. Such a reform has to begin with a rethinking of the role of Central and state governments and the private sector in higher education. No one will deny that our performance in primary education is abysmal. Whether the few successes (particularly of the IITs and IIMs which, interestingly, were outside the deadening hands of the UGC and ICSSR) in higher education (including its supply of highly skilled individuals to the rest of the world) would more than compensate the failure in primary education from a social perspective and thus rationalise the enormous resources spent on higher education, is arguable. Whether the outcomes for primary and higher education (including research) would have been any different had the Central government played a more active role in primary education is another open question. I am afraid that dreams of establishing world-class research universities and thriving centres of excellence in them and outside, would remain dreams unless at the very least they are kept outside of the UGC (as I understand is being considered already) and research becomes central to their functioning.

The second item in my reform agenda is to introduce the analogues of summer research support as well as sabbaticals and also to enunciate clear rules for consultancies, leaves of absence with or without pay, etc.

The expectation is that doing both will generate healthy competition for research within universities and institutes as well as between them.

The third item, which is probably extremely difficult, if not impossible to implement, but worth trying, is to loosen up much more than is currently the case of the salary grades and structures. Some of the privately-funded research institutions are less constrained by the UGC-ICSSR scales. It is very likely that a 'pan-territorial' pricing policy that mandates the same salary scale for all universities across the length and breadth of a country of India's size, would be just as inefficient and costly as the pan-territorial pricing we used to have for steel and probably still do for coal and so on. In the competition among universities for researchers, that salary is an important item is to be recognised and allowed rather than deplored.

The final item in my agenda is another very difficult one. It is to design a systemic approach for ensuring autonomy of research institutions, and avoiding neglect of research in areas (including basic research) not attractive to private funders who expect commercially applicable research funding with high short-to-medium run payoffs. For example, at Yale there is an office of cooperative research with responsibilities for university-private sector collaboration in research, the assignment of patents if any emerging from research, and rules for sharing benefits among the funder, the university and the researcher. The university also has an annual 'Conflict of Interest' reporting requirement which mandates each faculty to report any potential areas of conflict of interest between his/her obligations to the university and participation in outside activities. There is also an annual 'Activities Report', which is comprehensive and requires each faculty to report not only publications during the year, research accepted for publication, complete but yet to be submitted for publication and ongoing research, and also on teaching, participation in conferences and seminars, as well as *pro bono* activities. The report is deemed as an input to the annual salary decision as well as a signal for the university to expect competition for its very active faculty from outside. For brevity, I would not go into other checks and balances that are put in place to ensure that outside funding does not have undue and undesirable influences on university decisions, except to note that they exist.

8 National Perspective on Social Science Development in India

T.S. Papola*

Development of Social Science Research in India

The tradition of social science teaching and research in India is now almost a century old, beginning with the introduction of the modern university system of education in the country during the third quarter of the last century. Following the British tradition of liberal education, the education system in India incorporated social sciences as an important component of college curricula. It was natural in the beginning that the contents of social science teaching and research in India primarily aimed at dissemination and elaboration of the received theories and concepts of European, especially British social science. But soon, a trend developed, in a limited but a significant way, of questioning relevance and validity of such propositions and concepts and of asking specifically Indian questions, though still following the methodology and logic of British classical thinking. This trend also became, subsequently an integral part of the ideology of the national movement for Independence. While this trend continued on the basis of individual and isolated efforts, it could not grow on an organised and institutional basis due to the hostile attitude of the British government towards thinking which could foster, directly or indirectly, nationalist feelings. The mainstream social science teaching and research, therefore, continued to be positivist-theoretic and rather unquestioning in approach. Nevertheless, a corpus of social

---

* This paper was presented by Prof. T.S. Papola, at the conference of the Asian Association of Social Science Research Councils (AASREC), held in Sydney in October 1983 and also appeared in *IASSI Quarterly Newsletter*, December 1984. We are thankful to the author and Prof. A.K.Dasgupta, Editor-in-Chief, IASSI for giving consent to reproduce this paper.

science knowledge developed which combined with the growing body of factual information through official and individual efforts, on the one hand, and increasing strength and maturity of the national movement leading to the questioning of all things foreign, on the other, led to the emergence of an independent body of thought and literature, particularly during the 1930s and 1940s, mainly exploring a path for India's socio-economic regeneration and development after Independence. In this process, the exposure of the Indian intellectuals, both academic and political, to the socialist development in Soviet Russia, and rise of Mahatma Gandhi on the Indian political and intellectual scene emphasising *swadeshi* (indigenous) element in thought and action, played an important role in shaping the contents of new socioeconomic thinking.

After Independence, social science teaching and research grew at an unprecedented pace. There took place a manifold increase in the number of professional social scientists due to the expansion of the higher education system. The multitude and diversity of problems that surfaced themselves once the country embarked upon a programme of planed socioeconomic development provided tremendous scope for enquiry and research by social scientists. In terms of content and method, the holistic and transdisciplinary approach of the pre-Independence period gave way to the specialised and discipline-based studies, both on account of the need to study various problems in their specificity and the growing specialisation in the various social science disciplines into separate departments in the universities. Discipline-based social science research, with a strong empirical bias, experienced rapid growth. The questioning of accepted Western doctrines and propositions, which had started even in the pre-Independence period got further fillip as fresh evidence based on the experience of socioeconomic development in the country in its various sectors and aspects started coming up. The need obviously was felt both by development planners and policy makers and academic social scientists to carry out more and more empirical investigations. Researches resulted in throwing up a large volume of useful information, no doubt, which in many cases was fruitfully utilised to examine certain accepted propositions on relationships among socioeconomic variables. But most research attempts stopped short of formulating alternative hypotheses, propositions and theories. Most researches could thus suggest that the received theory did not explain a phenomenon, but little emerged by way of positive statement on its explanation. To a certain extent, it was an inevitable result of the dominant methodological framework utilised in most studies. The Indian social scientists for the first time had a large scale exposure to an interaction with the American social science tradition of quantitative variety. It helped bring precision and specificity in research work but, at the same time, the tools of research also brought with them the approach and framework of analysis which was not always found appropriate for dealing with the problems on hand. The scheme of variables envisaged as explanatory factors, chosen on the basis of an alien situation, proved inadequate, leaving a large part of the phenomenon unexplained. Rigorous efforts were made to improve identification and specification of variables with useful but still inadequate results. It seems that structural and institutional variables, which are not always easy to quantify, have a significant, if not a major role in economic and social processes in India, and the dominant mode of analysis based on quantitative techniques was not able to cope with them fully.

The above limitation notwithstanding, empirical-quantitative methods contributed significantly to the augmentation of research output, due to its relatively quick yielding nature as compared to the historical-deductive approach. Rapid expansion of the higher education system and multitude of researchable problems surfacing in the process of planned socioeconomic change, combined with the appeal and popularity of the empirical quantitative method, led to a fast increase in the volume of research, as is reflected in the published volumes of the results of the ICSSR stock-taking exercise of Surveys of Social Science Research carried out during the mid-seventies. The formation of ICSSR itself, with the promotion of social science research as its main objective, helped considerably in the process of acceleration of research output.

Social Science Research and Teaching

The large volume of useful information on different socioeconomic aspects thrown up by research studies succeeded in exploring certain myths about Indian society. It also brought out evidence to question several theoretical propositions on the interrelationships among socio-economic variables and, in many cases, provided direction for formulating alternative propositions. All this advancement of knowledge has not however, been adequately reflected in the teaching of social sciences. A manifold increase has taken place in the faculty and enrolment in social sciences in the ever increasing number of universities and colleges and practically all university or university level institutions, numbering over 120 now, offer courses in most social sciences in their campuses and in numerous colleges affiliated to them. There are today over 1000 postgraduate departments in social science disciplines in the universities, colleges and institutions, and most of them have been established during the last few decades. In a large number of these institutions, particularly colleges located away from metropolitan centres, however, research activity is virtually non-existent. This is one reason why classroom teaching in social sciences has not been able to absorb the new information and findings generated by research. But the syllabi and textbooks in social sciences have also been slow in picking up new research findings due to various reasons. There seems a general inertia to change the contents of courses; most standard textbooks used are foreign and those written by Indian scholars also get patterned after them, with hardly and significant effort towards genuine indigenisation. And also, the research findings themselves are not always of such definitive nature as to get included easily in the syllabi, textbooks and classroom instructions.

The cleavage between research and teaching in social science seems to have been accentuated to a certain extent by recent developments in the organisation of research necessitated by the need to augment research output in various socioeconomic aspects of development. Earlier, most research work was carried out in the universities by their faculty engaged in teaching as well. Today, there are three major sectors in the field of social science research in India: universities, non-university research institutions and the government. In recent years, university system has come under serious stresses and strains of various kinds, the most important being the overcrowding of the institutions of higher education. As a consequence university research has got confined primarily to the doctoral degree research, where again, the increasing numbers have started telling upon the quality. In any case, doctoral research has its constraints in terms of its capacity to deal with contemporary issues with the required degree of comprehensiveness. There is also a tendency on the part of the university community to look down upon research on topical and policy issues as 'inferior' to the more fundamental, philosophical and theoretical research. On the whole, the growth of university research in social sciences has not kept pace with expansion of the university system, and research themes have also generally ignored the swift pace of changes taking place in society.

A large part of social science research today is going on in organisations established either exclusively or mainly for conducting research. Most of these institutions of social science research have come up during the last two decades in the wake of the somewhat restrictive atmosphere of the university system for promotion of research on the one hand, and increasing realisation on the part of social scientists and policy makers of the increasing need for research on various aspects of economic development and social change taking place in the country on the other. These institutions have an advantage over the university system in terms of time their members can devote to the research problem on hand and relative flexibility of the administrative procedures they follow. Of late, they seem to have scored over universities in terms of research output and variety of research themes. Many of them receive regular assistance from the government, quite a few within the framework of the ICSSR; but all of them get most of their research funds from governments or their agencies. In view of the absence of regular teaching in their scope of activities, researches in these institutions do not get directly incorporated in classroom instruction, except in a limited way and with a time lag after the research results get published.

The governmental research system has gone beyond data collection and occasional descriptive reports. Various departments of the Union and the state governments have their research wings undertaking regular and occasional studies on subjects of immediate evaluation of their schemes and programmes. It is presumed that such studies serve very useful purpose as inputs in policy formulation and implementation. Most of this research is, however, highly specific in scope and empirical in content, and is often for 'official use only'. Therefore, its contribution and usefulness towards enriching social science disciplines in teaching and independent research is highly limited.

The Foci of Social Science Research in the Context of Planned Development

It is significant to observe that the needs of policy and programme formulation, implementation and evaluation have led to increasing realisation of the importance of and greater responsiveness to social science research by the government and official agencies during the recent decades. It has been reflected in the governmental support to research institutions and research studies through financial assistance, organisation of discussions and seminars on government initiative on various themes of policy relevance and research interest with substantive participation from the social science academics and involvement of the social scientists, particularly economists, in policy and programme formulation either by way of appointment of academics in official positions or of consultations in formally constituted committees on various subjects. Particularly in the Union government, practically every ministry and department has social scientists on its staff, most of whom have earlier been teachers or researchers in academic institutions for shorter or longer periods.

This encouraging trend notwithstanding, it would be unrealistic to assume that social science research is being directly used by the government. That is not possible; nor would it even be desirable from the viewpoint of a healthy growth of social sciences that research is undertaken primarily with policy measures in view. But a large part of research on socioeconomic aspects of development results in conclusions with implications for development strategy and policy; and it is not always made use of by the government. A hiatus exists between research and policy formulation insofar as most of the research is ignored by the policy makers as 'academic', and to a certain extent the researchers also fight shy of working on issues of direct policy relevance; and findings of their researches are often too guarded and qualified to be directly useful to administrators and policy makers. Unfortunately, it does not seem to have been adequately recognised that there is an inevitable and direct relationship between analytically sound scientific research and rational policy formulation; no research devoid of academic or analytical rigour could be good research, and any research cannot be useful for policy formulation without being good. The dichotomy between academic research and useful research is, therefore, false. There are, no doubt, indications that such a realisation is developing among policy makers as well as social science researchers.

In India, the processes of planned socioeconomic development and of development of social sciences have gone together in the post-Independence period. Inevitably, therefore, the themes and content of social science research have been mostly related to the problem of socio-economic change. In fact, the basic objectives of planning, namely, rapid growth of the economy, self-reliance and social justice have been the main foci of social science research during the last three decades. Instigations into conditions accelerating growth of agriculture and industrial output, social and economic implications of the process of rapid industrialisation, relationship between social structure and growth in rural areas, spatial dimensions of development, role of political institutions, particularly at the grassroots level, in the process of planned socioeconomic change and demographic aspects of development are some of the major themes around which most social science research has centred. Obviously, all these themes were directly related with the pattern of development envisaged through the instrumentality of planning. The fact of planning as a vital aspect of India's economic system was easily recognised and accepted by social scientists and the themes of their research started to incorporate increasingly the dynamic element of socioeconomic processes. Thus, economic studies have now growth and change as their main foci as distinguished from the static aspect of stability and equilibrium emphasised earlier. The sociological studies of, say, the caste system, shifted from their ritual and formalistic aspects to the changing relatives accompanying efforts for planned social and economic development and anthropologists' studies have shifted emphasis from the portrayal of typical characteristics of villages and tribes to their changing structure, power relationships and emerging stresses and tensions.

After about 20 years of planning, sometime during the middle 1970s, the question of poverty and inequality despite the achievement of considerable growth in output, came up as the main themes of national debate on public policy and development strategy. The social scientists in India responded to these trends by concentrating on the equity and distributive aspects of development programmes. A large number of studies on poverty, income distribution aspects of new technology in agriculture and of the emerging pattern of industrial growth, and on the problems of specially disadvantaged groups were undertaken to highlight these aspects. At the same time, the issues of emerging social tensions on regional and communal lines were also becoming a source of anxiety to all, and social scientists' response to this situation was reflected in their research efforts to investigate into the historical, economic and social roots of such trends, on the basis of studies at a macro level as well as micro studies of specific occurrences.

Thus, the major themes of social science research have emerged as responses to questions posed by policy and strategy of development on the one hand, and emerging socioeconomic and political trends on the other. The social scientists have mostly followed the lead given by developments taking place at the level of national policymaking or in different aspects of social life. The lead-giving task of social science research has been rather limited.

Ideological Parameters of Social Science Research

It is not only that the research foci and themes have mostly followed the pattern of national concerns and priorities; the national ideology has also influenced social science research to a large extent in terms of certain parameters. The Directive Principles of State Policy enshrined in the Indian Constitution on democracy, freedom, secularism, equality and social justice are accepted by mainstream social scientists in India as desirable goals; they are rarely questioned and are taken as given parameters of research on economic, social and political issues.

Similarly, a system of planning to manage development is also generally accepted. Researchers may focus on the need for improvement and reorientation of the planning system, but rarely question its necessity and desirability. That the traditional social structure based on the caste system is unjust and needs to be changed in a more equitable direction; and that untouchability is a social evil and needs to be eradicated, are accepted values in social science research. Objective studies investigating into the causes of communal and regional tensions have harmony and national integrity as their ideological framework. Similarly, the need and desirability to modernise the social and economic structure of the country is implicit in most social science research, though there might be differences among social scientists as to what 'modernisation' should mean.

Thus, certain overall parameters of national ideology are explicitly or implicitly accepted by social researchers, with little or no serious questioning of their desirability. Even questioning of their feasibility has the exploration of means of achieving them as its implicit objective. The social scientists have, however, not always accepted the politically dominant ideology of the party in government in respect to the routes and strategies to achieve the national goals and priorities. It is difficult to recall any policy measure which did not evoke critical comments from social scientists. Though it may not necessarily be due to the dissenting voices of the social scientists, it is interesting to observe that most social and economic policy measures in India endeavour to strike a balance between extremes: ideology of industrialisation is pursued along with emphasis on agricultural and rural development, large scale industrialisation is sought to be counter-balanced by small sector development; positive discrimination in favour of minorities and disadvantaged groups is combined with efforts at integrated development; tribal development programmes are a mixture of preservationist and integrating measures; and public sector hegemony is intertwined with promotion of growth in private sector. Such attempts at balance may be the result of the compulsions of the objective conditions obtaining in the society and economy, but they do provide scope for debate, discussion and research on alternatives by social scientists.

Relative Roles of Social Science: The Primacy of Economics

The major concerns of India as a politically independent nation have been economic in nature: underdevelopment, poverty and unemployment. It has been assumed that most social problems could also be tackled only with measures of economic development. Social scientists have, by and large, accepted these premises, notwithstanding some questioning of the validity of this 'deterministic' approach. Some evidence has been thrown up by sociological and anthropological studies to the effect that economic growth not only does not resolve all the problems but also leads to emergence of new problems. Yet, the overall priority to economic growth has been recognised, and resolution of old and new problems is mainly sought within the economic domain, by varying the pattern of growth.

It is inevitable, therefore, that economics attained the major importance in terms of relevance to the problems of Indian society. Among various social sciences, economics had the fastest expansion in terms of teaching facilities, faculty and enrolment, as well as priorities and resources available for research. Economics would account for almost one-third of the total university and college faculty and enrolment in the seven major disciplines recognised as social sciences by the ICSSR and the University Grants Commission. The research studies sponsored and financially supported by important national agencies like the Planning Commission almost all have economic themes, and even of those supported by the ICSSR which deals with all the social sciences, a substantial proportion is in the subject of economics.

It is being increasingly realised, no doubt, that many of the important issues needing investigation (e.g., education, national integration) should be tackled in a thematic rather than disciplinary manner; and efforts are being made by institutions to study them on a transdisciplinary basis, utilising the knowledge and expertise of scholars from different disciplines. Yet, since the university system follows in teaching the disciplinary division as generally recognised in Western social science, with little scope for interdisciplinary interaction, such efforts often tend to suffer from the lack of analytical rigour. Thus, while disciplinary division is essential for specialisation and rigorous analysis of certain specific problems, it seems to prove inadequate in dealing with some of the important problems of the society. In fact, a view seems to be emerging that most of the crucial problems facing the Indian society, even including slow growth of the economy, or dynamics of the caste system, which were considered to be the exclusive domain of economists and sociologists respectively, are complex and not amenable to diagnosis, explanation and solution on the basis of a single discipline-based analysis.

Issue of Indigenisation and Relevance

Researches in different social sciences have won wide recognition both on account of the new information they have provided on the socio-economic processes in India and of the fresh insights and propositions they have advanced for their explanation. Most of them have begun with the dominant theories developed in the West but in the process of investigation, significant modifications have been introduced, sometimes to an extent that the models look predominantly indigenous. Elaborately detailed specifications and significant modification of assumptions of the basically Western models of growth, have led to improved understanding of the growth process in a developing country, emphasising structural rather than purely linear nature of relationships between investment and output. Similarly, the uniqueness of the meaning of 'modernisation' has been convincingly questioned, emphasising the context-specific interpretation of the phenomenon and its processes.

Significant advances made in conceptual and interpretative aspects of research on specific social phenomena, however, do not add up to what may be termed as 'indigenous' theory of economic and social change. One wonders if such a theory is feasible or even desirable. Given at least a minimal universality of causations in socioeconomic phenomena, the claim of indigenisation of a theory would very much depend on the meaning of the terms 'theory' as well as 'indigenisation'. The fact that certain concepts and propositions developed in a particular land due to its advantage of chronological precedence of educational and scientific development, does not necessarily make these concepts and propositions 'alien' in other lands. The framework of analysis, in terms of the number and relative importance of different variables, could and does differ with the objective socioeconomic conditions of countries and regions, and also due to differing values of the systems to the extent that study and research in social sciences can hardly be value-free. In this sense, indigenisation could best be interpreted in terms of inclusion of locally relevant variables in the model or framework of analysis, their specifications to suit their local contents, and definition of the purpose and direction of research in conformity with the accepted value system. Indigenisation would thus imply relevance, in terms of the capability to explain, predict and prescribe in the specific national context. In this sense, social science research in India can be said to have achieved significant advance during the last few decades.

The social science community in India has, however, developed a healthy sense of dissatisfaction and inadequacy in terms of relevance of their research efforts; and the process of introspection and self-examination is on. Several discussions have been organised in recent years to review the past and ongoing research in social sciences in this perspective. This question as to how theoretical rigour and social relevance could be combined in research has been a concern of individual scholars and national bodies like the ICSSR. Reasons for a relatively slow process of synthesis lie partly within the educational system and require research. First, teaching in social sciences has very little fusion of theory and facts. In fact, the two aspects are taught in separate papers and with differently based material. For example, syllabi have separate papers on principles of economics or Indian social system. The contents of the former are theories and propositions without any reference to facts and are mostly based on the standard British or American textbooks. The latter have primarily descriptive and informative orientation, and here the Indian textbooks or sources provide the teaching material. The students hardly have an opportunity to relate one with the other, except income advanced courses at the postgraduate level in a limited way.

Secondly, much of the social scientists who had an opportunity to learn to synthesise theory and facts had it mostly in the institutions abroad; and such training, though generally useful, had the handicap having been based on an alien empirical environment. Such Western trained scholars had the advantage of strong analytical rigour, but in the absence of adequate empirical understanding of the Indian situation, it took some time before their research efforts at home could go beyond mere marginal manipulation of Western concepts to accommodate Indian data, to the building up of new theoretical constructs suitable to the needs of the Indian empirical context. Third, socioeconomic changes have been too swift in post-Independence India to allow time to shift the focus of social enquiry from what to why. Therefore, a large part of research has tended to be descriptive, throwing up useful information, but has fallen short of developing explanatory frameworks due to the highly complex and dynamic nature of the processes under study. While it is relatively easy to comprehend and analyse a static or a linearly changing situation, a situation of rapid structural changes in social relations requires a truly dynamic framework of analysis which is difficult to develop. After all, the changes taking place in developing countries like India involve not just growth or a transition but a transformation, and that renders the task of the social scientists really difficult.

These limitations notwithstanding, Indian social science has developed capabilities, as a result of extensive and intensive developments during the last three decades to deal with the emerging problems of scientists in any country. What is significant is that the institutional capacity, support and recognition of social science research has increased manifold in a short period. The problems on the teaching front, however, remain, as pointed out earlier, and rectifying the situation by restructuring courses in social science disciplines and ensuring greater interaction between research and teaching, therefore, constitute an urgent and essential step for a balanced and fruitful development of social sciences in India.

9 Social Science Research Capacity in South Asia

*Some Questions for Discussion**

Satish Deshpande

A number of issues emerged during the process of preparing the SSRC report on "Social Science Research Capacity in South Asia" that go beyond the confines of such a project. These issues are difficult to deal with for any small group of individuals because they stretch across many axes of variation. What is true for one region or nation may not be true for others; what seems crucial from the perspective of one discipline may seem unimportant from the perspective of another; and the problems of institutions like universities may be very different from those of research institutes, not to speak of variations in size, type of funding and so on. Even apart from the problem of variation, there are issues of broad significance that need to be thought about and discussed in the larger community of social scientists in South Asia.

The following themes and questions will surely be familiar to South Asian academics; I have also been thinking about them for some time now. However, the process of preparing the Delhi and northern India section of the SSRC report—especially in conjunction with the bleak picture painted there of the other countries in the region—seemed to invest known problems with a new sense of urgency.

(1) The 'decline and crisis' motif often provoked by our academic institutions is more a reflection of changes in the social context of the social sciences.

---

* "Social Science Research Capacity in South Asia: Some Questions for Discussion" has also appeared in *Economic & Political Weekly* 37(35), August 31- September 6, 2002, pp. 3628-3630. We are thankful to the author and the editor, EPW for giving consent to reproduce this article in this edited book.

Informal discussions on the state of social science research in India (comparisons with other South Asian nations cannot be made straightforwardly) commonly elicit narratives of the decline of once vibrant institutions and a sense of pervasive crisis in academia. However, it proves very difficult to take these casual anecdotal accounts into the realm of factual conclusions backed by evidence. Beginning with the difficulties of what to treat as decisive evidence, there are further problems of the lack of such evidence, or its inconclusive nature. What is undeniable in all these accounts is the crucial importance of contextual factors relating to the environment in which academic institutions function: whether or not there has been any real 'decline' in these institutions themselves, there has certainly been a major change in the social positioning of the academy. Thus, for the prestigious institutions in Delhi at any rate, the most critical constraints today are not material ones—there are teaching positions and research fellowships available, but it has become difficult to fill them at the desired levels of competence. To put it bluntly, vacancies at elite social science institutions no longer attract 'elite' candidates among either teachers or students, at least not in sufficient numbers.

This is clearly due to the fact that the academy in general and the social sciences in particular have fallen in general social esteem, both in absolute and in relative terms. Careers in the academy—even in once-glamourous universities and institutions—are now considered much less attractive than rival careers in management, banking, journalism, or even the newly professionalised and lucrative 'NGO' world. Moreover, in these changed times, the academy has lost much of its attractiveness even in absolute terms. Its favoured position in the past owed much to the broader context where socialism, planned development, nationalism and the general urge for progress carried meaning. By the same token, it has fallen in esteem today when the market, the individual and globalisation are the source of hegemonic ideologies.

One major issue that is always present either implicitly or explicitly in most discussions on the state of the social sciences in South Asia is the relationship of the academy here to the western academy. This is also an important aspect of the contextual changes that have altered the status of the social sciences in this region.

(2) The major crisis in South Asian social science research capacity is not so much in the production of research as in the production of researchers. However, the relationship between the regional and the western academy impacts on the production of both research and researchers.

Although it has been the subject of much public and private agonising over the years, our understanding of the relationship between the Indian and/or South Asian academy to the western academy remains surprisingly thin. It hardly needs stating that the older orthodoxies are no longer helpful—the western academy is not merely an extension of imperialism, nor is it simply the benign manifestation of a universal search for knowledge; at the same time, academic autarky is neither possible nor desirable. Moreover, assigning national identities has become much more complicated in the contemporary world with many academics (like so many other categories of globally mobile people) being able to lay claim to—and being claimed by—more than one national context. This is not to suggest that all these claims are alike or that nothing further needs to be said about them. But over the years, much of the energy that was once invested in the 'politics of location' has been dissipated in adjudicating contesting claims about relative privilege or marginality. By contrast, we still know far less than we ought to about the concrete mechanics of the globalised academy.

Who are the relevant 'stakeholders' (to use the current jargon), and what are their net gains or losses when, for example, a well-established professor at an Indian university moves to a western university; a promising graduate student at a western university decides to work on a South Asian subject; a western funding agency decides to invest in a South Asian research project; a South Asian journal obtains half its material from authors based in the West; a bright South Asian graduate student leaves for the West and spends the rest of her/his career there, or, alternatively, returns to the region with a doctoral degree? How, in short, does one go about estimating the costs and benefits of academic globalisation, and what is the net result of such a calculus today for a country like India or a region like South Asia?

Let me emphasise once again that tackling questions like these was not part of the explicit agenda of the SSRC report, which had the more preliminary objective of reporting on the current status of social science research institutions in South Asia. But they will have to be tackled at some stage of the enquiry given that the western academy looms large on the intellectual horizon of at least the elite institutions in the region. If a tiny minority of privileged, well-trained academics in South Asia now has a real choice about where to locate themselves, then we must try to understand the logic that governs their decisions and determines whether and to what extent they participate in local institutions. At a broader level, we need to renew our understanding of the criteria that qualify or disqualify institutions as 'local'.

It is surely significant that the mandate of the SSRC report was to focus on South Asian research institutions rather than research on South Asia. This is an acknowledgement of the importance of local institutions, something that Indian academics tend to take for granted. Because we have such a large national research establishment, Indians tend to forget that in many countries of the world, social science research is a largely off-shore venture dependent on the changing agendas of global institutions even when local personnel are also involved to a greater or lesser degree. We tend to treat this set of issues as already settled, as part of our common sense. This is especially true in the social sciences, where we have a vague sense that our research is more context-sensitive (and therefore less amenable to 'outsourcing') than the natural sciences. On the other hand, the developments of the past two decades—especially the emergence of a vast market for policy-driven short-term research projects dominated by NGO-style organisations—have created a menu of globally-portable 'prefab' methodologies that claim universal applicability. Given the complexity of the contemporary situation, it is doubly important to reopen all the questions associated with institutional location if only to remind ourselves afresh of what is at stake. In doing so, we must avoid being trapped within simplistic dichotomies that juxtapose monolithic notions of 'nationalist' and 'compradore' intelligentsias.

One of the interesting distinctions that the SSRC report draws attention to is the one between the production of research and the production of researchers. While both are obviously essential components of 'research capacity', the problems of the latter seem to be much more severe than those of the former. Despite the emergence of 'contract research' based on global tenders, there is still an obvious rationale for local research institutions, even if these take the form of 'regional' or 'project' offices. If nothing else, the constraints of sheer geography and the legal limitations imposed by nation states provide powerful reasons for the continued existence of regional research institutions. To continue in this minimalist vein, the resilience of state support and bureaucratic inertia also work towards ensuring the continued survival of research institutions, though this can no longer be taken for granted even in relatively stable environments like India. Thus, in spite of all the problems that have been discussed in the SSRC report, research institutions in South Asia continue to survive.

The picture is much more bleak when it comes to the production of researchers: every country, every institution and every discipline in South Asia (including the most privileged ones) is facing problems in this area. Indeed, with the partial exception of India, local doctoral degrees are more the aberration than the norm among influential academics in South Asia. This situation raises a parallel set of questions: Does it matter where researchers are trained? Should South Asian academics worry if most of their active researchers are being trained in the West, or if their own doctoral programmes are in decline? Given our history and our size, Indian academics tend to respond to such questions with a complacent sense of shock; we have yet to learn that rhetorical answers will no longer suffice. We need to reconsider the merits of the full spectrum of reasons that we used to (or still wish to) give to justify our doctoral programmes, ranging, for example, from the pragmatic ('we can't afford western universities') through the conditional ('our own universities are better suited to our specific needs than western ones') to the principled ('third world universities must be protected as ends-in-themselves in the interests of intellectual democracy'). Even more important than normative justifications are the practical means whereby we might reverse the downward trend in regional research training. When considering such means, it will be necessary to face awkward issues like the relative valuation of foreign *versus* domestic doctoral degrees, or the preferences of promising graduate students.

(3) The relationship with the West is not the only axis of asymmetry: the South Asian academic scene is marked by strongly unequal relations at the intra-regional and especially the intra-national level.

When speaking of the unequal relationship with the West, we sometimes forget that the national or regional entities that are juxtaposed against it are themselves riven by internal inequalities. While such inequalities may be particularly prominent in a large country like India, they are hardly absent in the rest of South Asia, and they need more careful attention than they seem to have received. There are two broad positions on this, one that sees elitism as the necessary corollary of excellence, and another that sees every instance of resource concentration as an instance of injustice. To say that each of these positions is justified in certain contexts is to state the obvious; we need to move beyond this level to address the subsequent questions: Just how much inequality is truly inevitable or should be tolerated? How do the different axes of inequality (across regions, classes/castes, genders, linguistic groups and so on) interact with each other, and which ones are more urgently in need of corrective interventions? What sort of correctives are desirable, which ones are feasible?

We also need to factor in the specificity of the third world context. In every region or nation in the world, the academy is both a job and a vocation, and many people enter it for the middle class lifestyle and status that it promises. However, in poor countries where such jobs are scarce, this aspect of the academy increases in importance, and a much larger proportion of PhDs are earned mainly to get or to retain good jobs that may have little to do with active research. (In most developed countries by contrast, a postgraduate degree involves significant hardship and sacrifices, and there are many other routes to a good job that are faster and less costly.) Moreover, countries like India also suffer from 'credential inflation'; because the number of desirable jobs is always much less than the number of aspirants, 'overqualification' relative to the job requirements is almost the norm. (Thus, it is possible to hire hardware engineers as programmers, MBAs as clerks, and so on, and PhDs are also part of this trend.) In short, the research establishment has to serve a more diverse set of (non-academic) social needs in South Asia than it does in the West. Any attempt to address inequalities has to be sensitive to these social needs; at the same time, it has to guard against degenerating into a patronising or cynical attitude.

This note began by mentioning that, of all the contextual changes that lie behind perceptions of 'decline and crisis', the most important is perhaps the lowered status of the academy in the eyes of the middle class elite that used to supply its most successful recruits. It seems reasonable to expect that the non-elite, or the not-yet-elite among the 'new middle classes' will seek to occupy the space vacated by the erstwhile elites. This may translate into a loss of momentum (or 'decline') in the short run because the new incumbents are not as well endowed with social and cultural capital as the previous ones. But the long-term implications are difficult to predict. Having opted for the West or having abandoned the social sciences altogether, will the old elites encourage, acquiesce in, or fail to protest the withdrawal of state resources from higher education, thereby precipitating the collapse of research institutions? (Incidentally, something like this already seems to be happening on a large scale in the primary education sector in India.) Will the populist pressures that are likely to accompany any major shift in the class-caste composition of the higher education sector lead to the further dilution of already weak academic norms and standards? Or will the broadening of the remarkably narrow social base of the Indian academy lead to fresh initiatives and new agendas that will revitalise the social sciences? (If this sounds wildly utopian, let us remind ourselves that we have already seen something of this with the change in the gender composition of higher education.)

There is no doubt that a number of messy issues will also get raked up when we get into the question of regional inequalities. Is research training or the doctoral degree to be considered a universal democratic right or a restricted privilege? How many researchers do we need? Does India really need the roughly 200 universities that grant doctoral degrees today? Where do we stop with regional equity—at the state level, the sub-state region, the district...? If we are to regulate the number of research universities, or the number of doctoral degrees, how is this to be done? At a different level, how is such regulation to be distinguished from other attempts to restrict entry and raise wages (by professional associations like the Medical Council of India or the Institution of Chartered Accountants of India for example)?

Finally, we come to the delicate question of international asymmetries within South Asia. As the SSRC report amply demonstrates, in academic terms, South Asia is not really a region at all: with the partial exception of the one-sided relationship between Nepal and India, there are no systematic academic linkages among our nations. This is certainly regrettable, even if the major reasons for this are also understandable. Are there any practical options for changing things, options that do not ignore the complications of regional geopolitics? The SSRC report has mooted the possibility of a regular South Asian conference that will bring together social scientists from the region. We need to think of other initiatives that might help us maximise possible regional synergies. Indian academics have a special responsibility here given the overwhelming size of our research establishment. Perhaps one way to begin might be to explore the reasons why institutionalised intra-regional exchanges have actually declined over the past couple of decades, even as our individual links with the West have been strengthened.

This note does not repeat the conclusions of the report itself, which is available in a summary and also a more detailed format from the SSRC. I am grateful to the other members of the SSRC team, especially the non-Indians, for valuable insights into other contexts. I must emphasise, however, that the views expressed here are my own, and do not necessarily reflect those of the group that worked on the report, nor of the SSRC.

10 Social Sciences in South India: A Survey*

M.S.S. Pandian

> The bourgeoisie has stripped of its halo every activity hitherto honoured and looked up to with reverent awe. It has transformed the doctor, the lawyer, the priest, the poet, the man of science, into its paid wage-labourers—Karl Marx.

Introduction

What follows is a quick survey of the resources available for and the constraints faced by social science higher learning and research in the region of south India. The survey is motivated by a desire to understand the current sense of crisis faced by social science institutions at the regional as well as at the all-India levels. The sense of crisis in social science institutions (both teaching and research) is fostered by at least three sets of factors. First, the state, in the wake of liberalisation and within a narrow and perverse logic of utility, is increasingly defining social science disciplines as of 'non-utility'. This has forced, for instance, history departments in a number of universities to reinvent their function as one of training students to be tourist guides. Second, as a consequence of this new characterisation of social sciences by the state, there is downsizing of state funding for social sciences. The systematic moves made by the Indian Council for Social Science Research (ICSSR) during the past decade to go back on its financial commitment to research institutions within its framework are a well known case in point. Finally, in the face of the assault by the state,

* "Social Sciences in South India: A Survey" has also appeared in *Economic & Political Weekly* 37(35), August 31-September 6, 2002, pp. 3613-3627. We are thankful to the author and the editor, EPW for giving consent to reproduce this article in this edited book.

social science institutions, mired by and large in a culture of non-performance and mediocrity, have failed to come up with an alternative logic to justify their very existence.

Against this backdrop, the present survey is divided into five sections. Section II maps out the institutional resources available for social science higher learning and research in south India. This is followed by two case studies in Sections III and IV. The case studies analyse in detail the Madras Institute of Development Studies (MIDS), Chennai, and the Institute for Social and Economic Change (ISEC), Bangalore. Section V details the key issues that have emerged through the survey and suggest a possible course of future action.

Resources for Social Sciences

South India is endowed with a reasonable degree of resources for social science higher learning and research, in the form of research institutions, libraries, documentation centres, archives and professional associations. Significantly, these resources are distributed quite evenly across the four states of Andhra Pradesh, Karnataka, Kerala and Tamil Nadu and the union territory of Puducherry.

Research Institutes

South India has four major research institutes within the framework of ICSSR—Centre for Economic and Social Studies (CESS), Hyderabad; Institute for Social and Economic Change (ISEC), Bangalore; Centre for Development Studies (CDS), Thiruvananthapuram; and Madras Institute of Development Studies (MIDS), Chennai. Of these four institutes, the latter three are well-known nationally and beyond.

The CESS, the youngest of the ICSSR institutes in the region, was founded by the Andhra Pradesh state government in 1980; and was recognised in 1986 by the ICSSR as a national research institute. It has also been recognised as a centre for advanced research by Dr. B.R. Ambedkar Open University and Osmania University, both located in Hyderabad. It runs a full-time PhD programme in economics and anthropology affiliated to the University of Hyderabad; and a part-time M.Phil and PhD programme in development studies affiliated to Dr.

B.R. Ambedkar Open University. The research focus of the centre is dominated by applied economics with an emphasis on the regional economy of Andhra Pradesh.

The CDS was founded in 1971 with the explicit agenda of promoting research in disciplines relevant to development. With a faculty of 26, it is the foremost social science research institute in Kerala. Apart from regular research, the centre runs an M.Phil programme in applied economics affiliated to Jawaharlal Nehru University (JNU), Delhi; a PhD programme affiliated to JNU and Kerala University, Thiruvananthapuram; and a postgraduate diploma programme in population and development affiliated once again to JNU. Sponsored by the United Nations Population Fund, the CDS conducts a policy-oriented training on population and sustainable development. Though the centre claims that it has established a tradition of interdisciplinary research, the main thrust of its research is applied economics with an emphasis on Kerala. The exception seems to be a couple of faculty members conducting research on economic history.

The ISEC, which was founded in 1972, is one of the five research institutions initially funded by the ICSSR. The main objectives of the institute are to undertake pure and applied research in social sciences in an interdisciplinary framework and to assist Central, state and local governments by providing advice based on policy-related studies. The MIDS, founded in 1971 as a private research institute, was reconstituted as a national research institute within the framework of the ICSSR in 1977. The stated objective of MIDS was "to undertake studies and research pertaining to development problems". We will have detailed discussions about the ISEC and the MIDS in a subsequent section of this survey.

Apart from these institutions that are funded by the ICSSR and the state governments, there are a number of research institutions in the region which are funded by non-governmental sources. The important ones among them are: Anveshi Research Centre for Women's Studies, Hyderabad; Centre for the Study of Culture and Society (CSCS), Bangalore; Institute of Development Alternatives (IDA), Chennai; and Madras School of Economics (MSE), Chennai.

The Anveshi, founded in 1985, is an important resource centre in south India for research on gender. Among other things, the centre has produced a two-volume *Anthology of Women's Writings in India*, which is considered a landmark in women studies in India. The research agenda of CSCS, established in 1996 and funded initially by the Ford Foundation, has been to understand culture in its most inclusive sense. Apart from individual research carried out by its faculty in areas such as visual media and gender, it also runs a media archives and a PhD programme. The IDA has been registered as a trust in August 1997 with the main objective of conducting research on developmental alternatives. Its research agenda encompasses gender, politics of governance, industrial labour, and agrarian change. It works in close collaboration with the V.V. Giri National Labour Institute, Noida and the Kerala research programme on local level development, Centre for Development Studies, Thriuvananthapuram. The Madras School of Economics, which has been planned as a centre of excellence for postgraduate education in economics in India, was registered in 1993 and started functioning in 1995. Though it initially received a capital grant of Rs. 3 crore from the Ministry of Finance, Government of India, and land for a campus on long-term lease at a concessional rate from the government of Tamil Nadu, it is mostly funded by leading Indian companies and financial institutions by their contributions to a corpus fund. Project-based research in areas such as environmental economics, energy and infrastructure economics and macroeconomic policy constitutes the important activity of the MSE. It runs a two-year M.Sc. course in economics in collaboration with Anna University, Chennai. Both Madras and Anna universities have recognised the MSE as an institution for carrying out PhD in economics.

Universities

South India is the home for several well-known and old universities. For example, Madras University was founded in 1857; Annamalai University in 1929; the University of Kerala in 1937; Osmania University in 1918; and the University of Mysore in 1916. Excluding the universities devoted for science and technology, the region as a whole has 40 universities—14 in Andhra Pradesh, 7 in Karnataka, 4 in Kerala and 14 in Tamil Nadu, and 1 in Pondicherry. Nineteen of these universities (or about half of them) were established either in 1980 or later on. The disciplines of economics, history and sociology dominate these universities. Of the 40 universities, 25 (62.5 per cent) have departments of economics; 24 (60 per cent) have departments of history; and 23 have departments of sociology. While 18 of them (45 per cent) have departments of political science, only 5 of them (12.5 per cent) have departments of anthropology.

Several of the university departments in the region have inadequate number of faculty members. Syllabuses used for the courses are often outdated by decades. Institutionally, most of the university departments do not have research orientation, though there are individual faculty members who do pursue research out of their own interest.

However, there are rare exceptions to this overall trend. The School of Social Sciences at the Mahatma Gandhi University at Kottayam is one such exception. The school was conceived as an interdisciplinary department to promote teaching and research in the frontier areas of social sciences. Currently, the school offers a PhD programme, two M.Phil programmes, and three M.A. programmes. Of the two M.Phil programmes, one is in interdisciplinary social sciences, and the other in natural history and human ecology. The M.A. programmes are conducted in three different disciplines—anthropology, economics and history—but with an inter-disciplinary orientation.

The school seems to have succeeded in offering a different kind of Masters programme, compared to other universities. First, it has a set of core courses common to all three streams. This comprises political economy, logic, and social theory. Second, it lays substantial emphasis on hands-on training. This is realised by two means. The school undertakes several research projects for the department of forest and wildlife of the Kerala government. The students take active part in these projects, particularly in conducting fieldwork. Besides, dissertation is a crucial component in the Masters programme. A student begins working on his/her dissertation at the beginning of the third semester and submits it for evaluation at the end of the fourth semester which gives a full year to concentrate on it. Being located away from the metropolis and the major libraries and archives in the state, is a constraint on dissertation work. The school seeks to overcome this by encouraging the students to work on topics for which untapped local resources are available (which are often unknown or inaccessible to metropolitan researchers).

However, running such an inter-disciplinary course is not without its difficulties. As a faculty member of the school puts it, "With the introduction of UGC National Entrance Test as a requirement for PhD fellowship, the Masters programme in general has become increasingly discipline-bound. This has rendered Masters programmes with interdisciplinary orientation as offered in the school less privileged. Reorienting the Masters programmes offered by the school along narrow disciplinary boundaries would have gone against the founding objectives and the larger orientation of the school. This would have also caused a disjuncture with the PhD and M.Phil programmes as these are conceived and conducted now."

Libraries

The libraries of the four ICSSR institutes in south India are of key importance in fostering social science learning and research in the region. The CESS library has a collection of over 20,000 books and subscribes to about 150 journals. As a participant in the World Bank Depository Library Programme, the library provides access to the Bank's research and data. The ISEC library has more than 1000,000 titles and 335 microfiche copies of periodicals. It subscribes to approximately 350 foreign and Indian professional journals. The World Bank, among other international organisations, has recognised the ISEC library as a depository library. It has also set up a data bank for storing both secondary and primary data collected for several projects carried out by the institute. The MIDS library has about 45,000 volumes and it subscribes to about 190 journals. The CDS library has, like the University of Kerala, a separate section for Kerala studies. The microfilm collection at the Centre for Development Studies has several old documents, census volumes and books on Kerala, while the Kerala studies section has mostly new books and reports, particularly from the 1970s.

Apart from these libraries, each of the southern states has an array of libraries catering to the needs of the social scientists. Perhaps the most important one in Andhra Pradesh is Vetapalem library, known also as Saraswata Niketanam, located in Prakasam district. It houses the well known Mackenzie collection. This library is reputed to be the best source for back volumes of Telugu magazines and newspapers, and also some rare books. Gautami library in Rajahmundry also holds a considerable collection of old Telugu newspapers, magazines and rare books. Of these two libraries, Vetapalem library is maintained better. Both these libraries are run privately with state aid. C.P. Brown Language Research Centre at Cuddapah is yet another important library in the state. Besides Brown collection, it also has some oral history collection. Apart from a good collection of books on women's studies, the library of Anveshi Resource Centre holds considerable material on women's movement in India, including clippings from contemporary newspapers, collection of books and articles written by women over the last 150 years, and 19th century women's journals.

The Sundarayya Vignana Kendram, founded in 1988 in Hyderabad, requires a special mention here. It has grown out of the personal collections of late P. Sundarayya, the Communist leader. Personal collections of others such as Bezawada Gopala Reddy were added to the collection later on. Personal papers of left wing political activists and writers mark out this collection as distinct. The papers of Sundarayya alone accounts for more than one lakh pages. The research library contains around 75,000 printed volumes in Telugu and English. The Kendram is also preserving a collection of books in Urdu under the name Urdu Research Library. The collection, considered to be only one of its kind in South Asia, consists of 30,000 books, journals, periodicals and manuscripts, dating from the 17th century.

In Karnataka, the Ecclesiastical Archives, located in the library of the United Theological College, Bangalore, is an important resource centre for social scientists. Founded in the late 1950s, the archive houses substantial collection of unpublished missionary society materials (mostly of the 19th and 20th centuries), private papers of Christian leaders in politics, back volumes of old journals (both academic and related to various Christian missions), etc. This well-maintained collection has an all-India focus. Part of the collection is in microfilms and microfiches. The archive is equipped with microfilm and microfiche readers and facilities for photocopying. The Media and Culture archives run by the CSCS, located in Bangalore, was initiated in 1998 as a project for electronically documenting material that would be useful for research on contemporary India. At present, the database consists of approximately 25,000 records in areas such as human rights/ civil liberties; history of radio and television communication; major issues and controversies in the fields of literary and news publishing; legal statutes, petitions and judgments on media; and key issues involving the Indian cinemas, including censorship controversies. Though this web-based collection is managed from Karnataka, it has an all India character.

In Kerala, the library of Kerala Institute for Research, Training and Development Studies of Scheduled Castes and Scheduled Tribes (KIRTADS), a state-run institution based at Chevayur in Kozhikode district, has over 10,000 books. Kerala Forest Research Institute (KFRI) based at Peechi in Thrissur, yet another state-run institution, has a vast collection of material on environment, in particular the forest ecosystem. Kerala Sahitya Academy, headquartered in Thrissur, has a vast collection of books in Malayalam and back volumes of journals. The Folklore Academy at Kannur has a good collection of documents, audio and video material relating to folk arts.

In the private domain, the libraries of Sri Chitra Hindumatha Granthasala, Vanchiyoor; Ulloor Smaraka Library, Jagathy, and the library at Malayinkeezhu, all in Thiruvananthapuram, and the Vignana Vardhini Library, Vypeen, Kochi, deserve special mention for collection of old books and journals. The public libraries in Kottayam, Ernakulam, Thrissur and Kozhikode are known for their old collection of books, mostly fiction. In addition, there are several institutions in Kerala which hold special collections. For instance, the Orthodox Seminary at Kottayam, the Catholic Church at Thrissur, and the churches at Niranam near Thiruvalla, Edathua in Kuttanad, and Kuravilangad near Kottayam preserve a huge collection of material related to churches, seminaries and missionaries. The records include daily journals and land transactions. The CMS College in Kottayam maintains the 19th and 20th century records and correspondence of the church missionary society. So far Tamil Nadu goes, special mention needs to be made of the Folklore Resources and Research Centre (FRRC), Palayamkottai; Roja Muthiah Research Library (RMRL), Chennai; and the Adyar Library and Research Centre (ALRC), Chennai. The FRRC was founded in 1987 on a generous grant from the Ford Foundation. Affiliated to the St. Xavier's College, Palayamkottai, the centre conducts research on varied aspects of folk life in Tamil Nadu. The research findings are published in the form of books (in Tamil) and in *South Indian Folklorist* (in English), which is a biannual journal. The FRRC archives has a sizeable body of folkloristic materials in the form of audio and video cassettes, photographs, slides, manuscripts and palm leaf manuscripts. The FRRC library holds over 10,000 books and 29 research journals.

The RMRL grew out of the private collection of Roja Muthiah Chettiar (1926-1992). The collection that contained nearly 100,000 items in Tamil, consisting of books, full-run of important journals and single sheet materials such as drama notices and wedding invitations, was bought by the University of Chicago and the RMRL was founded in 1995. Subsequently, the private collections of others such as Kovai Ayyamuthu, Gift Siromoney, A.K. Ramanujam and Milton Singer have been added to the collection. State-of-the-art preservation techniques and a very high degree of professionalism are the hallmarks of the RMRL. It is an indispensable institution for anyone working on the history, culture and politics of Tamil Nadu.

The ALRC was founded in 1886 by Col. H.S. Olcott, the president-founder of the Theosophical Society, Madras. The collection of the library at present consists of about 1,86,000 manuscripts, both palm leaf and paper, and some 1,75,000 printed volumes, excluding journals. The manuscript section includes numerous Sanskrit works besides manuscripts from Sri Lanka, China, Siam, Persia and other eastern countries. The printed books include old and rare indological works. The library also publishes a journal *Brahmavidya* since 1937 which carries papers on religion, philosophy, culture, Sanskrit and ancient texts.

In addition, the professionally-run libraries of the Dravida Munnetra Kazhagam (DMK) and the Dravidar Kazhagam (DK), two political organisations, have a wide range of materials including party newspapers and political pamphlets issued by different political organisations in Tamil Nadu. While the DK library holds considerable material belonging to the first half of the 20th century, the holdings of the DMK library starts mostly from the 1950s. These libraries are indispensable sources for anyone working on the post-colonial politics of the region.

The above inventory and description of libraries in south India is by no means exhaustive. In fact, they just give a flavour of what is available for serious social science learning and research.

Archives[1]

South India has four state-run regional archives. The Andhra Pradesh State Archives was founded, in its present form, in 1924. The historical records preserved in the archives include '*firmans* and *sanads*' of the Deccan Sultans, secretariat records of the former Hyderabad state (1853-1956), and secretariat records of the composite Madras state (1920-1956). The microfilm collections at the archives include such diverse material as the C.P. Brown collection, Gurzada Apparao's diaries, Kalahasti copper plates, and Telugu periodicals like *Sadhana Patrika* (1921-1950), *Krishna Patrika* (1902-1929) and *Andhra Patrika* (1914-1917). The archive offers full-time and part-time scholarships for research scholars.

The Karnataka State Archives, Bangalore, was set up in 1972 and preserves the records of the old princely state of Mysore, Bombay, Karnataka, Hyderabad and Coorg. It has a separate branch at Mysore housing the palace records and some other collections, notably the '*kadathas*' (oral history document on cloth) of the Yelandur Jagir. The Karnataka state archive has a rich collection of private papers and private collections of local political and cultural figures. In addition, it has a valuable collection of Persian records relating to the period of Tipu Sultan.

1. Some of the information used in this section is drawn from Raj (1999).

The Central Archives of Kerala state is located in Thiruvananthapuram. The most important collection available here is *Matilakam Rekhakal* that pertains to the daily transactions and administration of the Sri Anantha Padmanabha Swamy temple roughly from 14th to 19th centuries. The Direcorate of Archives at Thiruvananthapuram maintains the administrative records, primarily the proceedings of various departments of the Travancore princely state. These relate mostly to the 19th and 20th centuries. Besides primary sources, both the Central Archives and the Directorate of Archives, particularly the latter, have a collection of printed books, reports and manuals. The regional archives in Kochi maintains records of the Kochi princely state, while those relating to the Malabar district, which was part of the Madras presidency, are housed in the regional archives at Kozhikode. Besides, there are two important other state-run centres for historical source material. Both are located in Thalassery. The records room of the district and sessions court provides case records from 19th century as also village survey and settlement records of Malabar district for the first half of the 20th century. The revenue divisional office maintains the land records.

The Tamil Nadu State Archives at Madras, founded in its present form in 1909, functions as a central archives for the whole of the old Madras presidency region. This is so despite the fact that substantial parts of records have been transferred to other state archives in the region. It has a wide variety of historical material including secretariat and collectorate records. Over the years, it has established seven regional centres in the districts of Madurai, Coimbatore, South Arcot, Tiruchirapalli, Thanjavur, Madras and Salem. The regional centres are expected to centralise the distict-level records which are 30 years old. In 1973, the Tamil Nadu Council of Historical Research was founded as part of the Archives to strengthen its research component. It has so far given out 17 fellowships to promote historical research on Tamil Nadu. The 1970s also witnessed other developments, which strengthened the archives. Appointment of 12 librarians in 1979 and the inauguration of a modern research hall are the highlights of the period. In the 1990s, the research hall underwent further improvement and a new library building was established.

Documentation Centres

There are several small documentation centres in south India, almost all of them in the non-government sector. The most important one is the Centre for Education and Documentation (CED), an NGO established in 1975. The CED runs two reference centres—one in Mumbai and the other in Bangalore. Archived clippings from 10 daily newspapers, 32 magazines and 42 newsletters form the core of the CED collection. Its areas of emphasis are social justice, gender, human rights, environment, labour policy, development and social change. The reference facilities are used 9,000 times in a year by about 300 students and professionals. It charges a small fee for its services.

Among the documentation centres in Kerala, the important ones are Solidarity in Mananthavady, Wayanad, which concentrates on contemporary issues relating to tribals; and Samskriti in Pariyaram, Kannur, which focuses on the study of local, marginalised social groups, and on indigenous knowledge systems. Kottakkal Kanaran Smaraka Kalarividya Padana Kendram at Chombala, Kozhikode, focuses on the study of Kerala's martial arts and has a good collection of books and compact discs on *kalarividya*.

Professional Associations

Of the locally organised professional associations in south India, Andhra Pradesh Economic Association (APEA); Andhra Pradesh History Congress (APHC); and Tamil Nadu History Congress (TNHC) are the important ones. They have regular activities that bring together teachers, researchers and students.

The APEA was founded in December 1981 with an objective to improve the teaching of and research in economics by creating a forum of teachers, researchers and administrators. The association has over 300 life members. Since its inception, an annual conference on a selected theme, most often on a particular aspect of Andhra Pradesh economy, is being conducted.

The APHC was founded in 1976 and it brings together historians of the region in an annual conference. The proceedings of the conference are published. It has also organised district-level associations, consisting of lecturers in history, at places such as Nellore, Guntur and Cuddapah, to encourage micro-level historical studies by organising conferences and seminars. It is out of such an effort that a volume on the history of Nellore district (*Comprehensive History of Nellore District* [Nellore, 1995]) has been recently published. From 1989 onwards, the APHC is organising an annual Mamidipudi Venkatarangaiya memorial lecture. The lecture has been delivered by some of the best-known historians of India such as R. Champakalakshmi, R.S. Sharma, Bipan Chandra, Ravindra Kumar and Barun De. The resolutions passed in the annual sessions reflect the Congress's concern to enhance archival resources of the region and to improve the functioning of the state archives. In 1996, the Congress had 159 regular members and 59 life members.

TNHC was founded in 1994 "to foster historical studies and research at the regional level". Its members are mostly drawn from university and college teachers and research students; and its main activity is to hold an annual conference and publish the proceedings. It has so far held eight annual conferences. In order to get a feel of its functioning, I attended the eighth annual conference of the Tamil Nadu History Congress held in the University of Madras, Chennai, on October 13-14, 2001. The conference was remarkable on many counts. Attended by about 300 participants, most of them members of the Congress, it offered a forum for young historians to try their hand at writing professional papers, present them to an audience and establish connections with others working on related areas of research. In several of the papers, there was a visible effort to mobilise the latest scholarship and methodology—be its subaltern studies or post-structuralism. The result of such efforts is uneven and often lacking in understanding. Given the fact that the latest historical scholarship is at a discount in university teaching, these individual efforts and their dissemination through the conference is very important and deserves consolidation.

Local Social Science Journals

All the four southern states are marked by the presence of a vast sector of 'non-formal' academics who are not formally linked to academic institutions, but maintain a keen interest in scholarly writings and participate in debates of an academic nature. Most often this sector is a product of different social movements wherein social scientists too as public intellectuals participate. This intersection between the formal and 'non-formal' academics has given rise to a plethora of journals in local languages, which deal with an array of social science themes. The papers published in them exhibit a high degree of theoretical sophistication while engaging with local problems.

Let me give two instances from Tamil Nadu. *Aaraichi* which is published from the provincial town of Tirunelveli was a product of the mainstream left movement, though its constituency both in terms of contributors and readers is ideologically inclusive. Founded in 1969 by Nellai Arivu Kuzhu (Nellai Research Group) under the leadership of late Na Vanamamalai, a left intellectual, over 50 issues of *Aaraichi* has been published so far. The papers in the journal reflect a wide range of interests: sociology, history, anthropology, folkloristics and literary criticism. *Nirappirigai* is another social science journal, which is a product of the Dalit literary movement. *Nirappirigai* carries, among other things, high quality literary criticism,[2] local history with a subaltern perspective, and translations from English social science journals. The journal's engagement with contemporary debates in social sciences would be evident from the fact that it organised a two-day conference on subaltern studies in 1996, and the set of papers discussed in the conference were subsequently published in a volume in Tamil.[3]

Despite such intellectual vibrancy, which animates these social science journals in local languages, they are, as a rule, the result of the efforts of a handful of enthusiasts without any institutional or financial support. Given this, they survive for a few years and disappear. Even when they are alive and kicking, the regularity of publication becomes difficult. Let me illustrate this by giving a brief account of *Kerala Padanangal*, a social science quarterly in Malayalam, which is unfortunately no more around.

---

2. The following two papers, originally published in *Aaraichi* and subsequently translated into English, will vouch for the high quality of scholarship in the journal: A Sivasubramanian (1996). "'Fin-Levy' (*Thuvi Kutagai*) Agitation in Idinthakarai, Tamilnadu 1964-67", *South Indian Studies*, No. 2, July-December; and T. Paramasivan (1997). "The Temple Entry Event: Meenakshi Temple, Madurai, 1939", *South Indian Studies*, No. 4, July-December.

3. For an account of the conference, see Pandian (1997).

Kerala Padanangal, launched in 1993, was conceived primarily to bridge the gap between the formal and non-formal sectors of social science practitioners. The non-formal academics formed, as it was meant to be, the vast majority of the reader-subscribers of the journal. The rest were college and university students, teachers and researchers. Its former editor K.T. Rammohan notes, "editorial task was not easy. Most academics were trained in English-medium at the college and university levels, and never had any experience in articulating their ideas in Malayalam. Often, translators had to be engaged. The problem was compounded by the fact that Malayalam had not developed a language of social science. At one level, this meant a dearth of appropriate terminology. Sanskrit words or words of Sanskritic origin could not reach the target audience. Nor was it a preferred editorial option. Sentences initially thought out in English, even when translated into a non-Sanskritic Malayalam, were not quite readable." This is a statement of key importance. It tells us how the hegemonic presence of English as the language of social science practice in India comes in the way of dissemination of ideas at a wider level. Also, it makes difficult the necessary dialogue between different sectors of social science knowledge production. On another count, it points to the important need of evolving social science vocabulary in local language.

Despite such difficulties, *Kerala Padanangal* was run with much enthusiasm and hard work. The print-run of the journal was, on an average, 1000 copies and the subscribers numbered about 600. The journal closed down in 1997. The closure of *Kerala Padanangal* was necessitated by the logic of small-scale publishing. As usual with such publication both in Kerala and Tamil Nadu, it was brought out by a publisher whose main source of finance came from printing works undertaken. The priority of the publisher being job-works, often the journal could not be brought out in time and delays affected the regularity. The problem was compounded by the difficulties in distribution. About 400 copies were sold through established bookstalls and agents. This proved to be a major failure. While established book-sellers demanded as much as 40 per cent as commission, the agents agreed to lesser commission, but none ever paid back any money or paid very little. This worked as a drain on the publisher's resources. With a slump in the printing industry, the journal finally collapsed.

A promising aspect of this venture was that mail-orders for the back-volumes poured in after its closure, with the result that all printed copies have been sold out. What needs to be underscored is that the material cost of the whole effort did not need anything more than Rs. 60,000 annually. Still the journal had to wind up.

Case Study: Madras Institute of Development Studies (MIDS)

In order to obtain a detailed understanding of how institutions of social science higher learning and research function and the problems they face, we have done a detailed study of the Madras Institute of Development Studies (MIDS), Chennai and the Institute of Social and Economic Change (ISEC), Bangalore. Before proceeding to present the case studies, I need to mention that the data available for each of these institutions are of varying quality. Given this, certain aspects of each of these institutions are dealt with in detail and others briefly. In this section, an analysis of MIDS would be done.

Faculty

The MIDS, like most other ICSSR institutes, began with a small number of faculty members. In 1979-80, it had five members in the faculty. In the course of the past two decades, it has expanded its faculty strength, though at a slow pace, and today its faculty strength is 17. Though the institute claims that it is committed to promoting inter-disciplinary research, the distribution of the faculty members across disciplines show that it is primarily oriented towards economics. In its initial years, the institute's faculty was fully constituted by economists. This disciplinary monopoly over the faculty composition continued through the 1980s. For instance, in 1989-90, MIDS had one sociologist, the only non-economist in an entire faculty of 18. Things had improved in the 1990s and today the institute has five non-economists—one sociologist, two anthropologists and two political scientists—accounting for 30 per cent of the faculty (Table 10.1). Despite such diversification of the faculty across disciplines, the institute still continues to be dominated by economists.

Table 10.1

Faculty Across Disciplines, MIDS, 1979-80 to 2000-01

Year	Economics		Others	
	Number	Per cent	Number	Per cent
1979-80	4	100	0	0.0
1989-90	17	94.4	1	5.6
2000-01	12	70.5	5	29.5

Table 10.2

Cadre-wise Strength of Faculty Members, MIDS, 1979-80 to 2000-01

Year	Professors		Fellows		Associates		Total Number of Faculties
	Number	Per cent	Number	Per cent	Number	Per cent	
1979-80	2	50.0	0	0.00	2	50.0	4
1989-90	6	33.3	7	38.8	5	27.8	18
2000-01	8	35.3	7	41.2	4	23.5	19

The other feature of the faculty composition in the MIDS is that it is top-heavy with a large number of professors and a very few younger faculty members at the level of research associates. Over the years, the proportion of faculty posts occupied by the professors and fellows have increased and that of the associates have declined. While in 1979-80 the associates accounted for 50 per cent of the total faculty strength, in 2000-01 it has declined to a meagre 23.5 per cent (Table 10.2). As the vision document of the MIDS notes, "Injection of fresh blood, particularly at the middle and lower ends of the academic pyramid, is an urgent necessity" (MIDS, 2000: 6). The obvious reason for this trend is the lack of new recruitment to the faculty in the face of financial stringency. In fact the approved faculty posts for the MIDS by the ICSSR is 22. But for the recruitment made to the faculty in 2001, the figures would be even more disappointing. This is a matter of importance as it points to the larger story of lack of possibilities in academics for those trained in social sciences.

Research Output

The MIDS being a non-teaching institution with an exclusive emphasis on research, publishing research papers will index the level and the quality of the institute's academic activities. After all, "Faculty members [at MIDS]... set their own agenda of research, which gives them considerable autonomy and flexibility" (MIDS, 1995: 3). The faculty members of the MIDS have published in renowned Indian social science journals (such as *Economic and Political Weekly, Studies in History, and Contributions to Indian Sociology)* and in reputed foreign journals (such as *Journal of Peasant Studies, Dialectical Anthropology and Journal of Quantitative Economics*). Having said this, I need to add that the distribution of publications across faculty members is glaringly uneven, i.e., only a few of the faculty members publish. This is so even at the highest level of professors. A look at the publication history of five professors at MIDS who have spent 20 years in the faculty of the institute is revealing. For this exercise, I have taken only the standard social science journals and publishing houses. During the period 1980-1981 to 1998-99, the most productive of them has contributed 13 papers to journals or edited volumes and published two books. The least productive of them has contributed five papers to journals or edited volumes. During this period, all five of them together have contributed 57 papers to journals or edited volumes, and have published three books. Given the enormous amount of public resources spent on them, this level of performance can best be described as gloomy.

A discipline-wise break-up of the 156 working papers brought out by MIDS during the period 1978-79 to 1998-99, tells us that the institute's research output lacks in disciplinary diversity. Of the total number of working papers, 135 (86.5 per cent) fall within the disciplinary boundaries of economics; 14 (8.9 per cent) can be broadly classified as dealing with sociological issues; and 7 (4.6 per cent) belongs to history. This is a direct result of the dominance of economists in the faculty. The skewed distribution of the faculty members across the disciplines has its own negative impact on the possibility of collaborative work. Once again I have taken the working paper to index the degree of collaborative work. Of the 156 working papers, only 12 (7.7 per cent) were co-authored. And all of them were by economists. Though the degree of collaborative work itself is quite low in the institute, those who pursue disciplines other than economics are constrained by the fact that they do not have a critical number of faculty members in their disciplines to carry out collaborative research venture.

The MIDS has systematised procedures to evaluate faculty performance. First, every member of the faculty has to furnish every year a work report, which is perused by the academic council. In essence, this is a peer group review. Second, the work of every member of the faculty is reviewed by the academic council once in three years on the basis of the periodic work reports and a self-assessment report prepared by the faculty member concerned. This review is made by a committee of the academic council consisting of the director and two external members of the council. However, the evaluation procedures have not really worked. This is evident from the actual performance of the faculty in terms of their publications.

PhD Programme

The MIDS is affiliated to the Madras University Chennai, for its PhD programme. From 1979-80 to 1998-99, 36 students have registered for PhD at the MIDS. For a period of 30 years, this is indeed a small number. In several years, not even a single student has registered at MIDS. Of the total number of students registered, 18 have left the institute without completing their degree. In other words, the dropout rate of students is a high 50 per cent. Of the 13 students who have completed their PhD, 7 (54 per cent) work in academic jobs; 3 (23 per cent) are employed in non-academic jobs; and 3 (23 per cent) work in research projects without permanent employment. What needs to be underscored here is that despite a small harvest of PhDs at the MIDS, half of the former students with PhD degrees could not get academic jobs.

An internal note on the PhD programme, recently prepared to revamp the programme, identifies several reasons for this state of affairs. The smaller intake of students is attributed to the fact that the ICSSR insists on the clearance of the UGC-NET for ICSSR doctoral fellowships, while it pays a smaller fellowship compared to the UGC, "Many of the students who have passed this test often prefer to go to some other institution or university with better facilities."[4] In addition, the absence of a hostel facility for the students at the institute has worked against attracting students, in particular women students, from outside Chennai.

The training of the PhD students is also found to be lacking in many respects. First and foremost, the institute does not have any comprehensive coursework for the students and "the requirements imposed by the university—of having to pass a methodology examination for those without an M.Phil—more often than not degenerated into mere formality". Further, the programme "lacks a proper system for the continuous evaluation of the scholars. The PhD committees constituted for each scholar, more often than not, are seen as a requirement (stipulated by the university) or a formality to be got over with; they hardly provide continuous guidance or conduct regular monitoring". Also, with the majority of the faculty members not showing adequate interest in the PhD programme, just two of them supervise most of the students. This has led to an uneven distribution of workload and seems to have affected the quality of PhD supervision. It is the combination of these factors that might be accounting for the high dropout rate of students at the MIDS.

Inter-Institutional Interaction

The MIDS has been conducting an annual workshop for research scholars and guides since 1978. About 60 to 70 research scholars drawn from different universities and colleges in Tamil Nadu attend this workshop. In the course of the workshop, faculty members of the MIDS

4. After this survey was completed, ICSSR revised the fellowship amount to bring it at par with that of the UGC. However, it chose to reduce the period for which the fellowship would be given. In effect, the ICSSR fellowship continues to be less attractive than that of the UGC.

and invited resource persons give lectures and discuss the works of the research scholars. This workshop is an instance of the MIDS bringing into being and sustaining an institutional arrangement which gathers together social scientists from different educational institutions in the state. Of late, the workshop is organised every year in different universities and colleges in Tamil Nadu.

In addition, the MIDS has been conducting an annual interdisciplinary research methodology workshop since 1974. The workshop is designed to bring together social scientists from universities and research centres in south India. Till 1982, each workshop had a distinct individual theme such as poverty, regional planning, village studies, and caste and class in India. Since 1983 just one major theme formed the basis of the workshop for three successive years.

Funding

The principal sources of funding for the MIDS continue to be the ICSSR and the government of Tamil Nadu. In 1999-2000, the grant from the ICSSR accounted for 38.60 per cent of the total funds, while the grant from the government of Tamil Nadu (including the special library grant) accounts for 49.24 per cent of the total (Table 10.3). This reliance on the ICSSR for funding has been a source of acute financial crisis in which the institute is entrapped now. According to the silver jubilee document of the MIDS, "...since 1992 the ICSSR has been urging institutes funded by it to find their own sources of funding and has nearly frozen its grants. So the institute faces a deficit every year, which is getting accumulated over the years" (MIDS, 1995: 3). Often, both the ICSSR and the state government do not release the sanctioned grants. As on October 31, 2000, the unreleased grants from the ICSSR amounted to Rs. 11.03 lakh and that from the government of Tamil Nadu was Rs. 69.97 lakh.

From 1995-96 onwards, the MIDS is faced with substantial operating deficit every year. An internal exercise of the institute projects that, at the current level of funding by the ICSSR and the state government, the annual operating deficit of the MIDS would reach Rs.

17.37 lakh by 2004-05 (MIDS, 2000:27). To bridge its deficits, the institute is resorting to borrowing. As on November 31, 2000, its liabilities, including the debt of Rs. 96.26 lakh to be repaid to a commercial bank and pay arrears of Rs. 32.06 lakh to be paid to its employees, stood at Rs. 196.20 lakh (Ibid: 26).

Table 10.3

Pattern and Sources of Funding, MIDS (1999-2000)

Sources	*Rs. (In Lakh)*	*Per cent in Total*
ICSSR grant	24.74	38.60
Grant from government of Tamil Nadu	24.74	38.60
Special library grant	6.82	10.64
RBI chair	4.37	6.82
Internal revenue	0.93	1.45
Overhead from projects	2.50	3.90
Total	64.10	100.00

The reliance of the MIDS on the ICSSR and the state government for its funding is a result of its openly stated philosophy of research. As the vision document notes, "Most researchers at MIDS primarily set their own research agenda. Individual autonomy has meant immeasurable academic freedom...The strong individual ethos has conferred advantages on MIDS. Coupled with concern for quality this has engendered in the institute an attitude of healthy caution towards projects. The caution is dictated by a well-founded apprehension that excessive involvement with projects (more generally sponsored research) can deprive faculty of the creative leisure and indeed impetus for reflective research. It [projects] can have an especially deleterious impact on young researchers who [in pursuing projects] would find it difficult to obtain a secure foothold in a particular specialty" (Ibid: 2). As Table 10.3 shows, the funds from the projects accounted for a meagre 3.90 per cent of the total funds received by the institute in 1999-2000. However, over the period there is a small increase in the number of research projects taken up by the faculty of the MIDS. The balance between the locally funded projects and foreign-funded projects is shifting over the years in favour of foreign-funded projects (Table 10.4).

Table 10.4

Externally Funded Projects Undertaken by MIDS, 1979-80 to 1998-99

Years	Total Number of Projects Undertaken	Locally Funded		Foreign Funded	
		Number	Per cent	Number	Per cent
1979-80 to 1981-82	9	9	100	0	0
1989-90 to 1991-92	10	8	80	2	20
1996-97 to 1998-99	13	6	46	7	54

Library

Though the primary academic focus of the MIDS is development economics, the library collection is diverse. It stocks a fairly good number of books on history, sociology, political science, gender and cultural studies, apart from economics.[5] The journals subscribed by the institute also display similar disciplinary diversity. One of the critical failures of the library is its lack of effort to strengthen its minuscule and uninspiring collection of books in Tamil. Perhaps this is yet another instance illustrating the hegemony of English as the language of social science practices. The library is widely used by researchers, teachers and journalists. From January to December 1999, the library was visited by no less than 1,900 outsiders. Of the 1,646 visitors whose whereabouts could be discerned, 1,395 (84.7 per cent) were from the city of Chennai and 150 (9.1 per cent) were from other parts of Tamil Nadu, 75 (4.6 per cent) were from other states and 26 (1.6 per cent) were from other countries. Though the library serves mostly users from Chennai itself, visitors from other parts of the state is by no means insubstantial.

So far the MIDS library goes, the 1980s was a period of enthusiasm. The minutes of the library committee chronicles the efforts made by the institute to augment its collection—such as the formation of sub-committees to look into government publications to be procured, and representatives from the institute being sent to

5. This has happened despite the effort of the institute in the initial years to give a distinct economics-centred flavour to the library collection. For instance, the Library Committee of the Institute decided on October 17, 1981 that as a matter of policy, the library should acquire each year the complete works of an economist.

International Book Fair in Delhi. For instance, the 10th library committee which completed its tenure in December 1983, felt that certain sections in the library are very rich and certain others are not; and consequently a sub-committee was constituted for identifying areas where the library has to concentrate in future for acquisition.

But the dream of 1980s is in shambles today; even the decade of 1990s was one of lack of resources and unending despair. In 1992, the library committee was forced to bring out a note on the escalating cost of foreign journal sub-scriptions following the devaluation of the Indian rupee. Striking a note of caution, but simultaneously placing its concerns within the politics of uneven distribution of academic resources between the first and the third worlds, it noted, "[In preparing this note] We are solely guided by considerations of building the library stock of journals taking care of individual and collective research interests, keeping in view both the short-term and long-term budgetary restrictions, the non-privileged position from which we 'third world intellectuals' are forced to participate in the production of knowledge, and the highly contested nature of the decision-making on an issue such as foreign journal subscription." The note suggested that the institute should find means to exploit the price differentials between institutional and individual subscription rates which is very large for each journal; that half the subscription rate for any new journal that a faculty member wants to be met by the concerned member; that faculty members may sponsor individual Indian journals for the library. It also did an extensive classification of journals on the basis of research priority so as to cut down the number of journals subscribed. In 1993, the library discontinued several foreign journals with the hope that they would be re-subscribed when the financial situation improved. In the same year, a special annual grant of Rs. 3.5 lakh, with a 10 per cent increase every year to account for inflation, was given to the MIDS library by the Tamil Nadu government. While this came as a timely help, it could not help the library out of the crisis.

Apart from the inadequacy of the resources available, the library was affected by the uneven availability of the resources through the financial year. Normally, the ICSSR and the state government release the grant money during the last quarter of the financial year. This means that the library needs to bunch together its purchases at the end of the financial year or keep the booksellers waiting for payment for the books and journals bought on credit. For instance, the MIDS library committee had to note in March 1993, "the bills are not paid from the month of August 1993 till date...the present committee has decided not to buy books or at least not to place the bulk orders till the institute clears all the pending bills. And also as a precautionary measure we suggest that the future library committees consider buying books mainly in the last quarter of the financial year." The problem continued and intensified over the years. In 1995, the library committee acknowledged once again that "the delay in settling accounts with book-sellers is a source of embarrassment to the librarian in particular". And in an effort to overcome the situation, the committee suggested: "(a) subscription for journals will be the first charge on the available library budget; (b) up to September-October of a financial year only individual requests and government publications orders will be placed; (c) beyond October, depending on availability of resources, books on approval and those based on book-sellers' catalogues will be entertained."

The above account based on the minute books of the MIDS library committee tells us in plain terms that even good social science libraries are, in the face of escalation of costs, unable to maintain their past level of acquisition of books and journals. This has happened despite the fact that the MIDS has over the years increased its library budget. The outlay of money on books and journals has increased by 5.6 times between 1979-80 to 1998-99. While this looks like an impressive increase, one needs to remember that it is much lower than the overall increase in the expenditure of the institute. In fact, during the period under consideration, the overall expenditure of the MIDS has increased by 8.47 times. Given the inflation in the price of books and journals, the MIDS has to spend most of the increase in its library budget on journal subscriptions. As Table 10.5 shows, in the late 1970s and early 1980s the expenditure on journals accounted for 21.7 per cent of the total expenditure on books and journals. However, in the late 1990s, it has reached the phenomenal figure of 79.5 per cent.

The inflow of books to the library, in particular the ones published abroad, has suffered over the years. In the late 1990s, the inflow of the number of books to the MIDS library has become less than half of what it used to be in the early 1980s. In the case of books published abroad, the inflow to the library has reduced by 65 per cent during the same period (Table 10.6).

Table 10.5

Average Annual Expenditure on Books and Journals at MIDS, 1979-80 to 1998-99

Years	Books		Periodicals		Total	
	Expenditure (Rs.)	Per cent	Expenditure (Rs.)	Per cent	Expenditure (Rs.)	Per cent
1979-80 to 1981-82	96,432	78.3	26,693	21.7	1,23,125	100.0
1990-91 to 1992-93	1,70,600	43.6	2,20,973	56.4	3,91,573	100.0
1996-97 to 1998-99	1,33,718	19.5	5,53,346	79.5	6,87,064	100.0

Table 10.6

Annual Average Number of Books Added to the MIDS Library, 1979-80 to 1998-99

Years	Indian Books		Foreign Books		Total	
	Number	Per cent	Number	Per cent	Number	Per cent
1979-80 to 1981-82	319	39.0	500	61.0	819	100.0
1990-91 to 1992-93	375	52.4	341	47.6	716	100.0
1996-97 to 1998-99	196	53.3	172	46.7	368	100.0

Computer Facilities

The institute has 40 computers (13 Pentium, 11 AT 486 and 16 AT 386/AT286/XT machines), 9 dot matrix printers, 7 inkjet printers and 3 LaserJet printers. Further, it is also equipped with a scanner, a CD writer, tape drives, and zip drives. Most of the existing machines are lower end PCs. XT/AT 286, AT 386 and AT 486 machines account for 67.5 per cent of the PCs in the institute. It is not possible to load window-based applications in these machines. Since these machines are very old and out of tune with the technological advancement in PCs, it is difficult to maintain them. Given the paucity of funds, the institute has not provided individual PCs even for some of the senior members of the faculty. For the same reason, the latest versions of software are not available in the institute.

In 1996, the institute obtained a dial-up shell account for e-mail from the National Informatics Centre. Subsequently, the institute has configured a dial-up unix-to-unix copy protocol. Individual mailboxes have been given to the members of the institute. However, this facility can be accessed from only one machine. In 1999, the institute has configured a dial-up TCP/IP account for Internet and this also can be accessed from only one machine. Due to lack of funds, the institute could not network the computers in the faculty rooms. The faculty members have to come to a common pool to access e-mail and Internet facility through a dial-up system. The whole institute depends on just two computers—one to send and receive e-mails, and the other to access the Internet.

The computerisation of the library too is affected because of lack of funds. The institute's plan of computerising the library through LibSys software, which is widely used in Indian universities and institutions, had to be put on hold because the institute did not have the money to buy the software.

Case Study: Institute for Social and Economic Change (ISEC)

In contrast to other research institutes in the region, the Institute for Social and Economic Change (ISEC) is the only institute, which, from the beginning, had a multidisciplinary focus. Apart from economics, sociology has a big representation in the institute. Political science and education as disciplinary fields also have an impressive presence in the institute. It may be remembered here that M.N. Srinivas, well known sociologist, headed the sociology unit of the ISEC for a decade. Also, in comparison to the MIDS, the ISEC is a much larger institution in terms of faculty strength. In fact, the ISEC is the largest social science research institute within the ICSSR framework in the country. It is endowed with a 16-hectare campus, hostels for students, guesthouse for visitors, housing for the faculty and staff and a 300-seater auditorium.

Faculty

At the moment, the ISEC has faculty strength of 39. But for the resource constraint of the institute, the strength of the faculty would have been much larger. Out of the posts sanctioned by the ICSSR, 2 posts of professors, 9 posts of associate professors and 10 posts of assistant professors are kept vacant for lack of funds. Almost half of the current faculties of the ISEC are economists. While sociology account for 17.9 per cent of the faculty, education 7.7 per cent and political science 5.1 per cent. Interestingly, the dominance of economics has declined over the years. In 1982-83, economics accounted for 69.2 per cent of the faculty, and in 2000-01 it has declined to 51.3 per cent. On the other hand, sociology has steadily increased its share in the faculty. During the same period, its share has increased from 7.7 per cent to 17.9 per cent. Other disciplines have a fluctuating fortune (Table 10.7). In short, the ISEC has a better disciplinary diversity compared to any other ICSSR research institution in south India.

In contrast to the MIDS, the faculty members of the ISEC are better distributed across different cadres. In 2000-01, the professors account for a fourth of the faculty members. Their share in the total number of faculty members has declined from 28.2 per cent in 1982-83 to 25.6 per cent in 2000-01. Similar trend is witnessed among the associate professors too. During the same period, their share in the faculty has declined from 33.3 per cent to 23.1 per cent. On the contrary, the share of the assistant professors in the faculty has increased over the period. Their share was 38.5 per cent in 1982-83 and it has reached 51.3 per cent in 2000-01 (Table 10.8). Perhaps, the sheer size of the ISEC faculty (in contrast to that of the MIDS) might have contributed to this diversity—a diversity which allows space for younger social scientists.

Research Output

Since its inception, the faculty members of the ISEC have produced about 225 books, and over 2,500 technical articles. Of these articles, over 600 were published in refereed journals in India and abroad, 900

Table 10.7

Faculty Members and their Areas of Specialisation, ISEC, 1982-83 to 2000-01

Years	Economics		Sociology		Pol. Science		Education		Others		Total	
	No.	Per cent	No.	Per cent	No.	Per cent	No.	Per cent	No.	Per cent	No.	Per cent
1982-83	27	69.2	3	7.7	2	5.1	2	5.1	5	12.8	39	100.0
1990-91	20	62.5	4	12.5	4	12.5	3	9.4	1	3.1	32	100.0
2000-01	20	51.3	7	17.9	2	5.1	3	7.7	7	17.9	39	100.0

Table 10.8

Cadre-wise Distribution of the Faculty Members, ISEC, 1982-83 to 2000-01

Years	Professor		Associate Professor		Assistant Professor		Total	
	No.	Per cent	No.	Per cent	No.	Per cent	No.	Per cent
1982-83	11	28.2	13	33.3	15	38.5	39	100.0
1990-91	12	37.5	9	28.1	11	34.4	32	100.0
2000-01	10	25.6	9	23.1	20	51.3	39	100.0

articles in various magazines and about 1,000 articles were presented in seminars and workshops (ISEC, 2001: 7). We do not have detailed data on the distribution of the quantity and quality of publication across faculty members. However, as the director of the institute, Dr. M. Govinda Rao, mentioned in a conversation, all is not well with the research output of the institute. According to him, there are some who actively publish while most do not; and even the quality of publications leave much to be desired.

However, the research output of the ISEC is marked by a high degree of collaborative work. As in the case of the MIDS, I used the working papers published by the institute to index the degree of collaboration. Of the 88 working papers brought out by the institute, 46 (41 per cent) were co-authored. The availability of a critical number of faculty members in different disciplines and joint projects carried out by faculty members are mostly the source of collaboration.

The internal evaluation of the faculty performance, according to the director of the ISEC, has not really worked the way it was expected to. The institute is in the process of evolving a new scheme of evaluating academic performance of the faculty.

PhD Programme

The ISEC has an active PhD programme for which it is affiliated to the Bangalore University, University of Mysore, Karnataka University and National Law School. The doctoral students are allowed to register for their PhD degree only after they successfully complete a one-year pre-PhD course. In 2000, as a response to the complaints by sociology students, a separate module on sociology was introduced for them. Till then, a common course designed primarily for economics students was offered for all the students irrespective of their disciplinary interests. This tells us how economics continue to exercise hegemony even in a multidisciplinary institution like the ISEC. Increasingly, outside experts are being brought in to teach the students.

Between 1973 and 1996, 159 students have enrolled with the ISEC for PhD. Out of them, 81 (51 per cent) have completed their PhD. In other words, the dropout rate is a hefty 50 per cent. A conversation with the students at the ISEC gives us an array of reasons for this high dropout rate. Given the short duration of the PhD fellowship, most of the students, in a critical stage of their work such as at the point of completing their fieldwork or writing the thesis, are forced to take up part-time employment, often in research projects. The divided attention between the PhD work and the part-time job often leads to their eventual dropping out of the PhD programme. Of late, the disparity in different fellowships offered by the RBI, UGC and ICSSR, has led to the students leaving the PhD programme at the ISEC quite early. In a thoughtful comparison, Govinda Rao claims that the ICSSR fellowship is not even equal to the average earning of an informal sector labourer in Punjab, and wonders how it would attract bright promising students.

The ISEC has recently introduced a number of changes in their PhD programme, which is much appreciated by the students. The most important of them is two mandatory annual seminars, in July and December, where all the students present their work. As the students claim, it has improved their public articulation of ideas and has introduced certain regularity in writing out their work as they move along towards the thesis. In addition, the fact that the public performance of students is linked, though not formally, to the quality of guidance offered by the PhD supervisor, seems to have improved the interaction between the PhD supervisors and their students.

Inter-Institutional Interaction

In the ISEC, inter-institutional interaction most often takes the form of training programmes. It is one of the institutions recognised by the UGC to conduct refresher courses for the university and college teachers and such courses are conducted every year in the disciplines of economics, sociology and education. Under the World Bank-aided capacity building programme on ecological economics, the ISEC is a recognised centre for imparting training to teachers and government officials. The institute also conducts a refresher course in quantitative techniques and computer applications for teachers and researchers in social sciences.

Funding

Over the years, the role of the ICSSR in financially sustaining the research activities of the ISEC has almost become irrelevant. As the recent vision document of the institute notes: "...the share of the ICSSR support in the total budget of the institute plummeted year after year. However, the state government in recognition of ISEC's valuable research contribution steadily increased its support. Yet, as the state's own finances came under increasing pressure, the volume assistance fell short of the requirements. Thus, in 1998-99, the ICSSR funds constituted about 6 per cent of the total expenditures and the share of the state government constituted about 25 per cent of the total expenditure of the institute" (ISEC, 2001: 2). The figures clearly show that we need to rethink whether one can still call the ISEC and similarly placed institutions as the ICSSR institutions.

It may be noted that a substantial part of the institute's activities are supported by sources other than the ICSSR and the state government. The Reserve Bank of India has endowed a chair on macroeconomic policy. The Union Ministry of Agriculture has instituted an agro-economic research centre named Agricultural Development and Rural Transformation Unit (ADRTC). And the Ministry of Health and Family Welfare has established in the institute a population research centre. In addition, the ISEC takes up a number of funded projects to keep its core activities going as well as to upgrade the infrastructure. In 1998-99, sponsored-projects accounted for 46 per cent of the total revenue of the institute. This has a definite impact on the quality of research: "Although attempts have been made to ensure that projectitis does not adversely affect the quality of research it has become increasingly difficult to maintain the standards...taking sponsored projects to maintain the flow of funds and to get adequate access to computer and other facilities has become inevitable" (Ibid: 3).

Library and Computer Facilities

As we have noted earlier, the ISEC has one of the most impressive social science libraries in south India with a large collection of books and journals. The recent financial stringency has however impacted the library adversely. As the vision document of the institute notes, "there is a significant backlog in acquisition of volumes, subscription to some important journals has had to be discontinued and the plan for computerising the library has remained largely on paper" (Ibid: 3).

Almost all the faculty members at the ISEC have PCs, most of which were acquired through project funding. However, "the prevailing computer facility is inadequate and significant investment is needed to upgrade the facility...most of the machines are old, have low memory and need to be replaced. In fact, for 40 doctoral students, there are just five computers at present" (Ibid: 4). The institute has recently instituted a local area network, a dedicated line and a separate server to provide e-mail and Internet facilities.

Issues for Consideration

The at once intersecting and contrasting profiles of the MIDS and the ISEC as well as the general details of the social science resources available in south India bring into focus a number of pertinent issues for the future of social sciences in the region. My concern here is how to strengthen social science higher learning and research in south India by preserving and expanding the existing resource base for social sciences, strengthening the available institutional structures, and ensuring quality of teaching and research output.

Disciplinary Diversity

The social science in south India is dominated numerically by the single discipline of economics. As we have seen elsewhere, all the ICSSR institutes in the region, with the lone exception of the ISEC, is hegemonised by economists. This has not only led to the marginalisation of disciplines other than economics, but also has hampered the possibility of interdisciplinary research agendas. With the new emphasis on project-based research and non-state funding for social sciences, this divide is bound to widen. Both project-funded research and private funding most often favour economics over other disciplines. Madras School of Economics, which has been recently founded and financially sustained by corporate sector and private financial institutions, portend this.

Size of the Institutions

In the context of disciplinary diversity and a range of other issues, the sheer size of social science institutions in terms of faculty strength seems to be of critical importance. As we have seen, the ISEC is marked by a high degree of disciplinary diversity, a good deal of collaborative research and a lot of teaching and training. In contrast, the MIDS is lacking in all these aspects. If the ISEC could perform better in these aspects, it is, among other things, because of its large faculty size. In fact, the vision document of the MIDS identified 'inadequate faculty strength' as the reason for its failure to launch a long-term teaching programme (MIDS, 2000: 15). Further, the expansion of faculty strength is essential to accommodate younger scholars and re-energise these institutions by the infusion of new ideas. The fact that most of these institutions are not able, in the face of financial stringency, to fill up even the sanctioned posts is particularly worrying in this context.

Funding

As we have seen, social science higher learning and research in the region is crippled by lack of funds. This is, at an important level, the result of the ICSSR diluting its commitment to social sciences. For instance, the silver jubilee document of the MIDS notes, "There is no certainty about the quantum of ICSSR grants now. In such a situation, it is difficult to plan ahead; and the administration has to spend much of its time and energy to make both ends meet (MIDS, 1995: 9). Certain institutions like the ISEC are weathering the crisis by resorting to large-scale project-driven research, while others such as the MIDS, constrained by certain research ethos forged during past decades, are resisting project-driven research and are deeply in a financial mess. The crisis is felt by all the institutions in the region. As early as 1981, a document of the Centre for Development Studies, Thiruvananthapuram, noted, "We shall also need more funds—not so much on the capital account, as most of the basic overhead facilities will be established soon—but to meet staff expansion, maintain the rate of acquisition for library, and most importantly to meet spiralling of costs."[6]

Dr. A.R. Vasavi, given her experience as a researcher at the National Institute of Advanced Studies (NIAS), Bangalore, which is run on externally-funded research projects, identifies three key problems with project-based research. First of all, those with research funds have leverage over those without; they have access to facilities such as secretary, computer and other office related support. They are less accountable to the institute for their time and the type of work conducted. Second, funded research is valorised for its capacity to generate revenue (15 per cent overhead charges go to the institute) and is not really scrutinised for quality or orientation. Further, the sources of funding are not scrutinised either. Finally, most funded research seems to culminate in reports made to the funding organisations. There seems to be no pressure placed on the researcher to develop the reports further into academic outputs. According to her, "Contributions from such research to general development of social science is missing and is also not encouraged".

However, Vasavi also adds that funded research has its own positive sides. According to her, since most fundable research is directly linked to development themes and is based on field research, it offers an opportunity to challenge or overcome some of the distance between academic work and the requirements of public policy: "Speaking for myself, the need to write proposals and do research that can be funded has forced me to engage with NGOs and other agencies such as government departments and personnel, which I would not have otherwise. In some ways, the existing divide or the exclusiveness of the citadel academia can be challenged. Funded research has the possibility of bringing about positive and much needed linkages between academic institutions, government agencies, and civil society."

G.K. Karanth of the ISEC endorses Vasavi's opinion that researchers are forced to take up funded research to have access to basic research facilities such as research assistance, computers, and funds for fieldwork and travel. Talking about sociology in particular, he notes that

6. Centre for Development Studies (1981). *Centre for Development Studies: 1971 to 1981*. Trivandrum. p.21.

project-driven sociology has by and large remained development sociology wherein the emphasis is on development rather than on sociology. This has impacted adversely sociology as a discipline. We may note here that this is a concern which is around for a long time. Referring to funded research sponsored by the developmentalist state, M.N. Srinivas noted in the 1950s, "The government of India has an understandable tendency to stress the need for sociological research that is directly related to planning and development. And it is the duty of sociologist as citizen that they should take part in such research. But there is a grave risk that 'pure' or 'fundamental' research might be sacrificed altogether...The pressure in favour of applied research is real, and besides, funds are not available for 'pure' research. Soon 'pure' sociology might disappear from this country...."[7]

There are others who find state funding as the source of many problems plaguing social sciences. Govinda Rao is definitely for state-funded public good research. But simultaneously he feels that most often state funding is used as a free-riding vehicle by social scientists. For him, the lack of quality of research output produced in the ICSSR institutions signals this. Sharing his experience as someone who has done project-driven research and undertaken consultancy, he notes that it is possible to produce high-quality research papers, publishable in refereed journals, out of project work. In addition, project research, particularly the ones done for the government, can give access to data, which are not normally available and could be used for further research.

In short, we have a range of opinions about state and project funding for social science learning and research. Given the validity of all these arguments, it is difficult to take a pure and simple position on this. Perhaps what one should try is to arrive at a balance between state

7. See Srinivas (1963). Expressing similar kind of anxiety, Andre Beteille wrote in the early 1970s, "There are certain types of research which government might need to have done urgently, and it would only be fair for the social scientists to offer his services in such cases. But this is different from determining the priorities of research in general... The line between dependent and independent experts is likely to be thin, particularly when all or most such experts have to depend for financial support on government. And, if the main object of social science research is critical understanding, it is difficult to see by what right any committee of experts – dependent or independent – can determine priorities of research for others." See Beteille (1978).

funding and project funding for social sciences. However, such an enterprise needs to be informed by at least three factors.

First, one needs to ensure that private funding should guarantee the autonomous growth of social sciences rather than solely pursuing its own private agenda. Let me give an example. The first batch of 11 M.Sc. students completed their course at the Madras School of Economics in June 2000. The MSE announced in one of its brochures that two of the students have joined a multinational financial institution and one a private sector national bank. And one of the PhD students on completion has also joined a multinational financial institution. The statement about how the students of MSE are useful to the corporate sector may have been directed at its corporate sector donors. However, this also indicates the kind of pressures that may be brought on social science institutions by private funding sources.

Second, certain social sciences, as they have constituted themselves as particular disciplinary domains with specific ground rules, need a higher degree of 'state-support' than other social sciences. Here the following description by Andre Beteille is of help: "...it would appear that the social sciences might perform at least two different functions, those of social engineering and of critical understanding. Among the social sciences, economics might concentrate more on social engineering although political economy in the wider sense of the term has much to contribute to critical understanding. History and political science would contribute to critical understanding than social engineering. Sociology and social anthropology might contribute a little of both" (Beteille, 1978: 141). While social sciences which are attuned to social engineering are the ones which can bring in projects, the others may not. This means that there needs to be continued state-support for social science research, at least in the case of certain disciplines and certain areas of research.

Finally, if the current transitional moment has to be navigated with the least of disruption, then once again the state has to step in with increased funding before a balance between different sources of funding could be established. As the vision document of the ISEC succinctly puts it, "...social science research would still need continuing support for the following reasons: the transition from the present dependence on grants to self-supporting status would need time to avoid dislocation and distress to existing personnel. Social science research would have to strike a careful balance between activities yielding large returns and those—like PhD programme—where returns accrue to society and not to institutions. It may be difficult and also unfair to expect the institutions to fully cross-subsidise the latter activities by returns earned from marketable activities" (ISEC, 2001: 32).

It is not only that the continued support of the ICSSR is necessary for the healthy future of social sciences in the region, but it is also time for the ICSSR to evolve efficient and responsible procedures in dispersing the funds to the institutions. Bunching of the funds at the end of the financial year and not honouring to grant the sanctioned funds are a source of great difficulty for the ICSSR institutions. In this context, the following suggestion made by the MIDS is important: "The ICSSR could very well set the dates for sanction for the entire year; release the sanctioned amount in three or four equal instalments, and ensure that the last instalment is released well in advance so as to give the Institute adequate time to get the matching grant released from the Tamil Nadu government well before the end of the financial year" (MIDS, 1995: 9).

Ensuring Quality

The need to improve the quality of teaching and research in social sciences is an urgent necessity in south India. Existing evaluation procedures have not really worked. Govinda Rao feels that stringent evaluation of the performance of the faculty members is necessary. However, he also notes that one cannot have a unified procedure to evaluate performance since different members of faculty are capable of doing different kinds of research—pure public good research, project-based research, etc. He also adds that since legally it is hardly possible to remove non-performers from the faculty, pressure can be brought to bear on them only by publicising the evaluation reports to the whole academic community. According to him, this could be done by publishing the evaluation reports of individual faculty members in the annual report of the institute.

A related theme is how to evolve structures of rewards which are incentive-based. The current incentive structures are found to be rather inadequate. For instance, the MIDS silver jubilee document notes, "While the Institute has given its staff/faculty, Tamil Nadu government/ UGC pay scales, it has not been able to match the other service conditions including the allowances and leave encashment. The incentive structure is thus unattractive to the newcomers and to the existing members to remain" (Ibid). In such a situation, Govinda Rao says, we need to live with brain drain. In fact, the earlier efforts to bring back scholars from abroad to south India failed. Narrating the experience of the ISEC, M.N. Srinivas notes, "...the prime objective to bring back social scientists to Karnataka did not materialise. Scientists from abroad demanded modern equipment such as computers which the Institute could ill-afford at that time" (ISEC, 1997: 22).

While this is the overall context of incentive structure of the social science institutions, these institutions have also internally failed to reward the performers. As the vision document of the ISEC notes, "...like in other social science research institutes the structure of rewards is not strictly incentive based. Increments are given routinely and there is no way to reward better performing persons with greater financial rewards. Annual review of the faculty provides an opportunity to assess their performance, but this has to be linked to rewards to ensure accountability...." (ISEC, 2001: 17). Citing the case of the Research School of Pacific and Asian Studies (RSPAS) at the Australian National University, Govinda Rao notes that a pool of research fund distributed to the faculty strictly on the basis of performance could be a useful way of linking performance to reward. He adds that unless this fund is substantial enough, it will fail to ensure performance. According to him, allowing part of the faculty time for consultancy—say 45 days in a year—could also reward those who could perform.

Ensuring the quality of social science research is also linked to continuous research capacity building of the faculty. The divorce between teaching and research is identified as one of the main sources of inefficiency in social science practice. According to Govinda Rao, "Lack of teaching helps one to hide ignorance than to expand knowledge. On the other hand, the movement of the bright social scientists to research institutions have deprived young students of good teaching." However, Karanth feels that re-establishing the lost connection between teaching and research is difficult, though not impossible. Universities and research institutes have over time evolved as parallel power centres and this has been facilitated by the governing structures of teaching and research institutionalised in the entities of the UGC and the ICSSR. But he thinks that one needs to evolve mechanisms by which "we [researchers] involve them [teachers] in our work; and they involve us in their work". This would require renewed cooperation between universities and research institutions.

Libraries, Archives and Similar Resources

Though south India is endowed with a reasonably good degree of library and other social science resources, we need to mention that by international standards, it is quite meagre. What M.N. Srinivas noted of the situation in Karnataka applies to the whole region: "No scholar in the social sciences can really achieve research of international standards with the library resources at present obtaining in Bangalore, and indeed in Karnataka as a whole" (ISEC, 1997: 31).

Even these limited library resources are under great strain. We have seen in detail the crisis which is being negotiated by the MIDS library. The libraries of institutions that are financially better-off than MIDS, are also not immune to downsizing the level of purchase of books and journals. For example, in 1996-97, the library of CDS, Thiruvananthapuram, subscribed to 375 journals and proudly announced that, "This has been achieved in spite of the rising costs of journals" (CDS, 1997). However, such optimism was short-lived. In 1999-2000, the library committee of the CDS had to constitute a sub-committee "to evolve a strategy for the optimal use of the funds available for journal subscription". The committee recommended that subscription to 240 journals (126 foreign and 114 Indian) be continued (CDS, 2000).

The impact of resource crunch on libraries is not confined to the ICSSR institutions. S. Theodore Baskaran, the former director of the Roja Muthiah Research Library, Chennai (which is funded by non-state sources) notes that uncertainty in funding is one of the major problems in drawing up long-term plans for the library. Also the insecurity over employment leads to a quick staff turnover affecting the efficiency of the projects carried out by the RMRL. According to him, Indian corporate sector is dismal in responding to the needs of the library. Gautami library at Rajahmundry and Vetapalem library, which hold significant material for historical research on Andhra Pradesh, are under severe financial crisis to undertake microfilming of rare material. In other words, while funds can be mobilised for certain kinds of research from a number of international organisations, these organisations may not be responsive to the need of expanding the infrastructural resource base for social science research.

On another count, Baskaran notes that the best of the training available within India for preserving archival and other material (including the training given by the National Archives of India) is out of tune with the latest methods and techniques used in the first world. If the Roja Muthiah Research Library uses the most modern techniques and has a small band of people skilled in employing them, it is because the staff of the Library of Congress, Washington DC, and Wellcome Institute, London, trained them.

The state archives are faced with problems which are structural in nature. First, there is not yet an adequate realisation both by the state and the people who actually run the archives about the importance of archives as a critical resource for social science research. For example, despite holding a rich collection of material, Karnataka State Archives is yet to emerge as a proper institution fostering historical research. As a well-known historian who has used extensively the Karnataka State Archives, notes, "Due to the absence of a proper cataloguing system, scholars find it extremely difficult to use the archives. The catalogue exists only for the period between the late 19th century and about 1942. Thereafter it abruptly ceases. There is no catalogue at all for the Tipu records, or the Board of Revenue records. There are also a number of kadathas in modi-Kannada which are not catalogued. Generally, the conditions for scholars are rather poor since the archives is housed within the legislature building and many records are suddenly and arbitratrarily placed out of bounds. Furthermore, there is a continuous request for records from the legislature which gets priority over the needs of the scholars." The consequence of this has been disastrous for the historical scholarship on the region: "A number of scholars prefer to work on Madras presidency since the archives at Chennai is much better organised. This may have long-term consequences for scholarship on the region, which at the moment is under-researched."

Similar problems affect most of the archives in south India. The problem has been well-summarised by the director of one of the state archives in south India thus: "It is most often not the availability of resources which is the problem. With some effort one can bring together the necessary funds. But the real problem is, those who hold decision-making powers in archives structure do not know how to conceptualise the tasks of an archive."

Second, the state archives are headed most often by officials belonging to the Indian Administrative Service, without much of an academic inclination. And the post of the director of the archives which does not carry the normal bureaucratic authority is treated as a 'punishment post' within the bureaucracy. Given this, they often wait for an opportunity to move to some other post. Treating their tenure in the archives as a passage to elsewhere affects the functioning of the archives. A committee appointed by the Tamil Nadu state government in 1991 and headed by historian S. Gopal to revamp the state archives, suggested that the director of archives should be a historian holding a doctorate. However, this suggestion was not implemented. I may note here that often in the colonial period it was historians of eminence who headed the Madras archives. The first curator of the Madras archives, Herbert Henry Dodwell, began his career as a professor of history in the Presidency College, Madras. And B.S. Baliga, who headed the archives for a substantial stretch of time, i.e., from 1934 to 1958, finished his doctorate in history from the University of London.

Unless the state archives are brought under the control of historians, they are bound to languish in the region. Here too the choice of the historian is important. Most often, such appointments can turn out to be political. Perhaps, a structure of management wherein a historian conceptualises and blueprints the programmes of the archives and an administrator, who carries out the formulated programmes, can yield the best results.

Associational Life and Journals

The local-level social science associations in south India are performing a useful role. A number of them are very active. However, their functioning is hampered by financial difficulties. For example, the planning department of the Andhra Pradesh government supported the publication of the conference papers of the Andhra Pradesh Economics Association from 1984 to 1995, by a small grant. However, the grant has been suspended since 1996. As a consequence, the publication of the conference papers has been rendered impossible. The economics of sustaining such professional associations is evident from the annual accounts of the APEA for the year 1994-95, the last year when it received the planning department grant. Of its total receipt of Rs. 61,190.50 (including the previous year's saving of Rs. 8,915.50), the government grant (Rs. 38,000) accounted for about 62 per cent; and the receipts out of membership fees (Rs. 7,775) accounted for about 13 per cent. The story of the Andhra Pradesh History Congress is similar. The general secretary's report presented in 1996 notes, "Our organisation is facing a financial crisis, though it has not reached such serious proportion to declare bankruptcy. Our sources of income are only two, the membership fee and the sale of proceedings. Both the sources of income account for not more than three to four thousand rupees. If we want to run our organisation reasonably on sound basis we need Rs. 10,000. This is not a huge amount for the government or some other organisations to give us...."[8] The amount of fund required to sustain and expand the activities of these associations is rather small. But even such small amounts seem to be hard to come by.

The same is true for the journals in local languages as well. A small grants programme to support the activities of these associations and journals is a necessity. The story of the journals also brings out the need to develop social science vocabularies in local languages. Without

8. Andhra Pradesh History Congress (1996). XX Annual Session. Guntur. p.20.

this, the agenda of disseminating social science knowledge at the local levels is bound to flounder.

A Postscript

In the course of conducting this survey, my conversations with a cross-section of social scientists from different age groups and disciplinary backgrounds has brought forth three key trends in social science practices in the region. Within the framework of the survey, I could not pursue them systematically. As these trends seem to me to be of certain importance for the future of social sciences in the region, let me briefly account them.

First, south India is the home for a critical number of social scientists, mostly in their 40s with a great degree of self-confidence, whose work has been globally acknowledged. Most of them are located either outside state-funded institutions or feel constrained by their location within such institutions. Almost all of them are non-economists working in areas such as history, political theory or media studies—areas that are marginal to mainstream social science institutions.

Second, the activities of these social scientists are sustained, to considerable degree, not by institutions but by active networks. These networks facilitate, on the one hand, exchange of ideas, source material and books; and on the other, make possible conferencing, short-term teaching possibilities locally and abroad, and research collaborations. These networks are both local and global.

These two trends show that there is an incommensurability between the status of social science institutions and that of social sciences in the region. While good cutting-edge social science thrives outside institutions, institutions are, at least to a significant extent, in a state of crisis and decline. This story of incommensurability may have serious implications for creating future social scientists—which require revamped institutional structures and not merely intellectually productive networks.

Finally, the very logic of this network has more or less completely displaced Delhi as the centre of Indian social science scene. The networks not only have a global reach, but also have actively incorporated social scientists from places like Bangalore, Goa, Kottayam, Hyderabad, Madurai, Pune and Thirvananthapuram. The recognition for the work is no longer expected or sought from Delhi. It now comes from international academic centres (which 20 years back needed to be accessed through Delhi) as well as from the network of smaller local academic centres. In other words, there is a provincialisation of Delhi in the imagination and practices of this group of social scientists in south India.

References

Beteille, Andre (1978). "The Social Sciences", in Romesh Thaper (ed.), *Change and Conflict in India.* Delhi: Macmillan Company of India. pp.142-43.

Centre for Development Studies (2000). *Annual Report 1999-2000.* Thiruvananthapuram. p.64.

———. (1997). *Annual Report 1996-97.* Thiruvananthapuram. p.43.

Institute for Social and Economic Change (2001). *Vision 2010.* Bangalore.

———. (1997). *Silver Jubilee Bulletin 1972-97.* Bangalore. p.22.

Madras Institute of Development Studies (2000). *Vision 2010.* Chennai.

———. (1995). "1971-95: Silver Jubilee Document", Chennai.

Pandian, M.S.S. (1997). "Kumbakonam Encounters Subaltern Studies", *Economic & Political Weekly*, 22 February.

Raj, M. Sundara (1999). *A Manual of Archival Systems and the World of Archives.* Chennai: Siva Publications.

Srinivas, M.N. (ed.) (1963). *India's Villages.* (Bombay: Asia Publishing House, 1963 (1955, 1960). p.6.

11

Fourth Review of Indian Council of Social Science Research*

An Overview

A. Vaidyanathan

In recognition of the importance of social science research for development planning and policy, the Indian Council of Social Science Research (ICSSR) was constituted by the Government of India in 1969 as an entirely government funded national organisation that would promote social science research, but without placing it completely under governmental control.

Achievements

The most important achievement of ICSSR has been its role in creating and supporting 27 national institutes in different parts of the country with state governments as funding partners. These institutes are free to decide and implement their research agenda subject only to periodic external reviews of their overall performance. They are active centres of research on regional, social and developmental issues at the regional level. Since its inception, the Council has funded some 3,000 research projects by scholars from universities, colleges and research institutes; awarded nearly 400 research fellowships and 860 doctoral fellowships. It also provides a number of services (such as documentation, training in research methodology and use of computers and bibliographic assistance) to help young researchers.

* An overview of the main recommendations of the Fourth Review Committee of the Indian Council of Social Science Research has also appeared in *Economic & Political Weekly* 43(5), February 2008, pp.21-24. We are thankful to the author and the editor, EPW for giving consent to reproduce this article in this edited book.

Concerns

The functioning of the Council and its performance have been reviewed by external committees of scholars thrice in the past. The first review done in 1973 sought to provide a vision and a broad strategy for research promotion and also articulated concerns about the implications of the governance structure envisaged in the memorandum of association (MoA) for the autonomous and effective functioning of the Council. They were not in favour of any change at that point in time. The two subsequent external reviews—the second one in 1976 and the third in 1986, reviewed the activities and functioning of the Council in considerable detail, highlighted weaknesses and made remedial suggestions. But these were not pursued seriously either by the Council or the government. Meanwhile, there is a growing concern that ICSSR's impact on social science research has fallen far short of expectations. The Fourth Review Committee was constituted to review the performance of the ICSSR and to suggest ways of making it more effective. This paper is by way of a summary of its report (the full report is available on the ICSSR website). The disappointing performance of the Council is attributable in part to the sorry state of social science research generally and to weaknesses specific to the Council. Governments and public agencies, which have been the main source of funding independent scholarly research, continue to be sceptical of its value.

Social research is increasingly commercialised and driven by the interests and concerns of the sponsors as distinct from public interest. Commercialisation has led to the rapid growth of more lucrative opportunities for individuals, consultancies and non-government organisations (NGOs) in "research". The best of the graduates from premier institutions prefer to go to foreign universities and stay abroad after completing their doctorate.

The better performing students prefer to take jobs in information technology, financial services and even NGOs that offer salaries and career prospects which no academic or research institutions can match. The quality of postgraduate PhD students in social sciences, and the quality of their training have declined. These factors together have led to a decline in the supply of teachers in higher education. Even the best university departments are unable to attract high quality faculty.

Interest in and competence of academia for rigorous research on societal trends have also declined as the cumulative result of lowered standards for recruitment of teachers in colleges and universities and incentive systems that do not encourage, much less reward, quality of teaching and research. The report's survey of research articles in select social science journals showed that 40 per cent of authors were located in research institutes and only a third in universities.

Internal Weaknesses

Besides these systemic trends, ICSSR's performance has been severely impaired by external constraints and internal weaknesses specific to it. External constraints are the result of the basic features of its constitution, the manner in which it has operated and the availability of funds. The constitution of ICSSR, set out in its MoA, provides for a Council comprising ex-officio members representing various departments of government and academicians nominated by the Ministry of Human Resource Development. The chairman of the Council and its member secretary are also selected by the government. Formally, though created and wholly funded by government, the Council is free to make its decisions as an autonomous body. However, the MoA specifically makes these decisions and their implementation subject to government approval. Ex-officio government representatives presently constitute far too high a proportion of the Council membership. Appointments of the chairperson, member secretary and non-official members of the Council are all decided by the government. Lack of transparency in the criteria and procedures for these appointments and failure to observe the spirit of the provisions in the MoA have eroded the credibility of the Council as an autonomous and professional body.

The Council is funded entirely by the Ministry of HRD. While the quantum of grants has increased in absolute terms, they have been inadequate to meet the Council's commitments to meet the rising costs of the growing number of institutes it has sponsored. Allocations for projects and support services have been squeezed leaving little room for expansion. Inadequate budget allocations are compounded by arbitrary cuts and cash flow problems due to irregular release of funds. Grants to the Council are subject to stringent and rigid conditions regarding personnel policies for its staff as well as the terms of institutional grants, projects and fellowships. Cumulatively, these have severely constrained the Council's capacity to plan and consistently pursue a coherent long-term strategy and prioritise different activities.

The salary structures approved by government are inadequate to attract and retain qualified academics in professional/managerial positions. These positions are now mostly staffed through internal promotions. Ad hocism in recruitments and promotions, as well as the inability of the Council (for lack of ministry approval) to ensure parity in salaries and benefits with those of government, has meant that the morale and motivation of Council staff are low. Internal organisation and procedures follow patterns typical of government departments. The mechanisms for appraisal of requests for grants, assessing their performance on the basis of rigorous and professionally credible peer review have been lax and ineffective.

The Committee's Recommendations

The following are the main recommendations of the Committee.

(a) Crucial Importance of Autonomy:

Based on its detailed review of the Council's functioning and its extensive consultations with a wide spectrum of respected social scientists from across the country, the Committee is convinced that ICSSR can and must be enabled to play a leading role in promoting independent scholarly research. The report spells out measures to remove both external and internal constraints that currently impede the ICSSR's functioning.

Functional and financial autonomy of the Council is a necessary precondition. This requires major changes in its constitution to entrust overall governance of the Council to a governing body comprising eminent scholars drawn from different social sciences, and a limited number of government representatives. The governing body will lay down the general policy. An executive council will be responsible to oversee its implementation by the Council's chairperson and chief executive. The report suggests that the reconstituted body be called the Indian Academy of Social Sciences, and also spells out the criteria and processes by which these councils and executives will be chosen.

Subject to broad guidelines, the executive council should be free to decide, without any requirement to get government approval or clearance, all matters relating to the strategy of research funding; prioritising within different activities; mechanisms and procedures for giving grants and for monitoring and peer review of outputs; internal personnel policies and financial controls suited to the specific needs of the Council. Periodic peer review of the Academy's overall performance in relation to its mandate by a committee of eminent social scientists should be mandatory.

(b) Council's Mandate:

The Council's mandate should be to fund and support high-quality social science research of a kind that documents, analyses and interprets different (economic, social and political) aspects of society, emerging trends and important contemporary issues in a broader perspective and from multiple viewpoints. This has a crucial role for generating more knowledge and better insights which, in turn, helps policy makers, facilitates informed public policy, public discussion and a deepening of democracy. It should at the same time, address the task of enlarging the pool and improving the quality of researchers and enlarge its support activities.

This calls for a significant expansion in the scale of its activities. Substantial increase in quantum and assurance of funding is therefore essential. Knowledge-generating research of the kind that the Council is expected to support calls for liberal public funding. While private sector and international funding agencies are unlikely to be interested in supporting such research, the Council may be left to decide whether and on what terms it accepts offers of funding from such sources.

The Committee has suggested that a mere 0.1 per cent of public sector plan outlay be earmarked for social science research. Since it covers practically all aspects of economy, society and politics, it would be appropriate that the government as a whole, rather than any individual department (as is the case at present), take the responsibility for funding.

The increased resources should be used to expand all major programmes (research institutes, research projects, fellowships and support services) and achieve a better balance between them. In order to be effective, the restructured Council needs to reorient its strategy for research funding along the lines indicated subsequently.

The Council should play an important role in increasing the pool of qualified researchers, by increasing the number of doctoral and research fellowships and bringing stipends on par with those of the University Grants Commission (UGC), and taking a proactive initiative to encourage and support, in collaboration with UGC, selected research institutes and universities in different parts of India to organise and conduct intensive and structured pre-PhD courses and specialised research methodology courses in social science.

The Committee also recommends a substantial expansion and reorientation of its research support activities for: (a) expanding access to the library resources and reducing costs by using computer networks in collaboration with other organisations; (b) continuing reviews of current Indian research in different disciplines and also of current state of knowledge in the thrust areas of research; (c) translating reviews of theoretical work and reviews of literature on selected themes into major Indian languages for wide distribution to college teachers and students; (d) facilitating access to and use of the rich material in regional language newspapers and periodicals; and (e) revival and reorganisation of the data archives unit.

(c) Changing Strategy of Funding:

At present, the bulk of research funding goes to the 27 national institutes. Inadequacy of grants to meet rising costs of even existing staff and facilities has forced them to depend increasingly on sponsored projects. This makes it difficult to pursue sustained work on specific themes. More importantly, under the current system, the magnitude and periodic revisions of grants to institutes are not related to their performance.

Funding for independent research projects is not only quite small (both in absolute terms and relative to those of institutes) but highly fragmented in terms of scope and objectives. The Council has not implemented suggestions to promote research around selected themes. Laxity in refereeing of proposals, and peer review of the output of research has resulted in inordinate delays and poor quality. Very little of the work is published.

In order to remedy this situation, the Committee has recommended that while projects and programmes on topics of individual researchers' choice should continue to be eligible for funding, a substantial part of its resources should be earmarked to projects/programmes relating to selected broad areas/themes. The aim should be to promote sustained, multi-institutional and interactive research on selected themes. The themes, to be chosen and changed periodically, should reflect contemporary social and economic concerns which are widely recognised to be important. Funding departments could indicate the broad themes on which they would like to be researched. However, the elaboration of the specific agendas and modalities of implementation should be decided by the Academy through a credible and transparent consultative process along the lines spelt out in the report.

Funding should be on a liberal scale with greater flexibility for grantees to decide, subject to broad guidelines, appointments, remunerations and other personnel matters. At the same time, there should be effective incentives for timely completion of research and ensuring its high quality.

Such a strategy calls for major changes in the Council's current policies and practices for research funding. The Committee has suggested that the Council should not support any existing or new institutes on the present pattern. In respect of existing ICSSR institutes, the present system of recurring grants should be changed. Specifically, the quantum of block grants to be given to each institute be kept at roughly the current levels without any commitment to meet the rising costs of the core staff. But all of them, along with individual scholars or groups of them in other institutions (including universities and colleges), will be eligible to seek the Council's funding for individual projects and thematic research programmes including especially multi-year research programmes/projects. Proposals should spell out clearly the objectives, methodology, expected outputs and time schedules of their components. Decisions on funding will be based on recommendations of a transparent and rigorous peer review of proposals.

Final reports should be reviewed by independent scholars at the end of the programme with reference to the stated objectives, the quality of analysis and adherence to time schedules. Publication of results in refereed journals and as books/monographs, as well as rating the overall performance of institutions on this basis should be given much greater attention and weight in assessing performance than is presently the case.

The Council should rationalise and simplify monitoring systems, leaving grantees free to decide matters relating to their internal administration and utilisation of grants without having to obtain its approval. Focus should be on getting strategic and substantive information on the utilisation of grants and progress on programmes for which grants are given.

Renewal of research grants to institutions should not be automatic. In order to ensure accountability in terms of both quality and meeting time schedules, each grant should be based on a fresh review of the programme proposals, taking into account earlier performance.

(d) Internal Administration:

The internal organisation and administrative procedures of the Council should be thoroughly restructured to encompass a manifold increase in the scale of operations, significant changes in its mix and professional leadership of high quality. The Council should be free to determine and adapt personnel policies (staff structure, emoluments, qualifications, recruitment, evaluation and promotion criteria) in the light of its specific requirements.

The main job of the professional staff is managing research programmes and projects, rather than actually doing research. They should be trained in one or more social sciences and given special training in research management.

Open competitive recruitment should be the basis for selections. Serving employees should have the opportunity to compete for these positions, by availing of special training at the Academy's expense to upgrade their skills.

The organisation should be made flatter, with a reduced number of administrative and support staff, by introducing computers for internal and external communication, maintenance of accounts and other records.

Conclusions

The Fourth Review Committee of the Indian Council of Social Science Research has attempted to provide an overview of the current scenario and challenges facing social science research in India. Its recommendations seek to broad base the funding of the ICSSR, reconstituted as the Indian Academy of Social Sciences; give it the autonomy proper to an institution seized with the task of promoting social science research; and professionalise this institution and strengthen the peer dimension of its functioning, thereby restoring some of its eroded credibility. Above all, these recommendations are intended to further the larger purpose of encouraging independent social science research oriented to generating knowledge.

12 The Near Future of Social Science Research in India*

Partha Chatterjee

It is important to make the ICSSR truly autonomous, but the question is whether the Review Committee's detailed plan for autonomy is desirable and feasible. One could also consider alternative plans to the Committee's proposals for introducing accountability in the research institutions.

The Fourth Review Committee of the ICSSR has made recommendations on the future organisation and funding of the ICSSR itself as well as of the institutes within its network.[1] But since the time the report was submitted in March 2007, official statements have announced a massive increase in the outlay for higher education in the Eleventh Five Year Plan and the setting up of several new Central universities. This comes in the wake of the recommendations of the Knowledge Commission for the establishment of 1,500 universities in India in the next decade. Whether social science research will be affected by this enormous increase in the state expenditure on higher education has not been considered, for understandable reasons, by the ICSSR Review Committee. But it must be borne in mind today in discussing the report, because it indicates a significant change in the background conditions.

The ICSSR

One suggestion of the Committee to augment the public funds made available to the ICSSR is to change the present arrangement of funding

* This paper has also appeared in *Economic & Political Weekly* 43(5), February 2008, pp.38-40. We are thankful to the author and the editor, EPW for giving consent to reproduce this article in this edited book.

1. "Restructuring the Indian Council of Social Science Research", *Report of the Fourth Review Committee* (ICSSR, March 2007).

through a single source, namely, the Ministry of Human Resource Development (HRD), and instead encourage various ministries of the Government of India as well as the Planning Commission, which are users of social science knowledge, to provide research funding to the ICSSR. The suggestion is commendable, but it is doubtful whether the other ministries will agree to provide anything more substantial than limited, project-specific grants. The reason is a simple fact of life of the institutional politics of state bureaucracies. The ICSSR is known to be the baby of the HRD ministry, and neither ministers nor bureaucrats belonging to other ministries will find any incentive in patronising it when they know they will have no institutional control over it. It will require a huge transformation in the prevailing bureaucratic culture to change this mindset.

The second, and perhaps the most radical, recommendation of the Review Committee is to reconstitute the council of the ICSSR in order to make it genuinely autonomous. At present, the Council consists of 18 social scientists nominated by the Government of India and 6 government representatives. The chairman and the member secretary are also nominated by the Government of India. A key recommendation of the Review Committee is to institutionalise a genuinely autonomous Council by having it elected by professional social scientists themselves. They suggest a detailed plan of nominations through a collegium of senior social scientists. But the primary issue is not the alternative plan of constituting an autonomous council but whether autonomy in this sense is indeed desirable and feasible.

Strange as it may seem, there are many who would argue against autonomy in this sense. They will point to the fact that where funding comes from government, and innumerable bureaucratic hurdles, big and small, have to be cleared on a daily basis to keep the channel of funds flowing smoothly, it actually helps to have government nominees on the governing council of an organisation. It ensures that ministers and bureaucrats take an interest in the ICSSR and, when necessary, appropriate members of the Council can be mobilised to seek the ear of the minister. The downside of this arrangement is equally obvious—undesirable political interference and the appointment of government nominees of dubious academic standing.

It is impossible to support this argument on grounds of principle. There is no question that whatever the sources of funding—government or private—the apex organisation of social science research in the country should be autonomous not only in a nominal but a real sense. It ought to be run by a council of reputed and respected social scientists whose collective wisdom will reflect the most advanced research perspectives and the best disciplinary practices of the academic profession. Unfortunately, the erosion of autonomy of institutions of higher education in India has not been merely a one-way process of aggressive incursions by politicians and bureaucrats. Academics have been equally guilty of inviting the intervention of politically powerful figures to sort out their institutional problems or furthering their professional interests. Eminent social scientists, emerging as institution builders, have used their proximity to or influence over ministers and bureaucrats to raise funds and buildings for their organisations, and political authorities have been invited to intervene in professional disputes within academic institutions.

It was entirely possible, even within a formal structure of government nominations, to ensure the emergence of a universally respected convention that, irrespective of political or ideological views, only eminent social scientists would be nominated to an apex academic body such as the ICSSR. Unfortunately, at least from the early 1970s, that is to say, during the lifetime of the ICSSR, such a convention has been observed largely in the breach in institutions of higher learning in India. Such is the perceived dependence today of academic institutions on the organs of government that many social scientists have argued, in conversation if not in print, that a middle-level member of the IAS would be a more effective facilitator as the member secretary of the ICSSR than even the most imaginative and committed social scientist. Besides, many will also point to the dismal record of self-governance in the national professional associations of economists, historians, sociologists, political scientists, etc.

Such being the prevailing conditions, the prospects of the Review Committee's recommendation for constituting a genuinely autonomous governing council of the ICSSR becoming a reality in the near future are not bright. Nevertheless, it is a cause that must not be given up. Now that a committee of eminent social scientists led by A. Vaidyanathan has, in an official document, mooted the proposal, it is vital that it be discussed and propagated in order to create a strong opinion that social scientists of the country are prepared to demand and operate a truly autonomous ICSSR. There must be public criticism, whenever necessary, of unacceptable political interference or bias in the governance of the ICSSR, so as to keep up the pressure on Government to respect the academic autonomy and professional standards of the practitioners of social science. At the same time, it should also be acknowledged by us that it is unlikely that the formal system of government nominations will end any time soon. One must, then, fall back on other plans to revive the health of social science research in the near future.

The ICSSR Institutes

The ICSSR does not itself do any research. The institutional research it supports is largely carried out in the ICSSR network of 27 institutes located all over the country. The reality that is apparent from the Review Committee's report is the enormous disparity in the capacities and performance of these institutes. Only half a dozen or so ICSSR institutes are today genuinely viable as research and training institutions in the advanced academic disciplines of the social sciences. The Vaidyanathan report documents this, but does not discuss in detail what ought to be done with the rest.

I think a useful distinction could be invoked here between the academic and the applied social sciences. There is a large field today of the application of social science knowledge in government policy, non-governmental activism, market research, journalistic reporting, etc. These involve fairly standard theoretical frameworks, survey designs and techniques of data analysis that could be administered even by relatively small organisations of reasonably competent social scientists. These studies could be commissioned by government departments, non-government agencies or corporate firms. More importantly, such organisations could offer training programmes in the basic social science research methods and techniques that could attract many who are interested in acquiring these skills as professional rather than academic qualifications. This would require the designing of relevant and attractive professional courses instead of the utterly irrelevant academic courses on research methodology. But perhaps that is a challenge that many of the smaller ICSSR institutes might accept.

The Review Committee report also points to the perennial problem of accountability of the researcher. In terms of both quality and quantity, the academic research output of most ICSSR institutes is very poor—by no means enough to justify the ever-increasing burden of salaries and allowances. The Vaidyanathan Committee suggests that the core funding of all ICSSR institutes be frozen at their current levels and that they be asked to apply for additional time-bound project funds. Thus, additional research personnel will be recruited only for the period of each project. On satisfactory completion of a project, the institute will be eligible to apply for more funding of a similar kind. This will ensure, the report argues, better accountability, both of the researcher in relation to the institute and of the institute in relation to ICSSR.

This plan has merit, at least in theory. If one tries to sit down with concrete details, however, many problems begin to appear. Since the approval of a project grant usually means the beginning of the time period of the project, the institute will be under pressure to recruit the researchers to carry out the project as quickly as possible. This will mean that proper procedures of search and selection will not be carried out and hasty appointments will be made simply to get the work going. This will not create conducive conditions for the building and nurturing of faculty based on a long-term institutional vision. In other words, the plan may serve to discipline the poorly functioning institutes but will hurt those that have built their distinct identities and academic reputation.

It may be worth considering two alternative plans. One is to actually engage in an exercise of evaluating and ranking the institutes by performance and potential. This could be done by a committee of reputed social scientists who will use a set of declared, and more or less objective, criteria to make their evaluations. Based on their rankings, the ICSSR may vary the level of funding for each institute. If this exercise is carried out periodically, it would provide the incentive to institutes to improve their performance to qualify for a higher level of grants or strive to maintain their standards so as not to be demoted from their current levels. A process of this kind has been initiated by the University Grants Commission in the university system and the results have not been insignificant.

The second plan is to seek to connect the ICSSR and its institutes with the imminent expansion of the Central universities. If indeed dozens of new Central universities are to come up in different parts of the country, the ICSSR institutes could offer to provide some ready-made components for these new institutions. It will require some innovative thinking in designing new postgraduate and doctoral-level courses, but these fledgling universities could well be open to such proposals.

All this requires some dynamism and enterprise, both at the level of the ICSSR leadership and among the social scientists in the institutes. But it seems very likely that, for better or worse, the face of higher education in India will change quite rapidly in the next few years. I think it is time to think of the opportunities as well as dangers of the near future.

13 A View from Abroad*

Michael E. Lamb

I am keenly aware of my inadequacies and limitations while commenting on the report of the Fourth Review Committee of the Indian Council of Social Science Research (ICSSR). As a result, I begin these remarks with some caveats and words of warning. Most importantly, readers should bear in mind that I am in no way an expert on Indian social science, and know the history and function of the ICSSR only as they are described in this report.

As chair of the International Advisory Committee of the Economic and Social Research Council (ESRC) of the United Kingdom, I read the report in preparation for recent meetings with the ICSSR designed to explore, establish and/or strengthen bilateral programmes that might promote mutually rewarding collaborations between Indian and British social scientists. I found the report to be an invaluable resource because it provided a historically rich and detailed context for understanding better the Council with which the ESRC is developing programmatic relationships. I would like to believe that my enhanced understanding facilitated our discussions and will help ensure the development of links that enhance the quality of social science research in both our countries, to our mutual benefit as well as that of the international community of scholars more generally.

Unique Report

The report deserves admiration because it is, in my experience, unique. In addition to providing a historical context, the report provides an

* This paper also appeared in *Economic & Political Weekly* 43 (5), February 2008, pp. 40-41. We are thankful to the author and the editor, EPW for giving consent to reproduce this article in this edited book.

insightful and sympathetic analysis of the ICSSR that is as sensitive and searching as it is constructive. Whereas most commissioned reviews of this sort provide self-serving accounts in which critical comments are muted or stated in code, this report is noteworthy for its candid identification of the problems facing Indian social scientists in general and the ICSSR (and its affiliates) more particularly. Although I cannot in any way vouch for the accuracy and validity of the observations made and conclusions reached by the authors of this report, I was struck by the authors' willingness to identify the problems that arise when independent scholarly analysis is neither adequately funded nor respected and when, perhaps as a consequence of the former, social scientists and their analyses become commodities and hawkers.

Especially but not exclusively in developing countries and nations embracing new economic systems, applied research by social scientists can be of enormous value, benefiting the discipline, the academic community and the country or region in which it is undertaken. I have long argued that the distinction between applied and basic research creates a false dichotomy obscuring the reality that all good social scientific theories need both to be grounded in the real world and to make empirically testable predictions, just as all good applied research should both be grounded in and help further develop the theoretical aspects of the relevant disciplines. Rather alarmingly, the authors of this report suggest that the prevailing situation in India falls far short of this ideal. I cannot judge the validity of this assertion, but I fully share the authors' concerns and fears about the risks that arise when social scientists become guns for hire, tailoring their conclusions to flatter those who commission their efforts while ignoring their professional responsibilities to place their findings in the context of other scholarly work, both empirical and theoretical and to make it available for peer criticism, evaluation and integration.

Work for Hire

The politicisation and commercialisation of scientific research is by no means unique either to India or to the social sciences. The misuse of biomedical research findings (including the mis-reporting of the results of clinical trials for new drugs) continues to warrant considerable concern in the UK and the United States (US), for example, where the Blair and Bush administrations, respectively, have also been criticised for misusing the results of social science research and for suppressing scholarly messages and messengers that and who raise unwelcome questions or reach critical conclusions. According to the report on the ICSSR, however, the current situation in India is more alarming and problematic because work for hire has, for many social scientists, become the "only game in town", rather than being a potentially lucrative diversion.

In the absence of a motivation to value the approval and respect of one's academic peers, the report suggests, the scientific quality of the analytic work can only decline further and the credibility of Indian social scientists will be damaged similarly. For this reason, the report merits careful attention, because diminished respect for social scientists and the social sciences cannot be good for India or for the Academy.

Fortunately, the authors of the report do not merely identify and document the magnitude of the problem apparently facing Indian social science. Indeed, the report is distinguished also by the clarity and thoughtfulness with which it considers and recommends possible solutions to the perceived problem.

Recommended Funding

Specifically, the report identifies the need for major increases in public funding for social science research, increases that will make future funding levels high enough to ensure that the community of Indian scholars can afford to conduct rigorous research—both basic and applied—without needing to tailor their questions and answers to suit the parochial interests of their patrons. To ensure that increased funding actually serves to energise and rejuvenate the social science disciplines in India, the authors of the report also emphasise the need to make funding decisions completely transparent, determined solely by peer evaluations of research proposals on the basis of their intrinsic quality, insulated from even the appearance of political interference. The authors of the report claim (with good reason, in my opinion) that such support for investigator-initiated scholarly work will increase the quality of the scientific endeavours attempted, and I would expect it both to improve the quality of commissioned (i.e., not publicly funded) research while enhancing the credibility and social standing of social scientists in India as well.

Of course, to make the case persuasively in a fiscal environment wherein the competing demands for necessarily limited public funds invariably exceed the supply, the social science community, led by the ICSSR, needs to make the case that a vibrant social science community will serve the country and its citizens more broadly, not only the narrow interests of social scientists themselves. Doing so will require not only judiciously advertising instances in which high quality social research has informed decision-making and thereby proved its value, but may also require demonstrations of a willingness to differentially reward high quality and withhold support and funding from mediocrity and failure. The authors of the report suggest that the Council has not, in the past, been at liberty to exercise such discretion in many of its funding decisions, which have always been made with an eye (or two) on political considerations. For the report to have the desired effect on the government, however, the ICSSR will be forced both to embrace the requests for increased resources, and to acknowledge the need for a new pattern of expenditure, with quality of work rather than past funding levels determining future allocations. In the absence of such a commitment, it will be difficult to justify the desirability of increased national investment in social science research.

The ESRC is seeking to build closer relationship with the social science community in India because it recognises the mutual benefits that follow when scholars work with and learn from those whose cultural and academic backgrounds and skills differ from their own. We know that the collaborations we foster between Indian and British social scientists will be most successful and productive if the Indian community is energised and enthusiastic about the scholarly and professional opportunities and rewards available to them at home, because that will give them enhanced standing in relation to their peers elsewhere. By the same token, we in the UK need social scientists around the world who continue challenging us to raise our game. Thus, we too have a stake in the quality of Indian social science and look forward to continued profitable collaborations and contacts in the years ahead.

14 Social Science Research in India

A Summary of Discussions

R.S. Deshpande and Khalil Shah

Introduction

The V.K.R.V. Rao centenary celebration was appropriately planned by hosting a seminar on social science research at ISEC in Bangalore from the 6th to 8th of July 2008 as a tribute to the great visionary, whose contribution to the society as a statesman has been well recognised nationally and internationally.

The seminar was inaugurated on the 6th of July 2008 by eminent guests—His Excellency Shri Rameshwar Thakur, Governor of Karnataka; Shri B.S. Yeddyurappa, Chief Minister of Karnataka; Prof. Sukhadeo Thorat, Chairman, University Grant Commission (UGC), New Delhi; and Shri S.L. Rao, Chairman, ISEC. At the onset, Shri S.L. Rao welcomed the delegates followed by the inauguration ceremony by releasing a book '*The Passionate Humanitarian: V.K.R.V. Rao*' and guests speech by Hon. Shri. Rameshwarji Thakur and Shri. B.S. Yeddyurappa. His. Excellency Shri. Rameshwarji Thakur presided over the function and Prof. Sukhadeo Thorat gave inaugural address to the seminar. Finally, Prof. N. Jayaram, Director, ISEC proposed the vote of thanks.

The Seminar on Social Science Research (SSR) included seven technical sessions spread over three days. The themes for various sessions were:

1. Evaluating vibrancy and accountability of SSR.
2. Changing structure of SSR: interdisciplinary, multidisciplinary and emerging challenges.

3. Role and functioning of public domain SSR.
4. Project-oriented research *vis-à-vis* long-term research.
5. Mismatch between resource availability and demand.
6. Autonomy of SSR institutions.
7. Inter-institutional cooperation and dependence among SSR institutions.

Technical sessions were held in the presence of an eminent chairperson who briefed on the theme for the session. Paper presenters were then invited to present their views which were then followed by an open session giving scope for interactions. Each session had two rapporteurs.

In the first session on "Evaluating vibrancy and accountability of SSR", three presentations were made by Dr. T.C.A. Anant, Dr. A. Vaidyanathan and Dr. V.M. Rao. The session was chaired by Dr. Samuel Paul. These papers dwelt upon several issues such as funding of research projects, project grants by UGC and ICSSR, efficiency in conduct of research, transparency, quality of research, corporate responsibility, and relationship between university and research institution, agency base research and innovation.

The second session on "Changing structure of SSR", had four presentations by Dr. Ravi Kanbur, Dr. V.R. Panchamukhi, Dr. U. Sankar and Dr. Michael Walton. The session was chaired by Dr. U.R. Rao. The papers touched upon several aspects related to the changing structure of SSR such as multidisciplinary research, qualitative and quantitative techniques, dimensions that need change, research methodology and innovativeness, econometric modeling, use of remote sensing data, linkages between theoretical and empirical works, economics and anthropology.

Dr. Yogindar Alagh chaired the third session on "Role and functioning of public domain SSR", wherein Dr. M.V. Nadkarni, Dr. Narayanan Nair and Dr. John Crowley presented their papers. The papers presented focused on issues related to networking particularly between research institutions and policy makers, public and private domain research with regard to transparency, dissemination of research findings, local research capacity building and non-conventional mode of research, difference between academic research and policy research.

The fourth session was on "Project-oriented research *vis-à-vis* long-term research". This session was chaired by Dr. Mihir Rakshit. Dr. T.K. Oommen, Dr. Sugata Marjit, and Dr. P.K. Bose presented their papers. The session began with getting into the dilemma whether project-driven research is also knowledge-driven. The session further focused on topics such as short-term time-bound research and long-term research and their relative advantages and suitability, issues related to skills and finalisation, utilisation of research findings and conclusions, institution and individual research.

Dr. A. Ravindra chaired the fifth session on "Mismatch between resource availability and demand". Mrs. Lakshmi Venkatachalam, Dr. Ravi Kanbur, Dr. Mihir Rakshit and Dr. G. Thimmaiah presented their papers. These papers focused on issues related to demand for research, capacity building to conduct research, need for research before taking up a scheme, for implementation by the government, developing communication within the process at different steps, enhancing participation of people at district levels and bridging the gap, exchange programmes between research institutes and universities, causes of unfilled vacancies in research institutes and fund constraints.

The sixth session was on "Autonomy" to discuss whether SSR institutions are bartering autonomy with respect to grantees, administrators etc. The session was chaired by Dr. C.T. Kurien and the two speakers were Dr. T.S. Papola and Dr. S. Parasuraman. The discussions were focused on issues such as financial, administrative and academic autonomy and accountability, sponsored research, collaboration between universities and SSR institutions, autonomy and creativity.

The seventh session was chaired by Sri. S.L. Rao on "Inter-institutional cooperation and dependence among SSR institutions". Two papers were presented in the session by Dr. George Mathew and Dr. Anjan Mukherji. The discussions dwelt upon topics such as interaction amongst research faculty, research staff, personnel of library and information centre for data/document exchange, sharing of infrastructural facilities, research collaborations, joint publications, research sharing and importance of cooperation.

All the above seven seminars had two rapporteurs per session. They are listed according to their sessions as follows: Mr. Kaushik Basu and Mr. Pradeep Mehta; Mr. Mainak Majumdar and Mr. Manojit Bhattacharjee; Mrs. Sancheeta Ghosh and Mrs. Priya Gupta; Mr. Indrajit Bairagya and Mr. Shyam Singh; Mr. Krushna Mohan Pattanaik and Mr. Manojit Bhattacharjee; Mr. P. Srikant and Mr. K.H. Ananth; Ms. Amrita Ghatak and Mr. Mainak Majumdar.

The outcome of the seminar in the form of proceedings are enclosed here in for policy makers to consider the suggestions and make provisions to implement the same for enhancement of productivity in the field of social science research for the benefit of people at large.

Evaluating Vibrancy and Accountability of SSR

Evaluating vibrancy and accountability should be reflected in any evaluative exercise that is undertaken after research by academic institutions. One should bear in mind the context and the nature of the activity that the institutions are engaged in. Evaluation becomes easier to deal when standardised products are used. The impact of any research that is being evaluated cannot be figured out in the short term. Time dimension is a very important aspect of the evaluation process. Things that may seem irrelevant at the time of inception may become extremely valuable 10 years down the road. On the other hand, advising the government that may come closer to the standard product concept and with limited time period may benefit some. As the nature of the activity is knowledge generation there is a need to be creative, develop non-standard products and the institutional setting should enable one to be more productive. Institutions should device certain policies in order to maintain high standards of research. A dedicated researcher needs to uphold the values, be creative and maintain the quality of research.

Evolution of ICSSR

When evaluating an institution like ICSSR, one needs to know how it has been evolved. It is very important to note that the public state supported dimension of social science research is very recent. In India, the Planning Commission tried to bridge the gap of knowledge by establishing a research programmes committee. These projects have been directed by ranking professors of the university departments who are busy, overloaded with government assignments. The projects were delayed and did not have adequate manpower to execute them. The report of the committee of Planning Commission chaired by V.K.R.V. Rao documented the state of social science research in India and the need to expand the capacity to do research which led to the inception of ICSSR. The four roles which ICSSR defined were responsive role, promotional role, coordinating role and networking role. The lack of advocacy role was one of the major limitations of ICSSR. The responsive and promotional role remained as the core activities of the Council which created an imbalance in the roles. The lack of the coordinating and networking roles had major consequences which resulted in institutional imbalance. In 1973 and 1974, the government transferred the funding to ICSSR.

The ICSSR is also seeking to promote research within the university system and the bulk of its funds go to university departments in affiliated colleges for promotional research. The programme grew in size where 60 to 80 per cent resources are allocated to the institutes under ICSSR. One of the major drawbacks is the possibility of multiplication of institutions if recurring and non-recurring grants become available from the Centre. Since a large number of institutions and NGOs were claiming for grants, it was necessary for ICSSR to come up with a framework to determine the criteria for funding. The second problem is that these institutes explicitly by original mandate were not universities and thereby needed to be affiliated to universities to design and run PhD programmes. The institutes followed and incorporated the weakness of the universities' disciplinary structure into their own PhD programmes. In the current structure of ICSSR and UGC, it is physically or logistically impossible to coordinate and derive any major benefits. The structure of ICSSR does not provide any role for a huge community like social science association. There is a greater need for coordination between research grant schemes so that the projects get greater mileage from each other.

Concerns of Social Science Research

The two major contributors to social research are the practical needs of the policy and the individually done research. Social sciences deal with a variety of problems and issues where there are great levels of value loaded assessments, analysis and diverse disciplinary perspectives. The most important criteria in any social research is that it should produce professionally competent, rigorous and analytical treatment of focused social issues. There are some problems which may involve the operational decisions of managers, departmental executives etc. This may require some research such as polycentric research which addresses issues that relate to policies.

The public funding to a large extent is spent on collection of lot of data. India is one of the most enviably positioned countries, in terms of the data research. However, until recently, very little of it was available in the public domain; the researchers could not access it. Over the years the situation has changed, with the data collected; papers are produced without giving details about how the data were collected, what was the design, what are the kind of errors in the data or what kind of biases there might be. This brought in constraints to cross-examine and interpret data. Knowledge-based research process is demand-driven. Initially, the main source of demand was the public sector.

The committee's individuals who produce reports are either not available in the public domain or the analysis is not open to public/ professional criticism. The other institutional worrisome issue is the proliferation of private institutions. Commercialisation of research is a major destruction involving problems of lack of transparency, strict professional peer reviews, criticisms in normal academic processes of journalism particularly where the data is unavailable as it is confidential and a privilege of its client. This impedes really good academic research. Various departments in the Ministry have funds for research and they commission projects. However, it appears that these departments do not give importance to either know or are concerned about the results. The state government spends very little funds on projects except those on consultancies for design of projects and evaluation. The second component is on the institution itself which sets up and control projects. These are not subject to any rigorous academic and scholarly assessment. The third component is to institutes like the ICSSR etc., where certain funding which is provided for research is subject to rigid conditions. The processes and the criteria by which the proposals are invited, screened, evaluated and granted are not totally transparent. There is huge demand for students in social sciences in consultancy organisations, NGOs and in the IT and corporate sectors. Many students find opportunities abroad. Hence, the environment is not conducive to either attract or retain good people. It appears that the curiosity factor which is one of the major driving forces of creative research has totally evaporated now in research institutions. The problem of overdependence on government funding has changed but the change is essentially in terms of the NGO, the foreign funding agencies, international agencies etc., that has created a divided market and kept away good people from being loyal and involved in building institutions.

One of the interesting features about India is that with the exception of a few organisations like TATA, others have not really shown any inclination to commit funds for research. There is a big difference in the US and other Western countries. Though there is fund lobbying in research, it is observed that there is seriousness and research of a high order. These are some constraints that are partly responsible and get compounded by problems internal to the social science research structure. The ICSSR gets limited amount of funds and it does not get adjusted when costs go up. Hence, it is forced to find consultancy projects which involve a donor's agenda and in many cases it is found to be detrimental to pursuit of any knowledge generating research. The second serious problem is the question of autonomy. Autonomy means major review of the institutional design of whole set of institutions involved in social science research. There has to be an internal process where one cannot legislate these things. The institutions are free to decide on the details of the project based on their interests, their competence; they want to do, say what their programme is and its outcome. The other important issue is about interactions between the institutions. One is reluctance on the part of staff of the autonomous institutes to do any teaching. The other is, even when there are people who are interested to teach in universities, the response is extremely lukewarm. Since these problems cannot be solved by legislation, one way of countering this would be to collaborate in organising training programmes especially on linguistic aspects. There is a symbiotic relationship not only between research and teaching but also in involvement in policy.

Trends in Social Science Research

With the talent pool available at ICSSR, one may be able to build up some institutional arrangements for continuous monitoring. The first trend seen in the social science research are, growth in institutions, growth in the faculty and growth in the research output. Second trend is sophistication in technology and better internal means of communication. The third trend is specialisation. And finally, with globalisation there are no linkages of the social science research which is almost cutting across even the national lines. Due to globalisation, the faculty increase contacts and there are number of people who are on the frontier of the social science research. In addition to the positive trends there are some negative fallouts; the first thing is wastage. Out of some 10 papers that are received for publication in journals, 8 to 9 papers get rejected in the initial screening or soon after refereeing. The problem is the lack of quality work which cannot be corrected at that stage. Hence, there should be attempts to monitor the rejected papers for correction and improvement.

Departments of Research Methodology

Research process can be observed under two entities—replication and innovation. Replication is where one takes the existing methodologies on extensive mode. Innovation is considered as a means to improve existing methodologies. Innovation should feed the replication and replication should give the feedback to the innovation, indicating what kind of problems need to be attended to be renovated. With regard to the database situation, there are three things which are of importance. One is the official statistics. SSR community has put more pressure for obtaining reliable data from those agencies which supply. Second point is that at the top level, there is very little understanding of the processes going on at the ground level for the data collection. Finally with the advancement of computer technology, it is relatively easy to save the data and use it for future research. SSR community need to find out some way of preserving the past data and making use of it, that is retrieving and making use of it in their own future research. SSR community should interact and communicate to all the stakeholders in social science research, the policy makers, the other sciences, even other social sciences and the lay citizen.

Changing Structure of SSR: Interdisciplinary, Multidisciplinary and Emerging Challenges

One has to go much beyond to social science models and has to look at dialogue as an instrumentality for drawing inferences. As an economist, one would look at externalities and public good problem and the efficiency required which interpreting problems.

Issues of Interdisciplinarity

It is important to encourage interdisciplinarity, where one has to be as concrete as possible and the other will need to have sustained engagement. It is a known fact that natural sciences are successfully interdisciplinary while it is not the case in social sciences. Perhaps the attainment of great success was mainly because the objective was well defined, concrete and isolable. It is advisable to push forward this interdisciplinary engagement especially when one has a team of histological differences which are pulling one apart in different directions.

Revolution in Social Science Research

Social science research as a process consists of several entities, one, of course is the researcher himself i.e., role played by the researcher, his inherent capability, his aptitude, is research culture, his objectives, etc. Second, research theme, methodology and data that needs to be monitored. The third dimension is the research facilities within the institutional framework, the purpose, relevance of research and finally research output and its use. The actions of a researcher will have to be viewed in three phases: one is prior to becoming a researcher which implies the entire education system comprising postgraduate education system, the M.Phil. course, training programmes etc. Second is, during the phase as a researcher how he grooms himself and responds to the requirements of the society and the third is, as a beneficiary of the research career. All these phases are very important to define and understand the complexities of the role of the researcher in the research process. Research careers are chosen by most as a last resort and thereby, the supply of good research assistants is so limited in the practical world. Also, the grooming of the potential researchers at the post-graduate level are also very poor.

Multidisciplinary Research

Multidisciplinary research in social sciences can be produced with the involvement of a sociologist, a psychologist, a geographer, an economist and a political scientist, each being trained in the other discipline to a certain extent. It is not just enough to induct different broad angular segments of the matrix but there is need for total revamping of grooming in social science research and involvement of universities. One of the main issues is the research culture, where papers are accepted without refereeing.

Autonomous academic institutions should be free from political interference. ICSSR is an apex body but still gets a lot of instructions from the political system. The *Nature and Purpose of Economic Activity* in 1964 by Dr. V.K.R.V. Rao gave a great vision to social science research. All social science research should adhere to three objectives: to satisfy the fundamental minimum requirements of the community of economic goods; minimum use of resources that is efficient; and not to hamper but foster and promote the end of all human activity *viz.*, development of human personality. In the two articles in the *International Income and Wealth Series I*, he refers to issues of comparing incomes and per capita incomes. He gives an account of how comparison is impossible and should not be done. He says that since bundle of goods are different, qualities are different, utilities are different, attitudes are different, lifestyles are different, the comparison is not correct and does not show anything. Even the purchasing power parity is totally analytically faulted because one cannot have the prices for goods in a comparable manner.

In multidisciplinary research, there is no synergy among the disciplines. Different people work together in a compartmentalised manner, the results are put together and there is no interaction or feed-back either in terms of conceptual level or any type of development of new tools or applications.

Sustainable Development

There are a lot of controversies about the meaning of sustainable development due to differences that exits between inter-generation equity and intra-generation equity. One must consider the economic, social and environmental benefits for sustainable development. The dynamics of the ecological process, about the threshold limits, the earning capacities, the two-way linkages between economies are very poor. A lot of research is needed in developing sustainable indicators.

The Barriers in Research

There are a lot of learning costs when there is a shift from one field to another field and many times, the scientists and technologists, they do not take economists or social scientists very seriously. There needs to be a constant promotion of the capabilities of an economist or social researcher. It takes a lot of effort on the part of the researcher in understanding their language, the objectives which requires a heavy investment and especially thereby, one foregoes benefits because it is easy to replicate papers on the area that has already been done. There is no incentive also for the people to shift to some other field on collaborative research. Another problem with publication is that most of the journals prefer sophistication; a standard model with minor improvement relaxing assumptions or econometric techniques will get high publication. But if one is trying to do something innovative, looking at the problem completely differently and looking at the new data but with simple techniques, then it is given least importance.

Social science research needs to emphasise on the design of new institutions, new methods of pricing economic reforms and globalisation. We need to have the flexibility, fellowships for scholars doing significant research in one discipline to go to another and interact, and a publication policy encouraging new ideas, promoting multidisciplinary research, new concepts and new diagrams.

Every researcher has to look into different disciplines in order to infer the policies and analyse them with the media of communication. The disciplines can be broadly classified into a 'micro area' where there are interactions with anthropologists and with sociologists to some extent. The other can be called a 'macro area' in which interaction happens with social scientists.

Role and Functioning of Public Domain SSR

Public Domain Social Science Research and Private Domain Social Science Research

The ultimate goal of social science research is to build up form and inform public opinion, encourage democratic debates and not merely serve the policy formation by the government but even the public and NGOs at large. In the private domain social science research, very often, any research is not allowed to be published. It is only meant for the sponsors of the research. There is a possibility of confusion because quite often, the government itself might sponsor research which is meant only for the bureaucrats. But one cannot be sure if it even goes to the government and the whole cabinet. It is sometimes not allowed to go beyond bureaucrats and the concerned ministry merely because it is sponsored by the government. The criterion of which is to be the priority for funding by an institution like ICSSR, it is this distinction which is more important than private funding or public funding.

Relationship between the Government and the Social Science Research Institutions

The government is the main change agent of the society for social and economic change. This assumption is yet to be tested and proved. Since the past 50 or 60 years, the state has been assigned its developmental role. Now that this developmental role has been assigned to the government, there has to be a greater collaboration between the government and the state and social science research. But at the same time, there could be other change agents like NGOs, social workers, etc., who would also need social science input and this social science research output should not be denied to them. There is a possibility of a problem in the relationship between the government and social science research institutions where the sponsors of the research, particularly the government department might try to influence the outcome of the research. Thereby, it is important to have autonomy in spite of the close relationship with the government.

The ultimate purpose is not to limit the audience only to the experts within the subject, but to reach the public. This policy is important even in private domain social science research. If data is manipulated to suit the government or the ruling establishment, then social science research will lose all credibility.

Capacity Building

Capacity building is another important role of social science research. Several social science researches have PhD programmes. At present, they are aligned towards mathematical and statistical techniques. The interdisciplinarity or interaction between different disciplines has to be built in social orientation and research programmes from the beginning and it will take on from there. Related ideas particularly logic and philosophy of social scientists need to be taught to broaden the vision of social scientists.

However, there are some criterions for assessing these institutions:

1. Scope for creativity in social science institutions.
2. Extent to which this idea of interdisciplinarity works at what level. To what extent this works in practice right from the level of project formulation, guiding PhD students, methodology and how it is implemented.

A few important questions were discussed:

1. Quality of research.
2. Agenda.
3. Dissemination of research.
4. Research globalisation knowledge generation.

Policy Process and Research System

There is a need to find an access between social science researches; if policy makers are made aware of social science knowledge then mistakes that contribute to the failure to alleviate human misery can be rectified. The key issue is the capacity of social science to contribute to important social problems. The point here is what kind of institutional structure offers the optimal trade-off or unoptimal trade-off? There are several local optima between two competing pressures:

1. The pressure of academic notion of quality. In a broader sense, only the peers of academics are qualified to judge the academic's work. This surely matters for career advancement and are equally embedded in the professional self-understanding of social scientists. One's hope for a good academic response causes the first pressure.
2. The pressure of policy-driven notions of relevance. It is based on a micro rapid response capability and immediate intelligent capability which is embedded in a time-bound logic of the political process.

The reason for UNESCO's concern in this area is the two-fold observation: The kind of nexus or interface that tends to emerge spontaneously in research systems that are strongly structured and adequately funded is suboptimum. This involves dualism which is embedded in the funding mechanism for research between academic research (indifferent of policy concerns) which is based on institutional funding and policy-oriented research (not necessarily indifferent to academic notions of quality but not defined in terms of those notions).

There are practical implications of which are executed in the various components of UNESCO's current activity in social sciences:

1. Strengthen national social science research systems (especially in developing countries). This research system should contribute to produce basic concepts in data, graduate training, international scientific exchange, public and policy awareness, and provide direct policy relevant input when required including institutional engagements in planning processes to bring together scientists and administrative specialists.

2. Develop tools and methodologies to make the existing social science knowledge base available to potential users and in this way, no one knows in advance as to who the potential users will be. The knowledge base has to be brought together as a whole and will be available to anyone who might need it. This is the current focus of UNESCO's programmes.
3. Establish a meeting ground where people can be involved in social science knowledge generation and use. One of the initiatives UNESCO has been seeking to promote is the establishment of a forum to bring together the ministerial level policy makers in the area of social development with academics and civil society representatives so that the issues of common concern can be identified and the relevant interfaces be developed.

Role of Public Domain Social Science Research

The research that goes into public domain must be readable, intelligible, and in a usable form. There is a horizontal public and a vertical public. The horizontal public here refers to the people of the republic of social science. The knowledge, work and information that is generated needs to be communicated to people or the vertical public. The main role is to educate, create and provide knowledge for the use of others. The focus has been on the government as a policymaking body and hence, a major user of the research. But increasingly, it is also being used by NGOs, civil society groups, commercial organisations even if they have not funded the research, and international organisations.

Project-oriented Research *vis-à-vis* Long-term Research

Majority of social science research that is carried out by a large number of institutes and universities are mostly project-oriented. They are very useful often but one problem is that, the data often are not available to the academic community. When a number of research projects have been carried through them the conclusions, generalisations, and advancement to the general body of knowledge or development of a new theoretical perspective are some of the issues that crop up. Most of these issues can be avoided if the research is focused on projects and their outcomes.

Dichotomies and Dualisms in Social Science Research

In social science, there are several dichotomies and dualisms that are being formulated like theoretical *versus* empirical, policy-oriented research *versus* theoretical research, qualitative *versus* quantitative, micro *versus* macro, fieldwork-oriented *versus* textual analysis, server research *versus* participant observation etc.; most of these dichotomies are simplistic, it is better to think in terms of continuity, the postulated continua.

The four goals that social science research normally pursues are description, explanation, prediction and prescription. Description is essentially an empirical task where the question can relate to micro or macro, done quantitatively or qualitatively through fieldwork or textual analysis, and that is the reason that dichotomies are not really sustainable. Description is a prerequisite for explanation where one cannot have a satisfactory explanation without description. Explanation is to pose the question (why and what) to find the reasoning behind it. Research projects can certainly produce a reliable description which is a stepping stone to successful explanation. The third goal is prediction which is impossible while getting through the problem. Prediction as a function of science will have to be kept in mind, and as it is well known in social science that a lot of probabilistic analysis take place. Explanations are prerequisite for prediction, thus the sequence is clear; description, explanation and prediction. Then comes prescription which as a function of social science research will not be endorsed by most social scientists. Knowledge for what is very important and therefore in the final analysis one has to prescribe based on the knowledge that has been produced.

Types of Research Projects

There are three types on the continuum of research projects that can be visualised. The first type is opinion surveys. The mass media now a days are full of opinion surveys where one knows the number of people interviewed, how the sample is selected—rural, urban, general-wise etc. They are providing information and they certainly provide the answers to the question but they are not producing knowledge. Then the second type is the project which normally evaluates the impact of economic development of social policy. They are not as instant as the opinion surveys or of short term. Usually, these surveys are done repeatedly over a period of time. The third type of project is explicitly designed to answer the 'why' question. This is the kind of research that institutions like the ICSSR or UGC or Anthropological Survey of India or Indian Institute of Advanced Studies etc., should be focusing. The division of labour among social scientists and the changing demands on social science research are two important factors to be considered.

Dichotomy between Projects *versus* Long-term Research

For project-oriented research most of the empirical work is done by social scientists, economists or political scientists with the exception of social anthropologists. Social anthropologists traditionally attached themselves to particular tribe, villages or urban neighbourhoods for an entire life time wherein collecting quantitative data from those pre-requisite societies was not feasible. Therefore, the qualitative data and participant observation of micro units have really become the birth-marks of social anthropology.

The earlier this dichotomy is abandoned, it is better for social science research in India. The mission of Western social anthropology was to help the colonial state to understand the native society so as to civilise it. In contrast, post-colonial national states wanted social science research to help efficient governments so that their citizens can be better governed. Hence, there was a need for quick massive research projects which were commissioned to collect data.

The real deficit of the project-oriented research is the manner in which the project research is done. Though the fund available is enormous, the problem in research projects generally are with the type of people who are employed to conduct the research. The first type of people is a large number of untrained persons who are instantly recruited to collect data, who do not have any knowledge on how to formulate questions or to administer them. The second are a team of people who analyse the data without having any feel of the field. The third level is the research administrators who are distant from the field and the analysis, but finalises the project report.

Social science research, project-oriented and long-term, is conditioned by several factors. One is the purpose for which data are collected and two, the subject matter of the theme of research. Three, the nature of society from which data are collected. Four, the segments of society from which information is sought. Five, the nature of the result designed which could be experimental or explanatory.

Need for Project Funding Research

ICSSR institutes have to have that responsibility to see whether the amount of money they are getting are enough to pay salaries for the positions that have been thrust upon them politically or otherwise. Most of the ICSSR institutes cannot fill up the vacant jobs because they do not have the money to pay their salaries. They do not even get the increments. This is for an institute which has a significant corpus fund, and well reputed, unlike many other institutes where salaries depend on projects. One does not have resources as promised by the Central government; some of the state governments have completely forfeited on their promises. Unfortunately, the institutes are at the receiving end. Project funding is the only source from where one can cross-subsidise good research. This is important that people appreciate it and an effort is made in convincing the government at different layers to fulfil their promises; without it the faculty members are forced to undertake project-funded research. There has to be a concerted effort to make research in social science and it does not mater what approach one takes.

There are two types of research, long-term and short-term research. Long-term research goes on for years funded by various kinds of governmental and semi-governmental organisations. A lot of time and effort is spent in collecting in-depth data but this data is never utilised and the reports produced are never read even by the agencies which fund this. The short-term research propositions have better possibility of reaching their goals. Short-term research can be divided into two groups. One kind is the normal science kind of approach where all the stages, the functions, division of labour that is utilised is known to everyone. Typically, this normal science kind of approach is uninteresting and makes no kind of contribution to the field of knowledge and is usually never read as well. On the other hand, the other kind of short-term research is more innovative in design and imaginative. Though this approach does not follow the conventional path, it may produce or suggest alternative ways of doing research, adding something new to framework of research. Every year UGC gets about 700 research proposals and ICSSR gets about 2000 research proposals; they are mostly short-term, small research projects. An institutional mechanism and administrative structure needs to be in place to select the few good proposals of academic research. The alternative kind of way of managing this is to have some real good social scientists evaluate the proposals and take that risk. The non-governmental kind of funding agencies have their own kind of experts and they employ professors from universities who are experts to evaluate the proposals. For example, Ford Foundation also finances research projects, but in their case they have their own kind of research agenda. They support only those kinds of programmes and also there is close supervision and monitoring of these projects. It would be beneficial to transform research project into research programme.

Is there a Mismatch between Resource Availability and Demand?

The competing forces is really the curiosity about the functioning of society in its diverse social, cultural, political and economic dimensions and be the practical needs of policy makers in managers in governments civil society, private sector, to reliable information and social analysis. These different forces manifest themselves in different combinations and disciplines; thus in academics, there has been a tension between the cries for relevance on one hand and the freedom and ability of an individual researcher to pursue his curiosity on the other. When one looks at the issue of demand and supply in research or research capacity at different levels, it is really dedicated to the multi reflex that are created by an enriched, enabling environment for social science research.

Periodic research for horizon scanning is very critical if one is going to be able to develop a sort of vibrant demand for research. There are certain reforms that are necessary in terms of horizon scanning for developing a very meaningful research agenda at various levels and it needs to be debated whether institutions are developing this sort of medium to long-term agenda for research. Discreet divisions of functions in terms of creating projects that deliver are needed. The most important question is whether one can integrate all of it concurrently to a continuous evolving process which would be a much more innovative approach with regard to a continuous demand. Secondly, the justification of fundamental research or long-term research which has really no immediate user orientation is also important.

Reforms Required in Research

One needs to have to have a proper combination of institutional arrangements, incentive structures and make sure that the society itself is able to communicate these priorities to the society at large. In terms of generating better demand for research, a lot depends on the government, because of the amount of funds available for developmental spending where institutions need to play a major role in terms of prioritising demand for research. One of the major reform is of course developing a sound statistical base that will drive a lot of interest in research. Secondly, a lot of reforms are required in the government which will in turn help to spur the demand for research. The third reform is the communication about the relevance of research. There is a need for designing new research products, not to just look at it in terms of long-term project research and short-term project research, but basically a wide variety of products that could be of use to the user groups.

Some Suggestions to Strengthen the Institutions

ISEC or other institutions in the state capital should continue to hold major conferences to have a systematic programme of inviting researchers in institutions that are in the districts. The second suggestion is for similar institutions in other states to actually go to the districts and to engage with researchers. The third suggestion is that strong institutions with reputation like ISEC, partner with other institutions to go in for projects jointly, crossing borders to institutions in other state capitals that are not as strong like ISEC.

Demand-Supply Imbalance

The fundamental problem in social science research is of course that of funding. There is a widespread agreement that the amounts required for proper research is not available from the government or from the usual sources. The quality of social scientists that turn out each year and who would be willing to join the universities and the research institutions are very few. One needs to have a plan wherein the medium and long run the need to produce enough social scientists, mainly economists to meet not only the green demand from the private sector, from the regulatory bodies from the domestic and international institutions, but also for the academic requirements.

The second criterion is the need for textbooks at all levels pertaining to Indian markets and economy. In social sciences, the textbooks which are presently available are written in the context of the Western economics of the developed countries. The teachers who are doing fundamental research can point to the conditions under which certain theories or certain approaches will be more relevant and others which would be not. The other problem, which has been widely discussed, is that of the dualism between the ICSSR research institutes and the university system. In order to have a programme to upgrade the research and training of social sciences in India, one needs to have certain roadmaps as to how to move towards that system over a period of time.

Mismatch between Availability and Demand of Financial Resources

The availability of financial resources in relation to demand from social science research always exceeds the available resources. In 1960, the number of universities was small. Suddenly the number of young people increased and a large number of universities were opened but resources available for these universities were inadequate. Facilities like libraries were not there and teaching faculty was not adequate. Universities were unable to do research because the universities had to cater to the mass of young people entering the university system. By the 1970s, it was realised that the university system was not in a position to continue both teaching and research. Hence, ICSSR was established to ensure that social science research did not suffer. In order to get over this, financial mismatch institutions will have to mobilise financial resources from multiple sources. Too much dependence upon government funds probably will not ensure high quality as it is not questioned.

Autonomy—Are SSR Institutions Bartering Autonomy with Respect to Grantees, Administrators, etc.?

What is Autonomy?

Autonomy or lack of autonomy in financial matters might exist, where one might not have any freedom to use resources according to one's will. There could be autonomy or lack of it in respect to administration, governance (whosoever happens to be in power) and funders. They might like to be involved in the governance themselves, and thereby, academic autonomy is the bigger question here. Academic autonomy is the main concern rather than financial and administrative concern. A certain degree of financial and administrative autonomy will have to be forgone if funding is dependent on someone else.

Relationship between the Government and Academic Freedom

Considering social science research in India today or sometime in the past for that matter, autonomy is not being eroded or bartered. One specific context here is in reference to the research institutes that are more or less regularly funded or which receive corpus funding from one or the other sources, mostly from the ICSSR and also, from the UGC. There are others which are funded by the Planning Commission and partly by the Finance Ministry. We do not have many serious problems of autonomy in terms of the academic freedom of choosing themes of research, expressions of opinions, and publication. The relationship between the states and the social science research institutions need not necessarily be adverse or confrontational as is often thought. It has to be complimentary and cooperative and this would lead to the enhancement of autonomy of the research institutions.

Ensuring Autonomy

Another issue is how does one ensure autonomy and what has been happening so far? One way could be to be independent financially; some institutions have endowments. Yet, most of the institutions would like to have or depend on core funding from certain agencies like the ICSSR, UGC, or the state government. It is natural for the funding agencies to give certain guidelines in terms of governance and administration. The ICSSR, for example, have their representatives and it nominated social scientists on the board of governors of the institutes. The idea here is to have a better liaison to understand each others' problems. In most institutions, the relationships have worked in this particular fashion and there has not been any great interference by the state government officials in the affairs of the institution.

The ICSSR has acted as an effective buffer between the funding agencies (the government) and the research institutes. Autonomy is concerned not only in terms of funding for institutions to carry out their own research agenda; ICSSR has not given away research agenda. Firstly, autonomy should decide your own research agenda. The second is not being questioned about the findings and research output. There could be a tendency of questioning to check if it is useful or not. Autonomy is good but it has to be matched with a certain degree of accountability.

Sponsored Social Science Research

Sponsored research comes with clearly defined objectives, ideas and processes. There are a number of accountability measures in place as also a timeframe. They follow up with the researchers in a critical manner because of the reporting systems. If the resources are strategically got and used, it can beneficial. But, when the question of autonomy arises, it is not about their interference in the governance system but it is the interference into one's own ideological framework, the value orientation of the institution, the research agenda, and how it can be taken further in terms of research and contribution to the knowledge base and policy.

First of all, there is a need to engage with the government. There must be proactive engagement to see how they can fund education and research. How can institutions and universities come together? Secondly, there are numerous opportunities for funds and not all the institutions and agencies come with similar ideologies and orientations. There is a need to realise the enormous knowledge-generating potential of our research scholars which can contribute significantly to knowledge generation. This is where institutions like the ICSSR and UGC can play a very important role. How should they enhance the research that is available and the funding available for M.Phil and PhD students? UGC is trying to reinvent itself to find resources to pay for the doctoral research programmes. It needs to push a little more harder to get the required funding. Autonomy and the future is all about safeguarding what must be done and how it must be done. How do we counter the forces that undermine ideological orientations? There is a need to look at sponsored research from another perspective—what kind of money, whose money, why money, and what can be done with it.

Some important issues that were addressed on autonomy are:

- If autonomy is to be used as a means to promote good research, does it fulfil its societal role if there is one?
- Is autonomy of the institute and autonomy of the faculty mutual and compatible?
- If autonomy is linked with good research, does the norms of good research tend to be discipline-specific?

Relationship between Teaching and Research and the University System and the ICSSR Institutes

Institutes including CSTS, the Gandhian Institute and the Kerala Institute were established earlier than ICSSR but were taken over by ICSSR for funding purposes. Then the idea of each state having its own institute came up. Today, the composition of these 27 institutions have different histories. These institutes are trying to find funds from a variety of sources and have difficulties of its own.

Why did the Original Institutions come out of the University System?

The universities in earlier days were focusing much on the teaching aspect and people were submitting research projects to RPC and other institutions. This was an extracurricular kind of activity and it was not a part of the university system. Therefore, those who were research-oriented moved out of the system and created institutional structures. A kind of a disjunction took place between those who were research minded and those who were teaching-oriented. Research and teaching should come together and this interface will bring a change in the whole orientation and profiling of the institutes which are working outside of the university system.

Autonomy as an external dimension, essentially consists of the nature and extent of external interference in both, the internal structures and administration as well as the choice of the research agenda. The fact is that the government's fund does affect internal autonomy of the institutes in respect of hiring, remuneration and also, in terms of the agenda of research. The ICSSR is the only source of funding. There is a serious question as to how far the donor agencies should refrain from dictating details of what has to be done in the matter of personnel policy, general guidelines and the choice of agenda.

Threat to Autonomy

The threat to autonomy in institutions is largely created within the organisation rather than from external environment. ISEC has external experts and their opinions are most important to them. With the ICSSR as a research institution, one cannot get into training and education in a significant way. If parallel large postgraduate programmes are introduced, it will affect the funding. The threat to autonomy from external funding sources is a myth and it is really the governance of the institution that needs to be checked. The other question is with respect to autonomy of researchers and institutions.

Integrating Research with Action

Autonomy is very closely related to creativity and to be creative, one needs autonomy and freedom. Social science institutions today need to respond to emerging situations, not just the research. Integrating research with action is a very important element and this should be considered as a new phase in research. It is important that the scientists or social scientists of institutions are able to assert their own area of autonomy. They cannot do so unless they are very clear as to want they really what to achieve and to what extent. It is quite possible that the institutions may not be able to support all their areas of interest.

Formally, the ICSSR's rules state that, an institution, to be eligible for funding from the ICSSR cannot (at the same time) be eligible to receive money from UGC. That is the clause by which the government has created the ICSSR and UGC. There have been many debates in the ICSSR Council about, what the research institution does and when this issue of starting PhD programmes in ICSSR institutions came up. People expressed reservations that this would dilute their focus on pure research. They concluded that PhDs are consistent if they function as research institutions. The main question here is how should these institutions be funded. Historically, there is no evidence to the fact that the UGC was ever involved in funding this. Research required creating something outside the university system as only specialised institutions focused on research. There have been instances where certain important findings were not being permitted to be published by both the government and private sources. ICSSR is a four decade old institution. Very little has been done in terms of strict review of both institutions and individuals.

If ICSSR and other funding agencies seek to determine the agenda of research as it is not free money for people to do whatever they want; it will have to be a programmatic and specific theme-based research. India should move towards a competitive grant system or contract system as compared to the prevailing system where there is actually no competition. Diversity in the sources of funding will promote autonomy and responsiveness of research. At present, the system relies exclusively on some sources which may not be desirable for promoting autonomy. The other side of autonomy is to increase the sources of funding and thereby the accountability. If we have multiple funding sources, then accountability pattern also changes.

Inter-institutional Cooperation and Dependence among SSR Institutions, UGC, State Agencies, etc.

Cooperation or collaboration between social science institutions from India has been mainly with foreign institutions. There are not many institutional cooperations and collaborations that have taken place between institutions in India. One of the major reasons for this is the limitation of funding. There is a bureaucracy here and there are bureaucratic rules and procedures in academic world which prevent this kind of movement taking place.

Harold G. Moulton in 1929 said that the trend in the social sciences was towards increasing specialisation and as one goes on specialising, one ends up being alone looking at that special area. Since the 1920s or so, there has been a growing recognition of the desirability of developing a new body of generalisations of broader social impact. This trend for generalisation in turn has disclosed the necessity of cooperation at two levels. One, cooperation among scholars trained in different divisions of the social sciences and possesses the complementary technical qualifications. Two, is the cooperation amongst institutions of social science research.

Cooperation must be conceived and carried out in specific rather than in general terms. Investigations that are of basic significance very frequently transcend the bounce of a particular division of the social sciences and they require for their handling the peculiar qualifications of workers in several fields. Therefore, cooperation between different divisions of social sciences on the one hand and between different institutions in the social sciences is a must and the cooperation of scholars drawn from different divisions of the social sciences in various institutions on the other, is the most important and fundamental to all. However, this cooperation has not happened in our country between social science research institutions. While looking at the social science scenario in the country, it is very obvious that there is hardly any co-operation whether it is an ICSSR institution or a UGC institution.

To ensure that there is cooperation and the best knowledge based research programmes that will benefit the institutes in an effective manner, some measures need to be taken as follows:

1. Research faculty should meet at least once in a year at the national and regional level.
2. Research personnel—Middle level and technical staff should also meet region-wise or at national level.
3. Sharing of infrastructural facilities should be encouraged.
4. Library and document exchange should be effective.
5. Sharing of research findings should be done for mutual benefit.
6. Research collaboration needs to be encouraged.
7. Joint publications (is possible only if collaborated research projects exists between institutions).
8. Emphasis be given for sharing human resource.

Social scientists have to take the responsibility to make collaboration and joint development between institutions more effective. According to Prof. Harold Moulton, "Cooperation in social science research between Institutions, if it is to be made effective, requires four basic prerequisites. 1) increasing modesty; the scholars, the researchers, the institutions, the heads of institutions must have increasing modesty; 2) great tolerance; 3) endless capacity to stand wear and tear and what often seems to be fretless discussion. And, finally, 4) infinite patience with fellow workers."

Cooperation among recipients and non-recipients is needed for effective research. Financial resources cannot be shared but its allocation may be flexible towards an optimal utilisation. One needs a better, flexible, cooperative administration and institutional structure without which even private initiatives will fail.

Findings and Suggestions

The seminar made up of seven themes, included the presentation of papers by eminent speakers. The remarks of the chairperson of each session and summary by the rapporteurs have all brought in many interesting findings. Some of the important findings are given below:

Theme 1: Evaluating Vibrancy and Accountability of Social Science Research

1.1 SSR in India has seen remarkable growth, sophistication and globalisation. However, its pitfalls are wastage i.e., findings are not utilised and the level of quality is reduced.

1.2 Presently, SSR institutes get majority of its resources through government, ICSSR and sponsored research. ICSSR also sponsors different programmes to scholars, seminars and projects for strengthening future research capabilities.

1.3 There is need to take stock of SSR carried out in the country from time to time. Its impact can be felt over long period.

1.4 Majority of SSR is demand-driven and hence there, is minimal emphasis on knowledge augmenting research.

1.5 It is found to be important to bring in a sense of creativity in research and enhance quality levels in SSR.

1.6 Considerable expenditure is incurred in data collection from the funds allocated to research but reliability of the data remains questionable and hence, there is need to improve quality of data obtained.

1.7 The quality of research is getting affected due to lack of transparency, criticism and peer review.

1.8 The non-availability of credible official statistics, and delay in its access to researchers have resulted in the quality of research being poor.

1.9 There is a growing concern on usage of research findings for decision-making purpose.

Theme 2: Changing Structure of SSR: Interdisciplinary, Multidisciplinary and Emerging Challenges

2.1 Multidisciplinary approach is becoming relevant and is gaining importance in SSR and there is a need for capacity building.

2.2 Presently, there is no synergy among different disciplines and the gap must be bridged.

2.3 There is a need to link between theoretical and empirical findings.

2.4 Multidiscipline approach brings in genuine methodological exchange and helps in creating new concepts.

2.5 In addition to quantitative techniques, the qualitative approach using case studies, focused interviews and group discussions are adding values and augmenting research findings.

2.6 The five dimensions that need to be focused which have implications due to the changing structure and research are the researcher, theme, methodology, data and research facilities.

2.7 Availability of bright graduates to take up SSR has been scarce due to better employment opportunities through campus recruitments.

2.8 There is a need to have a forum for quality in social science research (FOQUS) to provide consultancy and upgrade the research outputs.

Theme 3: Role and Functioning of Public Domain SSR

3.1 Networking between various institutional structures and research institutes and policy makers are recognised to be important.

3.2 Public domain and private domain SSR can be differentiated on the basis of transparency but not on the basis of funding.

3.3 There is a need to have indicators to judge social relevance of research.

3.4 Local research capabilities are to be built at district levels.

Theme 4: Project-oriented Research *vis-a-vis* Long-term Research

4.1 Opinion surveys and surveys conducted to evaluate the impact of social policies on economic development may be classified as short-term research.

4.2 Studies to answer the wide range of questions where there is absolute necessity to generate knowledge are recognised as long-term research.

4.3 Problems related to skills of people involved from design to data collection till the analysis stage needs to be addressed on priority.

4.4 SSR needs to focus on purpose, theme, nature of society, its segment and as well as the research design in order to have distinctive contributions from both short-term and long-term research studies.

4.5 There is a need to transform research projects into research programmes, i.e., handling research through institutes in preference to individuals.

Theme 5: Is there any Mismatch between Resource Availability and Demand?

5.1 Focus on research should be more on building of expertise and capacities among different stakeholder groups which would help to identify, prioritise, facilitate and then divert the nationally and regionally relevant agendas for research.

5.2 Institutional arrangements should be excellent/proficient to attract good aspiring students and professionals to take up careers in the field of research.

5.3 Action needs to be taken to create vibrant and balanced environment for demand and supply of research.

5.4 Institute and university interactions needs to be strengthened through exchange programmes for improvement of research outputs.

5.5 Mismatch between demand and supply of financial resources and human resources needs to be rectified.

5.6 Research work may be decentralised.

Theme 6: Autonomy—Are SSR Institutions bartering Autonomy with respect to Grantees, Administrators, etc.?

6.1 Autonomy in research needs to be addressed in terms of financial autonomy, administrative autonomy and academic autonomy.

6.2 Autonomy through legislation may not be of much use in reality. It needs to be earned rather than being given.

6.3 Autonomy makes sense only when there is accountability.

6.4 Both ICSSR and UGC can play a pivotal role for good collaboration between SSR institutions and universities through structuring M.Phil and PhD programmes.

6.5 Autonomy is considered as a good means to promote good research and not an end in itself.

6.6 Concern for individual autonomy also needs to be looked into while considering institutional autonomy.

Theme 7: Inter-institutional Cooperation and Dependence among SSR Institutions, UGC and State Agencies etc.

7.1 Bureaucracy needs to be removed for better cooperation and exchange of knowledge among institutes.

7.2 UGC, ICSSR, Planning Commission, Finance Ministry and state ministries need to take active role in promoting cooperation between institutes.

7.3 Cooperation amongst institutes can be built through research meets of faculty and staff from time to time and through exchange of infrastructure facilities like library, research collaborations, sharing of research findings, joint publications, resource trainings, etc.

7.4 Building appropriate individual characteristics/qualities amongst the research fraternity such as modesty, tolerance and patience would also enhance the level of cooperation between institutes.

7.5 Exchange programmes that facilitate better exposure to researchers and faculty needs to be encouraged to improve quality of research.

7.6 Remuneration to researchers should match with equivalent positions in industry in order to attract and retain highly talented human resources.

Conclusion

The seminar organised from 6th-8th July 2008 to coincide with Prof. V.K.R.V. Rao's centenary celebrations at Bangalore was on social science research. The objective of the seminar was to discuss various issues related to social science research carried out in the country.

The seminar had seven technical sessions wherein 20 papers were presented by experts involved in social science research. Themes on which these papers were presented included various aspects such as evaluation and accountability, changing structure, role and functioning of public domain, project and long-term research, mismatch between resource availability and demand, autonomy for institutions and inter-institutional cooperation among SSR institutions.

Each technical session started with an introduction to the theme by the chairperson followed by paper presentations and open house discussions. Topics related to the theme were discussed in detail and paper presenters expressed their views and suggestions. Rapporteurs have summarised each presentation and there was a good interactive session at the end of each session.

The seminar has brought out interesting points through deliberations which are noteworthy for consideration and implementation by policy makers and executers. Discussions in the seminar dwelt upon past experiences, current problems and envisaged issues likely to be confronted in future.

Though the seminar has met its objectives by raising many issues related to the theme, it cannot be considered as conclusive as these issues need to be continuously addressed for upgradation from time to time through such seminars and meeting involving all stakeholders.

Institute of Social and Economic Change, Bangalore

Centre for Development Studies, Trivandrum

Centre for Economic and Social Studies, Hyderabad

Centre for Multi-Disciplinary Development Research, Dharwad

Centre for Research in Rural and Industrial Development, Chandigarh

Council for Social Development, Hyderabad

Centre for Social Studies, Surat

Centre for Studies in Social Sciences, Kolkata

Gujarat Institute of Development Research, Gujarat

Giri Institute of Development Studies, Lucknow

Institute of Economic Growth, New Delhi

Institute of Public Enterprise, Hyderabad

Institute for Studies in Industrial Development, New Delhi

Madhya Pradesh Institute of Social Science Research, Ujjain

Omeo Kumar Das Institute of Social Change and Development, Guwahati

Madras Institute of Development Studies, Chennai

Indian Council of Social Science Research, New Delhi

Annexure

Oral Presentations

A-1

Addressing Regional Imbalances in Indian Social Science Research Capacity

Ravi Kanbur

The Problem

The sharp drop-off in institutional strength in social science research, from the national capital to the state capitals, and especially from the state capitals to the districts, is obvious to all those who are familiar with the Indian scene. I start from the presumption that this is a bad thing. It is bad from an equity perspective and it is bad from an efficiency and growth perspective as well, in a country where key aspects of policymaking and policy implementation are devolved to the state and to the district level, and further down. In such a setting, a localised capacity to conduct excellent social science research and analysis is important, for developing and implementing policies and interventions that help growth and poverty reduction, and for arguing against those that do not.

I do not wish to go into big picture structural questions—for example, whether the number of 27 ICSSR institutions is too many, whether the incentives for researchers and institutions are appropriate, and so on. These are important questions that need to and have been dealt with elsewhere. Rather, I want to focus on what can be done within the present structures and constraints, over a 3 to 5 year period. And I want to focus specifically on what the stronger institutions of social science research, like ISEC, can do. I am not suggesting that these institutions are not already doing the things I will discuss below.

Ravi Kanbur, T.H. Lee Professor of World Affairs and Economics, Cornell University, New York.

But I do want to suggest that they could do more, and do it more systematically and strategically. I also want to suggest that funders consider a special window for supporting such outreach.

Three Suggestions

There are three specific things that strong institutions like ISEC can do to redress the regional imbalance in social science research capacity.

First, systematically and as a matter of course, when they organise the big conferences that showcase their strengths, they could invite researchers and teachers from less strong institutions. For an institution like ISEC, this would mean identifying and inviting promising individuals from colleges, universities and institutes based in the district capitals. Participation of these individuals would have to be funded, since it is very unlikely that their own institutions will have the funds to make participation possible.

Second, systematically over the medium term but opportunistically in the short term, staff of institutions like ISEC could engage researchers and college lecturers by going to the district-level institutions and holding seminars and conferences on key issues. These events could, for example, disseminate ISEC research to the district level, or they could be tied in to the district-level planning process, or they could coincide with a data collection visit to the district, of which there are many.

Third, institutions like ISEC could partner with institutions in the districts, or indeed some institutions in other state capitals, on joint research projects one of whose major aims is capacity building.

Funding

All of the above three suggestions are doable within the present structure. What is needed for them to happen? First, a passion for outreach, a sense that it is an inherent part of the mission of the institution to correct regional imbalances in capacity. After all, Dr. V.K.R.V. Rao moved from building two very successful institutions in the national capital to building an institution in his state's capital.

Surely, it is incumbent upon the inheritors of his legacy to move further, to spread research and analysis capacity to the districts.

Without such passion and motivation, the outreach will not happen. But passion alone will not be sufficient. Therefore, second, the exercise needs to be resourced adequately. It is too much to expect from the currently overstretched staff to add this to their plate as well.

In fact, the first of the above suggestions—invitation to and financing of conference attendance—should not be particularly expensive since it mainly involves local travel.

The second suggestion—seminars, conferences and lectures in the districts themselves—will be intensive in staff time and this should be appropriately costed for preparation and delivery.

The third suggestion—joint projects between institutions—is the most expensive since it might involve the whole gamut of institute activities and overheads.

Adequate funding is the key to incentivise staff to take on outreach. I can imagine that committed researchers and teachers would prefer to do outreach for part of the time to earn their salary, rather than take on yet another data collection project with a ministry or other funding agency, with little in the way of intellectual payoff. But the funding has to be right.

Funders

How might funders like ICSSR take on board and develop these suggestions further? I propose two tracks. In the short run, ICSSR could work proactively with selected institutions to pilot these suggestions, or variants, and to fund these pilots. Learning the lessons from these pilots, the initiative could then be scaled up to a general competition, inviting institutions to make proposals on outreach activity, just as they would for a research or data collection project to a ministry or to the ICSSR. These proposals could be reviewed by outside experts in the usual way, and a selection made. The key, once again, is to provide funding at a level sufficient to make it attractive for institutions to go for outreach rather than their more conventional bread and butter activities.

Conclusion

This short note has made concrete proposals, implementable over a 3 to 5 year period, for using the strong social science research institutions in the state capitals to develop outreach and helps build capacity in district-level institutions and even some institutions in state capitals. These proposals can and should be considered within the current structures of governance and administration of Indian social science research.

A-2

Changing Structure of SSR: Interdisciplinary, Multidisciplinary and Emerging Challenges

Michael Walton

Thank you very much. It is a pleasure to be here. I will give some thoughts on the theme of research on interdisciplinary questions, rather than comment specifically on Indian institutions. I come to this as an economist who has been primarily concerned with policy questions, such as questions of whether kids go to the school, whether they learn there, what happens in the market place etc.

I suggest it is really hard to get a grip with many of these vital questions for development, either analytically or in terms of policy, if you do not look at what different disciplines have to say. There are two broad areas, in which I have had relatively intensive interaction with other disciplines. One mainly concerns what economists would call micro areas of behaviour, and involves talking with anthropologists and, to some extent, to sociologists. The other concerns economy, wide functioning, where I have worked with political scientists. As time is short today, I will focus on an example of engagement with anthropology on micro, or community-level issues, leaving aside economy-wise questions. This emerged in work with Dr. Vijayendra Rao that involved bringing together economists and anthropologists to debate on issues of culture in development (this was published in the book *Culture and Public Action* that we edited together).

The concept I am going to talk about is one introduced by the anthropologist Arjun Appadurai that he termed the "capacity to aspire".

Michael Walton, Former Prof. V.K.R.V Rao Chair, ISEC, Bangalore.

This was developed from two sources in his work. The first source was his own work of interpretation of the cultural behaviours of various groups and social movements living or working in the slums of Mumbai. He analysed changes in how they conceived of the scope for engagement with other groups in the world, and in particular how they could potentially negotiate with groups in authority, and conceive navigational paths for social change, as a product of their experiences and learning in social mobilisation. The other source is more methodological. As an anthropologist, Appadurai was concerned with an implicit division of labour between economists and anthropologists. Economists are concerned with future-oriented action, with how people conceptualise the management of risk and allocate resources and make decisions accordingly. By contrast, in this narrative, anthropologists are concerned with the residues of the past, understanding the group-based symbols, attitudes, forms of interaction where they came from. He argued that this division of labour is deeply misleading, with pernicious consequences over which discipline has anything to say about the future. Thus, in this account, economists know about future and thus have coherent views on policy. Anthropologists may have interesting things to say about the past but have nothing useful to say on the future or on policy. Appadurai fundamentally contests this perspective, arguing that the way in which individuals think of the future is itself a cultural, group-based and socialised capacity. These, essentially group-based processes are further embedded in implicit inequalities or power and social status. The capacity to aspire affects how individuals and groups behave in relation to the future concerns, whether in market interactions or who they interact with state agencies, including over very practical issues such as demands for water and sanitation. Furthermore, this is a concept that is unequally distributed across groups in a society, but one that can be formed, created, adjusted through a process of social mobilisation and social interaction.

This raises a fundamental question for economists, concerning the treatment of preferences. For economists, preferences, that shape attitudes and behaviours to leisure, risk, and the value given to the future, are just given. Most economics start where preferences end. However, these are of course formed culturally. In economic terminology, preferences are endogenous. Analysing this will require a bridge between concepts across disciplines and this will be an important area for future research.

This can present a challenge, and I can illustrate this with a couple of stories on the 'capacity to aspire'. In the process of developing the dialogue, Vijayendra Rao and I asked other people to react. In particular we asked an economic theorist, Debraj Ray, to read the paper and he developed an economic model around it, with interesting issues of social distance and societal polarisation. The aspect of the concept that he picked up on was the idea that an individual's capacity to aspire could be a function of the extent which she could bridge to reference groups in society and thus could be negatively related to the extent of polarisation in the society. This has allowed him to bridge from this concept to lot of other work that he and co-workers have undertaken in the analysis of polarisation, and its potentially negative consequences. However, a next step in the story concerns a research proposal I recently reviewed. This was developed by economists, with an interest in exploring the concept of the capacity to aspire, and how it works for poor. But they referred not to Appadurai's paper, but to the economic analysis of Ray. Economists are more comfortable working with the concepts of other economists! This story has not ended and is an illustration of where interdisciplinary communication can be useful and difficult.

Let me wrap up with a couple of points. First, I would reiterate that it is often important to engage in interdisciplinary exchange for purposes of effective interpretation and policy design. Second, while there may be epistemological difference over the nature of knowledge, I believe progress can be made through digging and exchanging over specific concepts and empirical work. All of our disciplines have implicit internalised ways of thinking. These shape how we react to other perspectives, and sometimes there may be very fundamental differences in thinking. Getting better exchanges can be helped by incentives, by funding practices, but will also depend on individual motivation and communication, and a willingness to open up, and work through differences in particular instances. Thank you.

A-3

Changing Structure of SSR, Interdisciplinary, Multidisciplinary and Emerging Challenges

V.R. Panchamukhi

Thank you Mr. chairman. At the outset, I would like to pay my tributes to one of the greatest stalwarts of the social science profession, Dr. V.K.R.V. Rao. I would call him as an Institution, not just as Institution-builder, because his ability and vision gathered a large number of stalwarts and intellectuals around him. He always had an eye on bringing bright people around him and that is how he could build three institutions. I personally came in his contact when I joined for my PhD course in Delhi School of Economics and since then I had had many opportunities of interacting with him from a distance and close quarters. I would also like to mention here that when I was the chairman, ICSSR, I took the initiative to revive V.K.R.V. Rao prize system in social science research and raised the award amount from a paltry of Rs. 5,000 to Rs. 25,000. Moreover, as an editor of the Indian Economic Journal, I thought of bringing out a special issue on V.K.R.V. Rao including some of his seminal writings and I should really thank Shri S.L. Rao, Dr. Deshpande and Dr. V.M. Rao for making me available some of his seminal writings. Well, coming to the issue being discussed in this session, I agree with chairman, Dr. U.R. Rao, who rightly mentioned that everyone has different capacities of experiences to talk about social science research, both as an insider and as an outsider, from the academic world and the policy world. Therefore, friends, whatever I say, I draw both as an insider and as outsider. As a researcher,

V.R. Panchamukhi, Managing Editor, Indian Economic Journal and Former Chairman, Indian Council of Social Science Research (ICSSR), New Delhi.

academician and formerly chairman of ICSSR, I could see lot of problems in social science research in the country. I would provide a few remarks on social science in India by availing my experiences and observations.

While talking about social science research, I would like to look at the social science research process consisting of five main pillars or entities. First, of course, is the researcher himself. Secondly the issues related to research theme, methodology and data. Third is the research quality. Fourth is multidisciplinary research. And finally, the fifth is institution and research facilities. I sincerely and strongly feel that there is need for revolution in each of these segments and it is very important for the future of social science, its institutional framework, its purpose, the relevance of research, the research output and its use. In research, at certain stage of life, researchers become extremely strong-worded and highly reflective. But, I think tinkering of the system will not do much because we have gone far away from the ideal formative best modality paradigm of dealing with all these dimensions. I would like to urge all of you to tell us how to deal with these issues instead of just listing them.

Coming to first pillar of social science research process, the researcher, I feel that we have hardly given attention to the role played by him, his inherent capability, his aptitude, his research culture and his objectives and so on and so forth. Ideally, the researcher will have to be reviewed in three phases. One is prior to becoming a researcher. This implies his performance in our entire education system, including post-graduate, M.Phil, PhD courses and training programmes. Second is during the phase as a researcher how he grooms himself and responds to the requirements of the society. And third is as a beneficiary of the research career. All these are very important to define or rather to understand the complexities of the role of the researcher in the research process. However, among these, last two phases are quite important for social science research. Talking about grooming the potential researchers at the postgraduate, M.Phil and PhD level, I feel, is very poor in terms of training of latest developments. The condition is quite pathetic. If you ask any student out of normal universities the questions like, what are the issues in WTO, what is sustainable development, what are the ecological imbalances or what are the current issues our economy or society facing, we do not get clear or even sometimes no answers. We produce PhD holders in agriculture by someone who has not seen the farm, produce a PhD degree in industrial economics by someone who has not seen or worked in industries. I think there is need for a total revamping of the approach to the teaching and grooming of the researcher to be eligible to deal with the problems of the society. It is now obvious that research career is no longer attractive relative to other careers. In recent times, corporate and business houses have started recruiting the bright students on campus and offer large amount of money. This has certainly impacted career in social science. The research career is left high and dry and it is now only left to the left-outs of those who are either not getting opportunities in corporate or continue to remain in social sciences out of their desire. Therefore, at overall level we still find shortage of good researchers. We quite often experience this not only during recruitment of good researchers in the institutions, but also at the level of research assistant.

Now, coming to the second pillar of social science process—the issues related to research theme, methodology and data, I think, we have a lot to discover about how things happen in regard to choice of the theme and choice of the methodology and validity of statistical data. I would refer to the august body, a way back in 1982, Institute of Economic Growth (IEG) had organised a seminar on 'Relevance in Social Science Research' to discuss the issues related the research theme. The papers presented were later brought together in the book having the similar title! That volume clearly pointed out that if we want the social science to be relevant, then we need to take research themes that are relevant for policymaking as well as for improving and adding to the knowledge box of the discipline. It clearly underscores on need for regular interactions between policy makers, researchers and stakeholders both before and after formulation of research proposals and output. On the other hand, to avoid moving away from the basic objective of the discipline itself, it also suggests research community to be conscious of whole process of knowledge generation. Now, we hardly have any such interaction between researchers in the social science and the policy makers and the stakeholders. Similarly, we have two basic problems with research methodology. The research methodology courses taught in Indian universities and social science research institutions varies both in terms of quality and their rigorousness. It is quite obvious that the methodology courses offered in many universities has been reduced to barest minimum of statistical data, quantitative techniques and regression analysis. However, few universities and SSR institutions have managed to offer comparatively good quality and extensive courses in methodology. This has further created new problems and arguments for distinction between quantitative and qualitative research methodology. It is a fact now that a significant proportion of our academic population is failing to understand the abstract and highly esoteric quantitative mathematical papers that are being increasingly published in reputed journals. Being an editor of a journal, I think complaints of these researchers are valid and we need to face the challenge of making the choice of methodology simple and useful. I also agree with the point made by Prof. Ravi Kanbur urging researchers to go beyond pure models to look at dialogue as an instrumentality for drawing inferences. I think, his suggestion is quite valid. However, simultaneously, there is also a need for looking at content, modalities, usefulness and continuity of research methodology courses offered by our SSR institutions. Moreover, we should also do something to discourage an emerging trend where the participants want a certificate to improve their biodata to get promotion in their services. About statistical data, yesterday, Prof. V.M. Rao was pointing out that there is a lot of data, but we hardly ask the questions over the measurement and validity issues. He is quite right as when I was the member of National Statistical Commission (NSC), i happen to meet all the producers of monthly statistics of production. To my surprise, I found them just repeating the monthly data without going to the field or collecting. I think, there are many places, where these things may be happening. Earlier, we used to have seminar on database issues in the Indian Econometric Society (TIES), but we hardly have any such public debates on this. I think, we must challenge the reliability, validity and timeliness of data.

Next, very important and widely discussed pillar of social science is quality of research. With regards to quality of research, I feel that the status of quality of research is not in better condition in India. You take any examples, whether it is formulation of research proposal or papers sent to journals for publication or for that matter PhD theses. Most of the research proposals applied for funding are so badly formulated. Similarly, when I get papers from authors for publishing in Indian Economic Journal, many of them are very casually written and poorly referred. Moreover, papers brought out in conferences are also badly written and we hardly do anything to help them. I think there may be something wrong with our education system for the past several decades. Apparently, I find some reasons for quality deterioration particularly of PhD, when the degree was made as compulsory for promotion. I think many will agree with me on the fact that in many universities in North India, there are ghost writers of PhD theses and we find same papers published again and again. The problem with our evaluation system is we do not have certain kind of weightage system to the type of papers published as we can find it in foreign universities. During my tenure as chairman of ICSSR, I visited Australian universities and I was told that they have a weighting system for the type of papers published and papers published in newspapers are given zero weightage. I do not know whether such awareness about the quality of research exists in our country and if it is, I don't think there would be mushrooming of the number without quality. There is also a peculiar thing, as an editor of Indian Economic Journal, I faced, that is getting referees are so difficult and apart from this, if I say to any senior person, head of a department or a very well established one that I am sending your paper to referee, he replies, "I will withdraw my paper, please do not send my paper to that referee." I think the issue is our research culture, whereas in foreign journals no paper is accepted without refereeing, without really having number of referees in the divisions. Therefore, I think, quality culture is also necessary and we must have a better sort of courses to make it fine. In fact, I had mooted the idea that the hostel in the ICSSR should earmark 5-6 rooms for the major social science associations so that the ICSSR could interact with the social sciences effectively. I shared this idea with Prof. V.M. Rao and we felt that there is need for some voluntary service like *Seva* or something which I call as forum for quality and social science research. What this will do, is that it will openly invite papers and research reports and offer suggestions to improve quality of the paper so that it becomes eligible for a conference, or for a journal. Of course, there will be a problem of time. But if we really want quality then i think we will definitely find time to offer such services. However, it is a big challenge as the number of such people is very small who would come forward and respond positively. In fact, nobody does it. Even the guides have no time to correct the papers in a proper way.

The idea of multidisciplinarity of research is not new. It has been there right from 1960s. I remember, I was in Bombay University when Dr. Tope was the vice-chancellor. I had organised a seminar on 'Multi-disciplinary research' but since then I think the scope and content of it has remained the same. Can we produce in social science a multi-disciplinary research by involving a sociologist, a psychologist, a geographer, an economist and a political scientist in a same team? I think each one will have to be trained in the other discipline to some extent. What I mean is particularly when we have to do something like Prof. U. Sankar has attempted in his paper on biotechnology and sustainable development, where one needs people from both physical science and social science. Moreover, the question is—are we allowing in our system a physical science graduate to do a course in social sciences? I am not sure. Of course, Indira Gandhi Institute of Development Research (IGIDR) in Bombay was trying to get technologists and engineers to work on social science issues. In that sense, if you really want multidisciplinarity within social science disciplines and between physical science and social science, we do need some sort of interdisciplinary training. However, we should also understand that it is not just enough to induct different broad-angular segments of the matrix and expect them to produce a multidisciplinary researcher, in a week or month's time, you cannot really. I think there is a need for total revamping of our grooming.

When we come to the institutions, I somehow differ with the point made yesterday that funds are not important. I think, with the limited funds, of course, I know that those funds are to be used effectively but the amount of funds that is available to social science research in relation to the one available to physical science, we cannot compete with them but still there is need for increasing the funds to the social science institutions. I would also like to add a word of caution on this enthusiasm to eliminate those institutions and those centres which are not doing well. I think, one of the objectives of the

ICSSR and UGC is to promote research culture, research infrastructure throughout the country and I found that a number of colleges have highly talented researchers but they just do not have access to information and also there was a talk about the researchers going project-hunting, what else can they do? One of the conditions of ICSSR funding is that 50 per cent will have to be met by their own resources and in most states when 2-3 institutions exists, the state governments do not come forward. In fact, I had proposed that ICSSR should take the responsibility of writing to state governments. My point is when we have done the exercise of identifying the institutions by rigorous search committee and expert committee; they should accept it and give the funds. We all know that how ICSSR was created. Thanks to Dr. V.K.R.V. Rao! Yesterday, it was mentioned, setting up of ICSSR become quite easy because when Prof. Rao became the Education Minister, the same report created by him earlier was put up before him to set up the ICSSR. But we also ignore the fact that one of the arguments in that process was that University faculties do not have time to conduct research, therefore, there is a need for separate institutions to encourage research in the country. That was also good enough to set up ICSSR. Let me also talk something about research and teaching. I feel we have become so much moved away from each other. Being both as a researcher and a teacher I feel that teaching and research has to be together. From experience in Bombay University as teacher for more than 15 years and IEG also for quite some time, I learned that teaching is essential to have some clarity on concepts and methodology. When I was chairman of ICSSR, we sent a letter to all the universities and institutions to say that we should have exchange arrangements in between us and also tie up with recognised ICSSR institutions for guiding PhD students. Many of small institutions have lot of difficulty in getting themselves recognised as PhD guides. My point is why not the university system accepts the modalities of ICSSR to establish its institutions. Of course, those individuals, we can identify whether they are eligible or not. But automatic recognition for making teaching and research flow with each is extremely important. We also took some initiatives and I think Yogesh Atal is one of the leaders in launching a National Social Science Policy. Then, P.N. Tandon was one of the members of our council and he brought the wisdom of the Natural Science Policy. In the Natural Science Policy, they do mention that there is a need for greater interplay between social science and the physical science, whereas we do not have any such 'Natural-Social Science Policy'. I think if we are demanding, as Vaidyanathan Committee wants, larger resources has to be allocated. We must create a national consciousness of the priority to be given to the social science research and make a 'Natural-Social Science Policy' announced. We had initiated it but it went off air because of various other reasons.

I also feel there is a lot of political interference. There are many places where a chief minister took chairmanship of the governing body or institutions received lot of instructions from the political system. I think these kinds of thing should not happen, if we want autonomy of the academic institutions. We are totally non-political and we should be left free. When we come to research projects, another new phenomenon we notice that of mushrooming of post office NGOs. At ICSSR, when we gave a project to a professor, we found that project was not located in the university but located in some fly by night post office address. When we asked the university to endorse this assignment to the professor, University said that we have no rules to know what professors are doing and therefore they decline to interfere in the matter. This is classic case which points out that there are certain systemic problems and there is no point in just pointing out that this is going on. I think we must raise it. Similarly, we also found a lot of game plan for cornering the seminar funds and research methodology funds.

Let me now talk something on the issue of indigeneous thoughts and wisdom as there is general feeling among the Indian academicians that we hardly give references to the indigenous wisdom. I would like to remind you that in Dr. V.K.R.V. Rao's own papers we find lot of wisdom which is not really referred to or attended even in the recent times, leave alone what I call indigeneous wisdom refereeing to Kautilya's *Artha-shastra*. I do not go that far off but even in the recent time; there are many papers which give a better insight than those emanating from the so called western world. In fact, there is time now to discuss as to what constitutes development and how we can remove the jargons like globalisation etc., without referring to the welfare of the people. The paper 'The Nature and Purpose of Economic Activity' written way back in 1964 by Dr. V.K.R.V. Rao, is so beautiful and perceptive in this regards. It says that all economic activities therefore, all social science research should have the following three sort of objectives: (i) to satisfy the fundamental minimum requirements of the community of economic goods; (ii) to occasion minimum use of resources that is efficiency; and (iii) not to hamper but to foster and promote the end of all human activity *viz.*, development of human personality. What a beautiful perception or vision! Similarly, in the conference on 'Relevance in Social Science Research', he does endorse the need for having multi-disciplinarity and he says that alone would be able to make social science useful. Fortunately, I had access to the beautiful writings of his *Income and Wealth* series. Two articles, one is international comparison of national income and another is distribution of national income, both these have very perceptive points. He gives beautiful account of a comparison technically, analytically and practically impossible. When we now make purchasing power parity (PPP) as a major modality for comparing incomes, he has a big dig on that also. He says, even the PPP is totally analytically faulted because you cannot have the prices for goods in comparable manner, when qualities are different, bundles are different. So he gives price index in all these things. I think some of these basic elements of wisdom ought to guide us on the future of research to make it more useful, more analytical than what we are engaged in. I think there is a sort of imitativeness, I mentioned earlier that we take up topics done elsewhere and lots of research has been done as somebody said yesterday. Same production functions tried with different data. I think that tendency is still continuing. In my survey of research in econometrics for ICSSR which I did quite sometime back, following was one of the observations—"Research is highly imitative and not original in terms of formulation of hypothesis, choice of methodology and drawing inferences." Thank you very much.

A-4

Role and Functioning of Public Domain SSR

John Crowley

Thank you for the opportunity to offer some thought on this subject. I am of being views of total outsider with respect to the specific issues of Indian social sciences; the theme on which I will be talking in this session is the nexus or interface between policy and research—the connection between various kinds of input to the policy process and structure and dynamics of the research system. The idea obviously is that the way in which the nexus or interface tends to arrange itself spontaneously within existing policy and research system, is not entirely as it might be, may be not the best. We can only be hopeful. And that some deliberate designs sensitive to some of the key issues are developing and they could improve the way in which the interface operates to the benefit of researchers, of policy makers and of course of the society as a whole. Let me try and explain this. I am assuming for the purposes of this discussion that the idea of nexus or interface between policy and research is not in itself problematic. In other words, it is not illegitimate for social science researchers to contribute to policy formulation. Research that is policy relevant is not *ipso facto* the bad research. Though, of course, there are purists within social science communities, who may think otherwise and it is entirely true that there is no lack of bad policy-oriented research but probably there is no lack of bad basic research either.

No one in social science is necessarily critical, still as oppositional, in the sense that necessarily rejecting the terms of reference within which policy maker conduct their activity. Though, it is an easily observed fact that many policy makers are eventually deeply suspicious

John Crowley, Chief Editor, International Social Science Journal, UNESCO, Paris.

of social scientists, far more than they are of physicists or biologists. And, of course, there is indeed no lack of critical social scientists who are so consciously oppositional. The problem comes less no doubt from the oppositional nature of the activity of some social scientists and the habits social scientists have. From the policy makers' point of view somewhat disagreeable thing is that to receive remarks from social scientists that, "these are not the questions to be asked" when one is put by policy makers. Policy makers are convinced that they have at least some access to relevant questions and they do not like to be told that because of the lack of knowledge on certain issues, also they are not at the best place to frame the questions. Furthermore, I am ascertaining for these purposes something that is not probably very controversial that the nexus between social science research and policy is not just possible because the features that might make it impossible, I am assuming not to exist. But it is necessary in the sense that specific policy failures can be traced to respond to social science illiteracy. If policy makers had been aware of social science knowledge that often is not cutting edge knowledge but it is only basic knowledge that is taken for granted by social science professionals. Then they would have avoided mistakes that have contributed to human misery or at least human misery could have been alleviated. This is the basic issue. Social scientists may derive some more benefits but the key issue is the capacity of social science to contribute to key social problems. The question therefore is what kind of institutional structure offers the optimal trade-off or unoptimal trade-off?

There are several local optima here between two competing pressures. First, the pressure of academic notions of quality based on some peer-review. Not in the technical sense of any particular evaluation mechanism, but in the broader sense, where only the peers of academics are qualified to judge whether academics have done their job well. These principles of peer-review in broader sense are of course embedded in institutional evaluation mechanisms. Therefore, they matter—for how social scientists conduct their professional life, for their reputation and career advancement and they are equally embedded in the professional self-understandings of professional social scientists. To be a good academic is to respond to those criterion or quality and to be judged in those positive ways one hopes by one's peer, that is the first pressure. Pressure drives institutional functioning of research systems, because it is powerfully present not just in the heads of the researchers but also in institutions within which they conduct their careers. The second pressure—is policy-driven notions of relevance, which is based somewhat on, one might call it rapid response capability and immediate intelligibility which is embedded in the time-bound logic of the political process. If a policy maker requires a six month time framework for the purposes of some policy emergency data on, say, some specific aspects of rural poverty, then a suggestion—that this really requires five years research programme! The first two years of which will be devoted to background research and conceptual clarification is likely to be met with, well, less than full satisfaction. But, of course, there may be very good reasons at the conceptual level to insist that the question can only be answered adequately if it is first professed by a phase of conceptualised clarification. Let me clear that here is real tension. A productive nexus is unlikely to emerge spontaneously because these pressures genuinely clash. It is also a matter of policy makers and social scientists, as the phrase goes, getting to know each other better and putting them in a room and encouraging them to talk will simply bring out the disagreement, it will not make it go away. The reason for UNESCO's concerns in these areas is the twofold observations. First, the kind of nexus or interface that tends to emerge spontaneously in the research systems that are strongly structured and adequately funded is suboptimum. It involves effectively a dualism, which is usually embedded in the programming and funding mechanism for research, and between academic research in different policy concerns (which tends to be based on institutional core funding) and policy-oriented research or at least the research that is designed to be potential policy relevant (which tends to be driven by different funding mechanisms invariably short-project based). The second observation is that in many developing countries neither the background structure nor the funding are necessarily adequate for even this kind of suboptimum dualism to emerge with the result that any attempt to increase the strength of the policy-relevant research delivery system will simply detract by draining away from the background system.

What then is wrong with this dualism, even it can be achieved? Three things are to be kept in mind. First of all, such dualism narrows the connection between research and policy to rather small subset of the available knowledge and energy within social science communities. Secondly, it restricts the nexus or interface epistemologically to those questions that policy makers ask themselves and to the terms that they used to frame them. The point is—the questions that policy makers ask themselves leave too much out. In particular, all professional social scientists know one of the things that politicians and policy makers broadly understood tend to leave out the historical and conceptual analysis of how the policy questions came to be questioned in the first place and therefore the reasons for which they might not continue to be questioned in the future. This reflexibility about questioning is something that is not built in the policy process. And the third thing that is wrong with the dualism is the mistakes the holistic nature of the social science knowledge develops from not trying to solve practical problems, though some bits of it may or occasionally may do so, but on the basis of ongoing conversation between theories, paradigms, data, disciplines etc. The same is true; perhaps more widely recognised and accepted, with the policy circles of mathematics, physics or biology. To put it more simply, dualism is parasitical. Usable policy-relevant knowledge depends on a vibrant self-sustaining background on non-instrumental social science knowledge production. The issue is therefore not to promote policy-relevant research but to establish and to nurture the channels and the processes that connect the knowledge base and the dynamics of social science as a whole with the policy processes. A number of practical implications follow from this diagnosis which is operationalised in the various components of UNESCO's current activity in the social sciences. I would like to emphasise, in conclusion. First, there is a need to strengthen national social science research systems especially in developing countries where background conditions may historically not have been favourable and a strong research system for these purposes is needed where one can perform the full range of its functions from producing basic concepts in data, to participating in graduate training, engaging in international scientific exchange, contributing to public and policy awareness in social science issues and of course, last but not least, providing direct policy-relevant input as required including through institutional engagements in collaborative planning processes to bring together within the same councils, boards or other agencies, social scientists and administrative specialists. These functions work better when they are combined and when they are kept separate, multiplicity tends to pull down. Also, there is a need to develop tools and methodologies to make the existing social science knowledge base, including the non-instrumental background basic social science knowledge base available to potential users. However, no one knows in advance who the potential users will be? Most of us may not know how little bit knowledge may turn out to be useful. That is why the approach has to be comprehensive. Second, the need of the future policy makers is self-defeating. It is more important to try and bring together the knowledge base as a whole in a way that it will be available to anyone who may need it. This is the current focus of UNESCO's most of the programmes in its so called 'phase two'. The key objective of this is to develop a software basis, including relevant indexing and searching tools to collate the international social science knowledge base in such a way that non-specialists can have access to it without the basing or grading or diluting it. This is an enormous challenge and we have only made limited success in addressing it so far. But, it is a long-term project and we consider that the reasons just explained are absolutely central to the key concerns. Third, alongside this kind of impersonal interface, mediated by software and by data bases between the knowledge base and policy needs, there is also a need to establish innovative personnel basis where people can meet. People involved in social science knowledge production and social science knowledge use so that they can discuss matters of common concern. I would underline in this respect that academics are not only the people who produce social science knowledge and policy makers are not the only who use it. There is an important role here for civil society organisations to participate in such forum for discussion. One of the initiatives that UNESCO has been seeking to promote in social development is the establishment of a forum at the regional level and potentially at global level to bring together the ministerial-level policy makers with academics and civil society representatives so that issues of common concerns could be identified and regionally sensitive and nationally relevant mechanism or setup to pursue these concerns can be developed.

The conclusion is very simple. The policy research nexus is not a special place or a special mechanism or a special function within social science research system. It is rather something that works best when it is built into the design of the system. The policy research nexus reflects itself in a range of different processes all the way from basic institutional design to priority setting, to the design of research programmes, to the selection of project funding, to the distribution of public money, to evaluation of individual projects and institutions and to the range of formalised or non-formalised processes by which potentially useful social science knowledge is put to work in the service of urgent social needs. Thank you.

A-5

Role and Functioning of Public Domain SSR

Narayanan Nair

Thank you for inviting me to participate in this very interesting seminar. I will be addressing the issues already discussed in the previous sessions from a user's perspective. I have five questions and will take ten minutes. I have no answers to these questions. But I am raising this with the hope that the participants of this conference will deliberate on these questions.

First, there was discussion about scientific quality of research in the earlier sessions: but what is the relationship between scientific quality and societal relevance: A piece of research can be excellent if it can be published in reputed journals. However, the target group of that particular research may not be using the research findings. Compare it with another piece of research of average scientific quality, the findings of it used by the users for improving their living situation. The issue here is: how one could compare the quality of the first with the second, on a larger social context? How to combine societal relevance and scientific quality?

Second, when we plan large research programmes, how will you set the research agenda? In a society which is highly heterogeneous, who is going to articulate the agenda? Is the demand of the poor going to get a priority in the research or that of the corporate sector. In the science, policy discussion, this problem of agenda setting is known as the Ganusha dilemma: who sets the agenda and whose agenda is articulated.

Third, communication or dissemination of research. We work most of the time thinking that dissemination of research takes place on a

---

M. Narayanan Nair, Director, Centre for Development Studies (CDS), Trivandrum.

linear path: you do the research, publish and it would be automatically used by the users. That may not necessarily be true. Therefore, these days we talk about alternative modes of knowledge generation and use. In this mode starting from the very conceptualisation of research to implementation and final dissemination of findings, you get the users involved. In this research process, the user community becomes very important. The methodology of participatory research, participatory action research etc., is one way of directly communicating with the user community. How can one get the users involved in the process of agenda setting, implementation and utilisation of knowledge into practical use? What are the ways in which you can get the user community involved?

The fourth question: in a stage of globalisation when people have access to knowledge from all over the world, local capacities are needed to absorb that knowledge for creative purposes. It means that whatever be the nature of the research system it could lead to broad-based research capacity building. If you want to make use of larger application of knowledge to improve the conditions of people in the remote areas, local research capacities needs to be enhanced. It requires enhancement of capacities of colleges, NGOs and large number of peoples' organisations. How can one do such broad-based research capacity building?

The fifth question: If you are involved in research process with user communities, you tend to cut across various power groups in the society. It could result in direct confrontation and conflict. What kind of ethics one has to follow in such research? Whose interests you will protect and who will protect you when there is conflict?

A-6

Project-oriented Research *versus* Long-term Research: Some Reflections

T.K. Oommen

The phrasing of the theme suggests that project-oriented research is short-term research, but it need not be. I will revert to this later but before that two prefactory remarks are in order. One, there are several dualisms or dichotomies in vogue in social science research (SSR): theoretical *versus* empirical, policy *versus* theoretical, raw empiricism *versus* grand theory, quantitative *versus* qualitative, micro *versus* macro, field-oriented *versus* textual, survey research *versus* participant observation, to list a few. Two, one has to be extremely cautious in endorsing these dichotomies because they are simplistic and misleading if not down right fallacious. Therefore, it is advisable to abandon them and postulate a series of continuum in their place, the advantage being that while recognising the polar opposites the connectivity between and through a set of intermediate points can be visualised. Thus viewed, we can understand the complementarity between project-oriented research and long-term research. Each of the research project on the same theme then becomes a brick in building the mansion of long-term research.

The postulation that project-oriented research and long-term research are complementary can be discerned in terms of the intended objectives/goals of SSR, which are basically four:

1. Description of the social phenomena. To arrive at a description of the phenomenon investigated we need to ask two questions. They are: (a) what is it?, and (b) How is it? Description could be about a micro or macro unit, it could be done invoking quantitative or

T.K. Oommen, Emeritus Professor, Sociology, Jawaharlal Nehru Univeristy, New Delhi.

qualitative data and based on field data or texts/documents, but a combination of these is often desirable. Description is essentially an empirical task.

2. Explanation of the phenomenon investigated. The answer to the question: 'why is it?' is crucial in SSR. Why did the phenomenon take its present shape of what it is? What are the processes involved, that is, how it has come to become what it is? The point I am making is that the 'why' question cannot be answered without answering the 'what' and 'how' questions. To put it pithily, description is a prerequisite for explanation. If through research projects we can produce reliable descriptions, they are indeed stepping stones for advancing explanations, which is the avowed purpose of long-term research.
3. Prediction is the third objective of SSR; asking the question, what will it be? is the route to get the answer. Prediction should not be taken literally; and it may not always be correct. Meteorological predictions are often incorrect. Geologists fail to predict earthquakes and certainly tsunami. And yet prediction is an accepted objective of research in physical and life sciences. In social science one can attempt probabilistic analyses, providing indications of future trends and administer early warnings. The relevant point here is that if predictions are to be attempted, explanations should be in place. Thus, one can see the sequence involved in description, explanation and prediction in SSR.
4. The fourth goal of SSR is prescription. Many social scientists may think that the task of social research is accomplished with description and explanation, and at best with prediction. But the question, knowledge for what (?) remains unanswered. That is, if knowledge is to be used for human welfare, for improving the 'quality of life', to recall that elusive phrase, we must add a fourth objective, namely prescription, to SSR. To prescribe is to pose the question: 'what it ought to be?' I am aware that there could be interminable debates on this goal of SSR and yet if knowledge is to be productively used/applied social scientists should venture into this arena. The dichotomy between policy research and theoretical research withers away in the context of prescription.

> The dialectics between description, explanation, prediction and prescription is thus clear.

It is necessary to identify the different types of project-oriented research before we proceed further. At one end of the continuum are instant opinion surveys. One comes across the results of many such surveys reported in media and these days they are invariably accompanied by a note on the 'methodology' used, referring to the sample size and its representative nature. These 'research projects' report on a wide variety of topics ranging from popularity of politicians, religiosity among scientists and acceptability of condoms by women. These reports do not produce knowledge in the strict sense of the term but they do provide information about social phenomena without which generation of knowledge about them is not possible. I am acutely aware of the scorn with which most social scientists dismiss the results of these surveys. But these surveys do provide answer to the question: what is it?, with regard to the phenomenon investigated. And, the findings of these surveys could help social scientists to formulate hypotheses, which s/he could test rigorously and reject or endorse.

The second type of research projects I have in mind are those designed to evaluate the impact of say, economic development and social policies. These research projects cannot be instant ones but should be carefully designed after taking into account the intended purpose of the measures evaluated. These projects cannot also be one-shot affairs but need to be repeated; continuous evaluations are called for. In this type of project-oriented research, it is not enough to ask the question, what is it? and find the answer but also to ask the question: How is it? How is it that some development initiatives and policy measures succeeded, while others failed need to be understood. Such research projects can help in abandoning ill-conceived measures, making mid-course corrections wherever it is necessary, and replicate the desirable ones. These projects often may not answer the 'why' question, but answers to the 'how' question help us to understand correlations if not causations.

The third type of research projects I have in mind are those explicitly designed to answer the 'why' question, that is, geared to explain social phenomena. Ideally, the Indian Council of Social Science Research, the University Grants Commission and similar bodies should promote such research projects, which are oriented to knowledge production leaving the first type to non-governmental organisations (NGOs) which are nothing but into information gathering and the second type of research projects to departments of governments. In fact, the data collected by the official agencies such as the Census of India, National Sample Survey Organisation, the Central Statistical Organisation, the Anthropological Survey of India do answer the 'what', 'how' and even the 'why' questions. The gaps existing with regard to relevant required information can easily be met by these organisations. Once descriptions and explanations are available to those in the academia, that is, those in research institutions and universities can proceed with sophisticated explanation as well as predictions and prescriptions.

Having identified different types of research projects and their usefulness it is instructive to situate the crystallisation of the dichotomy, short-term and long-term research, in their historical context. As I see it there are two factors which gave birth to this dichotomy. One, the division of labour that existed between different social science disciplines and two, the changing demands placed on SSR by the governments and states. Social science as we understand it to-day emerged in the West and the fact that SSR came to India from there, particularly from United Kingdom, social science research in that country decisively influenced SSR in India. The fact that some of the Indian social scientists who assumed academic leadership, got their initial training in the West also rendered them the victims of 'captive mind' to recall the seductive phrase invoked by the Malaysian sociologist, Alatas. I have dealt with this issue at length elsewhere and hence will not repeat it here (see, T.K. Oommen, *Knowledge and Society*, Oxford University Press, New Delhi, 2007).

The most telling contrast in the context of the present discussion was and is between economics and social anthropology. While British economists did utilise vast amounts of empirical data generated by Government agencies, social anthropologists invariably collected data directly from their specific research sites. Sociologists were not averse to field projects; an early example being the poverty surveys of industrial workers by Charles and Mary Booth and a recent one being the study of

Social Mobility in Britain by David and Ruth Glass. Political scientists were mainly engaged in text-centric analyses, both philosophical and constitutional, in the beginning but when they reinvented themselves as behavioural scientists they too took to research projects. That is economists, sociologists and political scientists did undertake project-oriented research and these researches prompted and stimulated long-term research. In contrast, social anthropologists did not undertake short-term research projects and the reason for this lay mainly in the nature of the universe of their research; micro units situated in other cultures. While Indian social scientists largely followed the British pattern initially and the American model subsequently, sociology in India was under the shadow of social anthropology until recently which partly explains the absence of project-oriented and survey research in Indian sociology.

European social anthropology was designed to study other cultures, that is, non-European cultures, invariably colonial societies, designated as traditional, tribal, peasant, primitive or savage. The fact that the researchers did not belong to the same culture and their native language was different from the languages of the people studied, called for long period of preparation as well as long duration as the effort was to understand the culture of the people as a whole. Long-term research was the logical offshoot of this and instances of social anthropologists attaching themselves to their 'fields' for a lifetime was common. As they studied micro units—tribes, villages, segments of urban population—collecting qualitative data through what came to be designated as 'participant observation' became the unique selling point of social anthropology. Since social anthropologists investigated preliterate societies those days and their studies were holistic in orientation, survey research, the usual tool of project-oriented research, was unsuited. Thus, a logical conjunction of collecting qualitative data, through the method of participant observation from micro units over a long period of time became the norm in social anthropology.

In contrast economists, political scientists and sociologists of Europe, invariably studied their own societies designated as 'modern', before the launching of the area studies programme during the Cold War period. While studying one's own society, it was possible to study only a segment of the population or an aspect of social reality as these are huge, invariably nation states, as compared with the tribes or villages in the colonies or in the post-colonial states. Economists, sociologists and political scientists of India followed this trail and project-oriented research became a feasible proposition for them. Ignoring the differing historical background in the trajectories of different disciplines, there is a persisting tendency to privilege long-term research and castigate short-term, that is, project-oriented research. Earlier we get over this fallacy of misplaced concreteness the better it is for Indian social science. Indeed social anthropologists of India can ignore the change in the historicity of context from the colonial state to the national state and the shift to study one's own society as against other cultures, only at their peril.

This brings me to the second point I want to discuss in this context. Anthropology, widely acknowledged as a child of imperialism, helped the colonial state to understand the native culture to administer the subject peoples. In contrast, the post-colonial national state wants to take the help of social scientists to govern better its citizens, at least that is the assumption. Indian state too needed vast quantity of reliable data to facilitate the process of economic planning and formulate social policies. While long-term research is absolutely necessary to generate knowledge, the country also needs the generation of time-bound reliable data and that is the justification for project-oriented or short-term research. Good governance of welfare states cannot be deferred till the results of long-term research are available. However, the widespread tendency to treat short-term or project-oriented research as an end in itself is the reason why many serious academics look down upon these research projects. If these projects are couched in appropriate theoretical frameworks invoking relevant conceptual tools, wherever necessary and possible, much of the stigmatisation associated with project-oriented research will disappear.

I have suggested earlier that each of the research project designated to investigate particular dimension of social reality can be treated as a brick in the production of knowledge house. For this, there should be a shared (not common) research design leaving enough flexibility to take into account the regional/local variations. It is quite possible that the ICSSR is already doing this, if not it is high time to initiate such a process. However, this is not unheard of in India. Examples are 'Field Studies in the Sociology of Education' coordinated by the National Council of Educational Research and Training in the 1960s and the all-India project to study bureaucracy funded by the ICSSR in the 1970s. The growing tendency is to undertake huge research projects with heavy budgets with an army of quickly recruited, untrained or undertrained research investigators who are often ill-equipped to do the required quality fieldwork. And, an intermediate set of desk-bound research analysts unfamiliar with concepts and theories draft the reports to be whetted and finalised by the top level research administrators who are mentally distant from the research-process collection and analysis of data. Once the project report is submitted to the relevant agencies, the project is treated as terminated and rarely efforts are made to reanalyse the data contained in the reports so as to add to the existing fund of knowledge. The anxiety to acquire finance to sustain themselves drives research institutes incessantly in search of new projects. The premature termination of the life of research projects, without rigorously analysing the data contained in the reports, is antithetical to the very process of their becoming building blocks in the creation of knowledge.

Let me conclude this short note by suggesting that social science research, project-oriented and long term, is conditioned by several factors: (1) the purpose for which the data are collected, that is, the type of questions for which answers are sought; (2) the subject matter or the theme of research; (3) the nature of unit from which data are collected; (4) the features of the segment of society from which information is elicited; and (5) the nature of research design. If SSR is done taking into account these considerations, the imagined estrangement between project-oriented research and long-term research will disappear because both have their distinctive contributions to make.

A-7

Project-oriented Research *vis-à-vis* Long-term Research

Sugata Marjit

Good afternoon, I shall try to give you some comments and some observations on the theme of the discussion. We are having a discussion on project-funded *versus* long-term research in social science. I shall raise a few points much more mundane and narrow than what we have been listening so far. I am not going to talk about the definition of good quality research or theory or policy. I am going to talk about from the perspective of somebody who has been associated with a research institute, a social science research institute under the auspices of ICSSR for the last 10-11 years and happens to be the Director of the institute for the last couple of years. I shall give you a perspective which is completely based on my experience and the experience is one of research administration, administration of an institution where you have social scientists who are capable of doing very good quality research.

The issue of good quality or bad quality research arises only when basic minimum amount of resources are guaranteed for the institutes. This observation has obvious relation with the Fourth Review (Vaidyanathan) Committee Report and these issues have been raised by the Vaidyanathan Committee regarding the utilisation of project generated funding for our long-term academic benefit. First of all we must understand why we have to do project related consultancy type research. I am very happy that I have been chosen to talk about it, where I can fully express my opinion. You see, the hypocrisy of government at various levels have been killing us. Let me give you an example. These are not the problems of universities, I beg to differ with many of you who are working in the universities because you do not have to think

Sugata Marjit, Director, Centre for Studies in Social Sciences (CSSS), Kolkata.

about the salaries you have to pay to the people at the end of the month. ICSSR institutes have to have that responsibility. They have to see whether the amount of money they are getting is enough to pay salaries to the positions which have been thrust upon them, politically or otherwise. Most of the ICSSR institutes cannot fill up the vacant jobs because they do not have money. In my institute, from 2004 onwards, there is a cap which is there for many other institutes. We do not even get regular increments which we are forced to fund through other sources. Government goes on announcing increments, but we are provided with fixed amount of grants. This is a blatant hypocrisy that I am referring to. If we pay wages and salaries, we do not have money to pay for our electricity bills. This is for an institute which has a significant corpus funds, is very well-reputed and fortunately is not like some other institutes where almost entire salaries depend on projects. These are some of the hard facts that we have to face up to before we go in depth into the analysis of what is good research, bad research etc.

We do not have sufficient supply of resources as promised by the Central government, the ICSSR, etc. Even if partial support is available, some of the state governments have completely forfeited on their promises and we cannot do anything about it. Our state government has been semi-generous. But this is not the case with all other state governments. Is this the way serious social science research has to be promoted and protected? Is this is the way that government should behave? So, project funding is necessary. You like it or not, you may be producing junks, but that is necessary. Project funding is the only source from where I can cross-subsidise good research. This is important that people appreciate it. There is some sort of concerted effort in convincing government at different layers that you cannot go back on your promises, you cannot have a research institute where you do not fill up 20 per cent of position and all the faculty members are forced to do project-funded research. Now, some of the disciplines cannot do that because it is impossible to get research funding in those areas. So there is, you like it or not, free-riding because there are social science disciplines who are capable of generating research project funding and there are other disciplines which cannot. But this is not the fault of the other disciplines. This is clearly the fault of the state of social science research funding in this country and we have discussed it many times in the ICSSR directors' meetings in different places. Given the fact that the project funding is a reality, I have to engage in that kind of a venture. Then the safest thing is to look at the projects which serve both the purposes as Prof. Oommen has said, we must be having a long-term perspective. But primarily, it is a question of cash flow problem. So, you are possibly getting huge amount of projects and before promised money comes for the next year and fresh increments are eventually announced, you are at least guaranteed of six months of salary to your staff members. Nothing really happens if this problem is not solved, the promises are not kept, promises that have been committed due to whatever reasons. Sometimes they have been committed very inefficiently, they probably did not need so many institutions, probably they did not need so many departments, but the government cannot go back on the constitutional provision, can they? But here they do. This is a kind of sacrilege that a political institution can commit and the government has committed that time and again. You create something with a lot of hypes, but when it comes to the issue of maintenance and growth you look the other way and go for some new ventures.

Now, there is the university system and there is this ICSSR system. The fact is that, how can you integrate the university with the ICSSR institutions because university is mainly a teaching organisation. Top class universities will have good research facilities or researchers but there are problems. As a follow-up of the Vaidyanathan Committee recommendations, noted social scientist Partha Chatterjee has been suggesting that there should be some integration between university and ICSSR for the survival of both, for the survival of ICSSR research institutes and also for the departments in universities. University departments are also in doldrums because in many universities social science departments do not have extra money to even host a conference in a year. Fortunately, as research institutes we can get some project money, we can cross-subsidise and we can have a couple of conferences or workshops and so on. So, more integration probably would help this university and ICSSR institutes.

The other point I would like to make is that project-funded research can be good academic research. But accountability varies between privately-funded and publicly-funded research. If you are acquiring a project from the private sector, they will breathe down your neck. The report will be properly discussed and entertained. I shall give you two contrasting examples and if we cannot fix these problems, these loopholes in our public system, then how can we talk about quantity or quality of good research.

I did a project for ICICI Bank eight years ago after I had joined Centre for Studies in Social Sciences, Calcutta (CSSS). It was an interesting project on measurement of non-performing assets (NPAs) and so on and I had a small team, we did that. Then we were called upon at least three times to Bombay to present in three different preliminary meetings, then there was a whole ICICI or whatever you know, gathering or something. There we had to present, people would ask questions we had to answer and we did it as thoroughly as we could. Similarly, once I went to the Planning Commission to get a project and I went to meet a member. While waiting I was given a cup of tea and I kept it on a table. Under the table there were a lot of undistributed old project reports. Policy consequences of these reports were never made public. I knew that, whatever I do, my report would also go there. Nobody was really interested. So I waited, said hello to that person, never asked for money and went back.

What I am trying to tell you is the following: there are certain core issues that have to do with the academic governance system, no matter who comes at the Centre and who comes at the state. There has to be an approach in which the governments will decide that core funding for social science research is important for them and for the nation. If that is not done, then actually we are talking at cross-purposes. Then I will go on searching for project money, I would not bother about whether it is good research or bad research. Hence, government has to prove its credibility by at least not going back on the promises. All the institutes have to have their posts filled up, there should be some minimum research money available for each faculty member and given general trend of inflation, general cost escalation has to be taken care of. If each institute has 25 faculty members and then there is no way to fill up 10 vacant positions and I am saving the money of 6 or 7 faculty members to pay the salary of the non-teaching staff, there is something seriously wrong. I feel that these are core issues which should constitute the prelude to the discussion that we are having here such as what is good quality research, what is bad quality research, what is theory, what is policy, and so on? This has to be recognised and credibility has to be demonstrated on the part of the governance system; otherwise I do not think it is going to work. Thank you.

A-8

Project-oriented Research *vis-à-vis* Long-term Research: Some Trends

Pradip Kumar Bose

Let me begin by pointing out that in contrast to long-term research the kind of research we generally posit is short-term research and both long-term and short-term researches can be project-oriented. It is not that these categories are exclusive, separate and distinct but there is considerable overlap between them. So my first point is that the framework of discussion is slightly confusing but I must add that often such confusions are productive in bringing about interesting results.

Now I will take up some of the issues which both Prof. Sugata Marjit and Prof. T.K. Oommen have mentioned in their presentations, namely, the funded nature of long-term projects and its consequences. Generally long-term research is funded by various governmental and non-governmental agencies, the research that is carried out basically amounts to collection of data, but much of these data are never utilised in writing reports and in any case, as Prof. Marjit has rightly pointed out, these reports are never read by anyone, not even by the agencies which originally funded the project. Against this background, I think, short-term researches have better possibilities, though I am not saying that these possibilities are always fulfilled. One of the important advantages of short-term research is that such research cost less money. Within short-term research, two distinct approaches can be distinguished: the first is the 'normal science' mode of doing research, where the standard steps are followed, everyone knows what has to be done, the usual function and division of labour are utilised, and research

Pradeep Kumar Bose, Visiting Professor, Sociology, Centre for Studies in Social Sciences (CSSS), Kolkata.

report is assembled and produced following the standard procedures. This 'normal science' approach in the end produces nothing, makes no contribution to the field of knowledge, and generally never read. On the other hand, I will like to give more importance to the other kind of research or research proposals, which are innovative in design, imaginative, and avoid the conventional route. But to recognise such qualities in a proposal we need competent judges. In my view such research programmes have better possibilities because they suggest alternative ways of doing research and can also provide new framework for research. This is a kind of research which a young researcher in our country can aspire to because, as I have just said, long-term research require greater financial support and generally granted to senior researchers with experience. It is a different issue altogether whether the senior academics are capable of doing justice to the research or not.

Prof. Marjit just narrated the problems of research institutes and I share his anxieties. Yesterday it was mentioned that in the institutes supported by ICSSR, the state governments provide only 13 per cent of the grant, and ICSSR gives 27 per cent. In such circumstances, the gap has to be filled by the institutes themselves, and generally they do it by taking all kinds of projects irrespective of their relevance to the institute or its faculty. In such institutes a promising bright researcher ends up doing routinised, uninteresting, boring research, because s/he is told that such work has to be done for the survival of the institute. Hence, the point is that why young, bright, promising researchers should feel attracted to such jobs or career prospects. What I fear is that this gap is going to be much wider in future and most of the time a researcher in these institutes will have to spend in this kind of useless research. I have seen many institutes which have, over time, become data-collection agencies because of their heavy dependency on project funds.

Yesterday we heard from the chairman of the University Grants Commission (UGC) and also from the member secretary, ICSSR that every year UGC gets about 700 research proposals and ICSSR gets about 2000 research proposals. These are mainly short-term, low budget research proposals. But the point is how do we select from these more innovative, better quality research proposals? What should be the mechanism? Do we have in India a mechanism which can single out quality research proposals which can eventually produce good academic study? Do we have any institutional mechanism or administrative structures for proper screening of proposals and promoting them? So the question is do we have any incentive mechanism for the worthy ones and disincentive mechanism for the useless ones? My answer is no.

The way a research administration function in India is that it receives proposals and passes them on to 'experts' for comments and approval. These 'experts' take their own time and eventually send their opinion. In other words, the research administration functions more like a post office. The reason for such a state of affairs is that the first thing a bureaucrat will do will be to guard him or her from any future blame. If someone complains that why such a stupid proposal was sanctioned, the concerned bureaucrat can always say that it was sanctioned by an expert. The alternative could be that a panel of reputed, productive, creative social scientists could be formed, who can take responsibility and, if needed, stick their neck out. The non-governmental funding agencies generally have their own in-house experts for screening, selection, supervision and monitoring of projects. In many cases such experts frame research agenda, often actively search out organisations and personnel for doing particular research. There is something to learn from such procedures. At this point, I must also say that close monitoring, practiced by non-governmental funding agencies, is sometimes disliked by competent researchers, they may not like someone breathing down their neck all the time. So I think if we create proper structure, recruit proper personnel and experts who have the capability and imagination to promote quality researchers, then young researchers with their short-term research proposals can do wonders and collectively they can improve the quality and standard of social science research in India. Thank you.

A-9

Is there a Mismatch between Resource Availability and Demand?

G. Thimmaiah

In this session, we have discussed the mismatch between the human resources available and the demand for such human resources in research. We have also discussed the demand for research and supply of that and also the regional imbalances have also been brought out. To complete the whole package, I would like to discuss the mismatch between the financial resources available for research and the demand for that. That would make the discussion which will follow more meaningful. The availability of financial resources in relation to demand from social science research—well in India as on today, the government spends a total of 13 per cent of the total expenditure on education and that constitute about 3.6 per cent of the GDP. Now what is surprising is that this 13 per cent which was 13.1 per cent has come down to 13 per cent from 1991, and in terms of GDP, which was 3.8 per cent has come down to 3.6 per cent. That is probably because the denominator has increased; it is quite possible. Now in any case, demand always exceeds the available resources. There is nothing strange about it. Let me once again bring back the university *versus* ICSSR debate which was raised by Dr. Anant yesterday, and has been repeated althrough the sessions. Please remember, in the 1980s, the number of universities was small. Suddenly the number of young people increased and a large number of universities were opened and resources available for this universities were inadequate. Libraries were not there, even teaching faculty was not adequate. Therefore, there was no question of the universities doing research because the universities had to cater to the mass of young people entering the

G. Thimmaiah, Member, Board of Governors ISEC, Bangalore and Formerly Member, Planning Commission.

university system at least in south India, in the wake of the social awakening of the day. So, by the 1970s, it was realised that the university system was not in a position to continue both teaching and research. They had to be satisfied with just teaching. So, ICSSR emerged because they did not want research to go down. ICSSR came into being to protect social science research and to continue so, both the systems continued in a parallel way. Now, I am glad that the Vaidyanathan Committee has recommended their integration and probably that will yield better results. Now the shortage of resources for social science research has been mainly because social science research has been mainly dependent, if not solely, upon government funds. Governments face many claims and they have to set priorities. In a country where illiteracy is still a major problem, how can we demand more funds for social science research. This is an issue. This was raised in the 1950s, 1960s; now things have improved. Literacy rate has improved and as a result, now in the 21st century, we should be in a position to demand more resources for social science research. This would invariably bring in the role of non-governmental resources, which means we have to go to the market, we have to go to the corporate sector and there is nothing wrong, I think in it. Ideologically, social science research (institutes) should not hesitate to get resources from non-governmental sources. They may include some sections of the corporate sector that fund research as part of their social responsibility as in the case of the Tatas'. We all know that. International institutions and other domestic corporate institutions outsource research. Prof. Kurien rightly pointed out such outsourcing helps; when projects are submitted, the social scientists in research institutions are exposed to evaluation process; his/their efficiency is tested outside. It is a part of evaluation of research ability, research quality which we should welcome. Here the issue of autonomy and the threat of influencing the outcome should be looked into and protected. So as long as autonomy is protected, I think we should welcome it. Even in public funding, there is fragmentation and too much earmarking. That is what Prof. Vaidyanathan mentioned in the morning session yesterday. Let me make a point on this. See fragmentation has got some positive features. It increases the total resources available. If you say the Government of India in the Ministry of Education alone shall fund the research, then the total amount available will be limited. Since it is coming from all other ministries, now the latest being the Finance Ministry which allocates Rs. 10 crore for research institutions all over the country which Dr. Manmohan Singh started and we benefited. So, if the Ministry of Health and Family Welfare provides funds, Agriculture Ministry provides funds—many and if all these different ministries provide funds and we can cater to their research requirements there is nothing wrong. The total available resources for institutions will increase. This is one positive feature of fragmentation. But I agree with him that earmarking of these funds for X,Y,Z purpose is bad. See in economics, particularly in public finance, we call earmarking as an inefficient act. So, that has to be safeguarded. Now where do we go from here. In order to get over this mismatch we have got to mobilise financial resources from multiple sources. Too much dependence upon government funds probably do not ensure high quality. Because they do not ask (questions). In fact, in the previous session, Prof. Marjit shared his agonising experience with the state government. Let me share our very happy experience with our Karnataka government. Both of them (Secretaries) are here. In fact, we never had any problem. We always showed deficit in our budget. That is intended to get more money and project. So that is a strategy, but we never had any problem. Whenever we had cash problem, we always approached and they have been obliging and have helped. In fact the culture of Karnataka bureaucracy is entirely different. They have a positive attitude towards research, educational institutions and practiced non-interference. So, I want to share our experience with our friends. So I must mention this. Probably, non-governmental funding which involves interaction or outsourcing may raise the quality of research provided it is not doctored or influenced. Finally, let me ask, when we want government funds for social science research, do you not have the responsibility to fulfil academic expectations? Let me share one or two of my experiences. Long ago, the Reserve Bank of India started providing RBI chairs to various institutions. Suddenly that chair was withdrawn from this institute. We also had that chair. I asked 'why they are doing this?'. One of the Deputy governors told us that a reputed national university in Delhi had a chair. They wanted to know what research the professor under that Chair had done. When the Reserve Bank asked him, he said, you can only give money; don't ask me to give you the report. That enraged; they went back and decided to do away with the Chair system and they began giving one or two crore for each institution. Do whatever you want. So this is not social responsibility. That is not research responsibility either.

A-10

Research in Social Sciences: Availability and Utilisation of Resources

Mihir Rakshit

A common complaint among social scientists in India is the paucity of resources available for research, especially of a fundamental nature. Over the last two decades funds provided by the government to universities and research institutions have primarily been for purposes of meeting the salary bill of the faculty and administrative staff, but lagged far behind the cost of books, journals, data collection-cum-processing and other infrastructural facilities. This has forced many institutes to increasingly rely upon the private sector to finance their research projects. However, since the agencies' major concern is not often advancement of knowledge regarding the working of the society or the economy, the projects do not by and large address the basic analytical and policy issues social scientists may (or should) be interested in. This is often regarded as the most important reason that, despite an impressive number of projects in social science research being undertaken in India, there has hardly been any worthwhile progress in developing a satisfactory framework for in-depth study of major economic and social phenomena in the Indian context.

Much more serious than the financial crunch bedevilling social science research is however the shortage of human resources. Large enough government grant may facilitate good libraries or provision of other infrastructural facilities; but in the short- and medium-run academic institutions taken together will find it next to impossible to recruit talented social scientists to fill up their vacancies. This

---

Mihir Rakshit, Director, Investment Information and Credit Rating Agency of India (ICRA) Limited, Kolkata.

shortage of qualified researchers is due in part to a quantum jump in demand over the last two decades. In economics for example perhaps more than 95 per cent of the top quartile of students[1] from reputed institutions are absorbed in industries or financial firms at astronomical salaries even before they formally get their degrees. Among the rest who opt for an academic career, practically all do their PhD abroad and hardly anybody comes back to Indian academic institutions. Add to that, the fact that among the large number of universities in India only a handful provide rigorous training in social sciences, and the yawning demand-supply gap in human resources for teaching and research is not to be wondered at.

A short-term solution to the problem of bridging the gap may consist in making academic salaries competitive in relation to those offered elsewhere. The medium- and long-term solution lies in raising the supply of good quality social scientists through expansion and upgradation of training facilities. These solutions may seem market-based and would no doubt be popular among the large majority of academics, but are by no means as efficacious or easy to implement as they might appear at first sight. The solutions entail a steep rise in resources devoted to social science teaching and research. In view of large externalities of higher education and research and the distortions arising from private funding noted earlier, the lion's share of the additional resources would have to be provided by the state. However, given the overall resource constraint, the case for a substantial increase in funding for social sciences at the expense of other disciplines or of primary education, infrastructural investment, social security and poverty alleviation, is by no means open and shut. Quite clearly, deciding on how much to spend on advancement of knowledge in a field requires a social cost-benefit calculus, involving an appraisal of: (a) the opportunity cost of using resources; and (b) the expected return on investing in the particular area.

For purposes of allocation of resources in a given discipline, the opportunity cost (or what economists call the social rate of discount) may be given to education planners and it is to the second that they

1. It is this group which constitutes the potential source of supply in academic institutions.

need to pay close attention. Keeping in view the importance of in-depth studies of evolving social and economic issues in the Indian context, the Vaidyanathan Committee (of which I was a member) has advocated a substantial step-up in government grants for social science research. The committee has also suggested some important changes in the prevailing organisational structure and funding of research. Since its terms of reference were limited to the functioning of the Indian Council of Social Science Research (ICSSR), the committee's report did not cover the general problems plaguing research in social sciences in India. My submission is that, unless these problems are resolved satisfactorily, the cost-benefit calculus does not perhaps warrant a significant rise in public funding of research in our discipline. Indeed there is a substantial scope for raising both the quantum and quality of research output through proper utilisation of resources currently earmarked for universities and research institutes. Improvement in efficiency of resource use also enhances the marginal return on investment in higher education and strengthens the case for additional government support. Hence, arises the importance of locating the major sources of inefficiency in the prevailing system of teaching and research in social sciences.[2]

The most serious source of inefficiency may be traced to the organisational structure of higher education in India. Because of historical reasons we have a three-tier system consisting of undergraduate colleges, university postgraduate departments and research institutes.[3] The resulting twofold dichotomy, between undergraduate and postgraduate teaching on the one hand and between the (primarily) teaching and pure research institutions on the other, has had a cumulatively negative impact on both teaching and research.

The need for exposing first year students to the best teachers can hardly be overemphasised. First impressions, psychologists suggest, tend to last the longest and unlearning wrong notions or abandoning ingrained modes of thought is an extremely difficult and time-consuming task. Hence, the enormous benefits of initiation to the

2. Most of the deficiencies highlighted here are common to all disciplines.

3. Some autonomous colleges offer postgraduate courses but are poor cousins of university departments and research institutes.

fundamentals of a subject the right way and the lasting damage that bad undergraduate teaching or shoddy introductory textbooks can inflict.[4]

Second and more important, ultimately what matters in advancement of learning and research is the keenness of interest of academics in their chosen field. In this respect the role of teachers at the introductory stage can be decisive. By sharing with the students the excitement of unraveling the core elements of a subject and the intellectual challenge the task entails, a teacher can instil in his charges a life-long passion for the discipline and make them feel an academic career worth pursuing. That in the 1950s Presidency College, Calcutta produced social scientists of the calibre of Amartya Sen, Sukhamoy Chakravarty, Ashin Das Gupta, Amiya Bagchi, Pranab Bardhan, Benoy Chaudhuri, Sumit Sarkar, and Sabyasachi Bhattacharya was perhaps due in no small measure to inspiring teachers like Bhabatosh Datta, Sushobhan Sarkar and Tapas Majumdar who chose to take courses primarily for the first and second year students. With the setting up of a large number of universities and research institutes, and undergraduate colleges being increasingly staffed with less talented teachers under the three-tier system, the poor state of social science research in India is by no means unexpected. Indeed, such distorted allocation of human resources in our higher education seems to have had a cascading effect and been a major factor behind both the paucity of qualified graduates and their overwhelming preference for a non-academic career.

No less damaging has been the dichotomy between the primarily teaching and purely research institutes. Even the best of teachers tend to lose their edge and enthusiasm over time unless he is forced to reflect deeply on the vexing and emerging questions in his discipline, and this is possible only if he is engaged in active research and inculcates the habit of rigorous thinking and sorting out complex issues. In countries like India in particular, it is of paramount importance that undergraduate students of social sciences be exposed to instructions by first rate teachers who are also top ranking researchers.

---

4. A major responsibility of teachers is to ensure that during their first two years undergraduate students are exposed only to good books and references; after that they should be able to distinguish between shoddy and quality writings.

To see why, consider the challenge of teaching economics in a developing country. With the availability of a number of excellent textbooks written by leading economists, teaching and learning economics have in one sense become much easier now than in the olden days. However, the books are written in the context of a developed economy. Nor do they generally spell out the underlying assumptions relating to the structural features of the economic system behind the analyses and arguments—features which are often liable to make the analysis inappropriate for emerging economics. Herein comes the role of a teacher. Not only should he inculcate in students the habit of arguing from the first principles and following the Cartesian method of "systematic doubt"—of not taking anything for granted unless backed by convincing evidence and reasoning, but draw attention to implicit assumptions of textbook economics regarding the nature of the market mechanism and the constraints faced by economic agents under the presumed institutional set-up. Not only does an awareness of the limits of the conventional approach in analysing important economic and social issues in developing countries can pose an exciting challenge and motivate budding social scientists, but its absence tends to have a distortionary effect on the nature and quality of research in their later life. Since this appears to be an important reason, at least in economics, for lack of progress in developing an analytical framework appropriate in the Indian context let me illustrate the problem with an example from my own experience and area of enquiry.

In all textbooks the role of monetary factors in the macroeconomy is discussed in terms of a model with only two financial assets, money and bond, the market for one being the mirror image of the other. The money (or bond) market is taken to clear through instantaneous adjustment of the interest rate (or the price of bond) and it is through its variations that central bank policies or other monetary factors affect output, the price level and other macro variables. Mainstream economists are not, to be sure, unaware of the multiplicity of financial assets or of credit constraint/rationing some borrowers are subject to even in advanced economies. But with close correlation among prices of different financial assets and the insignificance of credit rationing in relation to the volume of financial transactions, the textbook model is considered to provide a reasonably good approximation of the reality.[5] In countries like India, however, informal credit constitutes by far the largest category of finance; mobility of funds across unorganised money markets is extremely limited; and rationing of credit is pervasive. Under these conditions the textbook approach for examining the efficacy of monetary policy or of the nature of interaction between the real and financial factors is likely to be highly inappropriate. Nevertheless, research on monetary issues by economists in India is conducted almost wholly in terms of the mainstream paradigm. The reason lies, I believe, in most researchers' inadequate grasp of the fundamentals for which the disjunction between undergraduate teaching and research is largely at fault.

Poor training in colleges and universities is no doubt a serious handicap for an academic, but certainly not beyond rectification. But full-time research with very little or no interaction with students seems to pose an insuperable obstacle to both overcoming the deficiencies of early training and preventing intellectual stagnation. This seems to have been the case in most ICSSR and other research institutes. Compared to the college and university faculty new entrants in these institutes are generally better qualified. But over time research of the large majority of them tends to become routine, unimaginative or repetitive. The main reason seems to be that, for most academics teaching, especially at the undergraduate level, is the best way of deepening their understanding, identifying unresolved issues and critical gaps in the subject and keeping abreast of its major developments. No wonder, the social return on the substantial funds invested in the institutes over the last three to four decades has been so meagre.

The main policy conclusions of our analysis may be summed up as follows. First, there is an urgent need of doing away with compartmentalisation of higher education and moving toward a system where postgraduate teaching and research are combined with undergraduate teaching. Second, given the scarcity of resources and the enormous benefits of scale economies in higher education, it appears

5. Only in times of financial crisis do the glaring deficiencies of these models come the fore.

advisable to build up as soon as possible a small number of universities with first rate faculty and infrastructure. Entry of first year students in these universities may be on the basis of all-India admission tests; but there should be provision (as in the USA) for entry at subsequent stages of well-performing, motivated students from other, not so well-endowed, universities. Nursing a few institutions of excellence and allowing for mobility of students and academics across these and other institutes are expected to boost efficiency of resource use and rectify the two crucial, debilitating deficiencies of our higher education, *viz.*, poor quality of undergraduate teaching and the absence of any first rate graduate school for preparing students for an academic career. The rectification should raise the supply of qualified manpower and pave the way for socially productive utilisation of enlarged funds for higher education.

Third, outside the university system some institutes could be entrusted with the task of promoting collaborative research by groups of academics whose interests are similar or expertise is complementary: not only is interaction among researchers working in the same field highly productive, but in social sciences in-depth study in many important areas also calls for collaboration among specialists in theory, statistical methods and institutional arrangements. These institutes may also provide facilities to university faculty to work full-time for a while in order to complete the research they have been engaged in and prepare the final draft for publication. For this purpose it is necessary to: (a) drastically reduce the number of (pure) research institutes; and (b) ensure that, as in organisations like the National Bureau of Economic Research (NBER) in the USA, they have no permanent faculty and are entrusted with the responsibility of bringing together university teachers to undertake time-bound, joint research in some specific areas or help them take a break from teaching for purposes of full-time research.

However, for better utilisation of infrastructural and human resources, these tasks may be assigned to select university departments of social sciences with provision of additional grants. The reason is that, well-run universities can be an ideal venue for collaborative studies in particular fields as well as for rigorous interdisciplinary research. What is no less important to recognise, a faculty requires a break from teaching not only for intensive, single-minded pursuit of research, but also for gaining expertise in new areas and broadening his vision. This he can more easily do in a university endowed with a large number of experts offering advanced courses in different fields: interacting with them and attending their courses could be a most effective way of upgrading an academic's teaching and research capability.

Given the clout of various interest groups and the relatively rigid mindset of the powers-that-be, dismantling the present system and implementing the suggestions made above would no doubt be extremely difficult. But free and frank discussion relating to the organisational set-up best suited for higher education is essential for overcoming opposition to the needed reforms and formulating a roadmap for their implementation. This is what I have tried to initiate on the present occasion with some concrete suggestions for revamping the university system.

A-11

Is there a Mismatch between Resource Availability and Demand?

Lakshmi Venkatachalam

Ladies and gentlemen, let me first begin by saying that, it is a privilege to be here and share this platform. Let me also welcome Dr. Ravindra, our chairman, who needs no introduction of course, because he is known to all of us besides being an esteemed colleague of mine. So, with your permission, since the 'introductions' have been done with, I could begin.

I must congratulate the institute on taking up this very very relevant seminar on social science research as a tribute to centenary celebrations of Dr. V.K.R.V. Rao. When I was asked to partake in this session, I was really quite apprehensive and, I gave Dr. Deshpande a provisional acceptance because, quite frankly, I was quite diffident about making any expositions on the subject; I am not a researcher to begin with, and therefore I am conscious of my inadequacies and limitations in commenting on the demand-supply issues in social science research. My background is that of an administrator and my perspectives on this subject are therefore, largely informed by my experience as a practicing administrator. But hearing some of the speakers, in the last 24 hours combined with some very meaningful observations that I have come across in this excellent volume that has been put together on the occasion of this seminar, I have gathered some insights! So, I will begin with just highlighting some of the very important points which I think, impinge on the overall issue of demand and resource availability for social science research. My attention was first drawn to the Regional

Lakshmi Venkatachalam (IAS), Formerly, Principal Secretary, Planning and Statistics Department, Government of Karnataka.

Committee on Social Science Research which was set up under the chairmanship of Dr. V.K.R.V. Rao and this was addressed in Mr. Anant's paper stating that, when the rationale for setting up the ICSSR was being debated, it was said, and I quote, "understanding of the social phenomenon and human behavior, knowledge about social processes and its determinants are essential for designing policies to promote social change and to produce a dynamic society capable of absorbing and utilizing the scientific and technological developments for the welfare of human beings". So, the ultimate goal was creation of a dynamic society capable of absorbing and utilising the scientific and technological developments. So, we are really talking about promoting and creating a new kind of culture which would inform society, which would be able to take benefit of the advantage of various developments in science and technology. There was also a very interesting observation in the same essay about, how social science is being pulled between two competing forces and this idea, was to some extent, resonating in the last session when we talked about the need and challenge of long term and short term, project-oriented research. These competing forces are really, on the one hand what you would call the innate curiosity about the functioning of society in its diverse, social, cultural, political and economic dimensions and on the other hand, the practical needs of policy makers, managers in governments, civil society, private sector, for reliable information and social analysis. These approaches manifest themselves in different combinations, in different disciplines; thus in academia, there has been a tension between the cries for relevance on the one hand and freedom and ability of an individual scholar to pursue his curiosity on the other. There were some very interesting comments in Dr. Srinivasan's essay on the need for creating a culture of research. I thought the reference to what Jawaharlal Nehru said about scientific approach and temper was very relevant for creating this culture in research. So, ultimately when you look at the wider issue of demand for research of availability of resources in terms of research capacity at different levels, these are really created and nurtured by an enriched, enabling environment for social science research.

Now, on the demand side, I came across some interesting comments in a DFID paper, i.e., the Department of International

Development of the British government. The paper spoke of the periodic need for "horizon scanning" as a very critical input, if we are serious about developing a vibrant demand for research, and like the demand structure for any activity, you have to really segment the market for analysing the need for various types of research products and the wider question of long-term *versus* short-term projects, etc. Certain reforms are called for in terms if horizon scanning for developing a very meaningful research agenda at various levels is called for and the question to be really asked is how far the institutions are contributing towards developing this sort of medium- to long-term agenda for research. The other issues are identification of functional areas for conceiving research projects that deliver the required inputs to develop policy and strategic initiatives in the medium and long term. The question is whether you can integrate all of this concurrently, so that it becomes a continuously evolving process that creates its own momentum for generation of continuous demand for research. So, here we have to look at how we strike a balance, as I said in the previous session, a fine balance between the requirement for long-term research agendas and short term project-oriented research, and in the process, we really develop problem solving capabilities in society at large. The other thing of course is that if we look at the demand question, how do we justify fundamental research or long-term research which has really no immediate user orientation and can owe very little to popular demand, and therefore how do we find a place for such research which might not have immediate relevance, but will probably throw up issues in the long term, and I do believe that adequate funding for this kind of research is very important. On the supply side, I can only highlight that some of these issues have been dealt with very well in most of the reading that have been placed; my attention was drawn to Prof. Srinivasan's analysis of how you have to have a proper combination of institutional arrangements, incentive structures and finally make sure that the society itself is able to communicate these priorities to the society at large so that the society develops respect and honours people's research, and research becomes an aspirational profession. Many of the papers focused on how there are competing demands for people coming out of the universities and students are not getting attracted to research. I also would like to address some of the other reform initiatives needed for generating better demand for research. Well—a good bit of that does depend on government because, let us face it, with such large chunks of money going to developmental spending, we need to play a major role in terms of prioritising demand for research. There are two or three things that I can think of: one, is of course developing a sound statistical base. I think this itself is a major reform that will drive a lot of interest in research. Today, we know that the Central Statistical Organisation (CSO) an institution of the Central government, set up for statistics collection and analysis, is probably one of the best systems in the world. But its counterparts in the states have a mixed legacy and record. In this context, I am happy to state that, based on the recommendation of the Rangarajan Commission, a major project being now taken up for reforms of the state statistical systems and hopefully, with a lot of reforms especially in the area of social sector statistics, there will be much better dissemination of relevant statistics that will lead to demand and surge of research activity. The second thing is the reform of processes and this is where I feel, there are a lot of initiatives required in government which will in turn help to spur the demand for research. We have not in government stabilised a process by which we take up development schemes or investments in a certain area, based on proper analysis, of research as to where such interventions are fully justified. While in the Central government, appraisal of new schemes by the Planning Commission is inbuilt into the process, (no doubt there is lot of impatience with the procedure but, nevertheless it is followed) at the state government level, the situation is highly uneven. Indeed we have a situation where schemes are announced in the budget and then we start looking at why it makes sense to do so. So if we were to sort of internalise a process within the governmental system as it is being done much more vigorously in the private sector, where for any investment into new products there would be a strong research input to support why the investment is strategically necessary, I think it would create in turn demand for a variety of research products where institutions and universities can participate. Such a virtuous circle of research had policy development, leading to further research input predicated decision-making for major investments and further analysis of the outcome of such investment leading to further research creates a self-sustaining demand for research products. The third important initiative is communication about the relevance of research. I think very little of this is happening in the popular domain while a lot of things have reached the popular imagination in the last few decades with the advent of TV, but the relevance and priority for social sciences is still something that we have not been able to discriminate effectively. Finally, I would also say there is need for designing new research products that not to just look at it in terms of long-term project research and short-term project research, but basically a wide variety of research products that could be of use to the user groups.

On the whole, there is need for infusing a lot of excitement, through innovative approaches, into social science research and the current seminar will hopefully come up with some useful ideas.

Thank you Mr. Chairman

A-12

Are SSR Institutions Bartering Autonomy with Respect to Grantees, Administrators, etc.?

S. Parasuraman

Thank you Mr. chairman, Prof. Kurien, Prof. Jayaram, Prof. Deshpande and colleagues. It is indeed a great pleasure to be here for this commemoration of centenary celebrations of Prof. V.K.R.V. Rao. This has been a very interesting and very important conference for me. First, much of what I am going to say today here is from a note, which I had written two years ago to the University Grants Commission (UGC) on the status of social science research in India. Second, of course is my own engagement with University Mission Group, constituted for exploring universities of potential excellence in India. I think my understanding of the status of social science teaching and research in Indian universities largely goes to Deepak Nair who wrote on this issue in an article, appeared in *Indian Express* newspaper two years ago. Deepak Nair captures exactly—the problem with our universities and the social science teaching and education in the country. He talked about stagnant curriculum; quite rigid, difficult to deal with and difficult to bring in the cutting edge understanding about at once. Moreover, poor academic environment, lack of accountability and inadequate infrastructure are the major causes of why our universities are becoming sick. A few weeks ago when Prof. Narayanan and I visited to a university, to our surprise found that the facilities available in the social sciences buildings were much poorer than that of science. Looking at the state of social science infrastructure at this university, it emerged to us that why the toilets do not have water and why the

S. Parasuraman, Director, Tata Institute of Social Sciences (TISS), Mumbai.

classrooms should not have a proper blackboard, benches and other required facilities. I think much of what we observed and what the university staff and students talked about has a great deal of implications on the curiosity-driven basic research *versus* combining with that of policy research.

The review papers which we have seen and the presentations that were made yesterday and this morning points towards why do we do sponsored research or projects of that kind? Of course, financial matters matter us at the end of the day and it is all about resources that the institutes or universities have got. I think there are two sides to sponsored research. At one level, what Prof. Papola said that sponsored research on its own may not be bad. In fact, it has some good elements to it. That is what we found. As we know, sponsored research projects come with very clearly defined objectives, ideas and processes. These also set in place a number of accountability measures, have a time-bounded framework and keep following up with the researchers in a critical manner because of the reporting systems. These bring in a lot of discipline to the kind of work that researchers do and moreover fund the resource gap available to any institution for that matter. These resources are good if strategically got and statistically used. But it is only one side of the story. The most important part is when it comes to autonomy. It is not about the interference of funding agencies in governance system of an institution, but their interference into ideological framework and the value orientation of the institution, the agenda of institution as to what needed to be done, what is own research agenda of institution and how would that be taken further in terms of research and contribution to the knowledge base and the policy debate *per se*. In last few decades, ideology-based agencies' (either religious or economic) funding research projects have become strong and they are showing their presence across the world. Therefore, the two pertinent questions are how much these agencies have been or are able to interfere into broader ideological framework of an institution and kind of research initiatives institution would take. Do they have some agendas of research or processes that fundamentally alter the agenda and ideological framework set by an institution? Some evidences noticed in the recent years are not encouraging as decline of some of the institutions in the country must have affected by that. The consistent lack of the government funding, I think, worsened the problem further and this is where we have lost quite a lot of it. The consistent squeezing out of the state funding for social science research particularly created a vacuum and has been taken over by institutions oriented towards particular ideology. This situation manifests its gravity when Mr. James D. Wolfenson, chief of World Bank, said in 1995 that if one thought about development they come to the World Bank. I think, the concerted efforts of these funding agencies to redefine development and bring together the resources of the bilateral and multilateral institutions to feed towards the research of a particular kind have distorted the research agenda of many of our institutions in the country and that has been the singular problem we are facing at this particular point of time. Then, a fundamental question is how do we reverse this, when they control large financial resources for research in social sciences? Why do we want to do research if it is going to feed to a particular process, the ideas and agendas?

I think, we must proactively engage with our government and find ways for funding education and research in the country. There is no way that we can let our government to go off the hook. We must try to find answers for how can we do this and how institutions and universities can be brought together? There are numerous opportunities available for institutions for getting fund at least from agencies having similar ideologies and orientations. Each one of our institutions, have to have a perspective under research agenda; both short term and long term around which we would like to raise funds or bring in resources to do research—very important agenda of an institution. We have done this exercise in Tata Institute of Social Sciences (TISS). To strengthen capacity and to realise the enormous knowledge generating potentials of our research scholars, institutions like ICSSR and UGC can play a very important role and fund for M.Phil and PhD programmes. Though these institutions are trying to reinvent itself to find resources to pay for the research programmes, I think, we need to push them little more harder to get sufficient funding. So, friends, autonomy and the future all depend upon safeguarding—what must be done, how it is to be done, and how do we counter the forces that undermine our ideological orientations? These are the places where we need to be very careful. Thank you.

A-13

Inter-Institutional Cooperation and Dependence among SSR Institutions, UGC, State Agencies, etc.

George Mathew

Dr. Rao, Prof. Mukherjee, Prof. Jayaram and distinguished participants, the last two and a half days were extremely valuable and enriching for me. The issues relating to cooperation between social science research institutions, which we will be discussing in this session, have long been discussed and debated. As I remember, a long time back, I read a few proceedings included in a book called *The New Social Science*. The proceedings were part of a discourse on the status of social science research on an event to celebrate dedication of the social science research building on the campus of University of Chicago in 1929. I was especially intrigued by one presentation by the President of Brookings Institute, Dr. Harold G. Moulton. He made a point which, I think is still relevant. The point is, historically, the trend in the social sciences has been towards increasing specialisation and most of us go on to the extent of specialisation, where we are the alone, looking at that special area. His main argument was that a growing recognition of the desirability of developing a new body of generalisations of broader social impart in turn discloses the necessity of cooperation particularly at two levels. One, at individual level, where cooperation takes place among trained scholars in different divisions of the social sciences who possess the complementary technical qualifications. And second, among institutions of social science research. Moulton was of the view that, when cooperation takes place, the cooperatives must work together on specific problems in order to contribute in a really constructive way to

George Mathew, Founder Director, Institute of Social Sciences (ISS), New Delhi.

the solution of significant social problems and develop new theoretical generalisations of importance. Cooperation must be conceived and carried out in specific rather than in general terms. Coming specifically to the cooperation between institutions located in the same country or in different countries, he pointed out significant possibilities, which exist because investigations that are of basic significance frequently transcend the boundaries of a particular division of the social sciences and this requires help of the peculiar qualifications of workers in several fields. Therefore, we see a need for discourse for the cooperation in one combination or another among or across political scientists, economists, statisticians, sociologists, anthropologists, psychologists or even lawyers. Taking example of lawyers, he argued that the cooperation between a group of individuals interested in the same division of the social sciences will supplement one another in vitally important ways. This certainly makes clear to us that cooperation between different divisions of social sciences on the one hand and between different institutions in the social sciences on the other is a must and the cooperation of scholars drawn from different divisions of the social sciences in various institutions is the most important and fundamental to all. This was said 80 years ago.

Today, when we apply this to India, we do not find much happening in terms of cooperation, despite of many of us have been reading, studying and lecturing about how universities in US, European and many other countries are trying to build cooperation among social sciences. Then, the question is why this has not happened in our country? To my mind, being an outsider of ICSSR and UGC network and hence, independent in that sense, when I look at the social science scenario in the country, whether it is ICSSR institution or UGC institution, there is hardly any cooperation. I am open for correction but that is my statement. Even independent institutions which are not getting funds or within the ambit of these two, the question is still relevant to be asked that how much cooperation is between these independent institutions. You will agree with me when I say that it is impossible to get the cooperation in the abstract or in general terms. I feel, cooperation should be possible in the following areas and stating an eight-point programme, or eight areas of concerns. I am saying this because we are all sharing one concern, that is what I got from the deliberations of the last two and a half days. We want to create one of the best social science knowledge base and we all know that goal is not possible without knowledge sharing in a systematic way and that knowledge sharing at various levels is unfortunately not happening. Therefore, in a telegraphic language, I would like to say, eight areas which can be considered for cooperation between the social science research institutions—first, research faculty meeting. Research faculty specially seniors; why cannot we meet at least once in a year? As the chairman mentioned here, there is a meeting taking place in the state. Fine, but Karnataka is one of the 28 states and 7 union territories. What about the national scenario? Two-times meeting may be difficult. But once in a year, may not be three days but at least one day, could be possible. We know, there may be many problems. This is a possibility and the research faculty can meet and share things like, what they are doing, what are their concerns and what a wonderful and rich social science ferment we can create in the country.

Second, the research staff meeting, i.e., the technical staff; it is not the seniors and all but what about the research staff at the middle level and technical researchers? Why cannot they also meet region-wise or nation-wise and also if big national meetings are not possible, exchange basis between these technical persons and they see what is happening in other institutes or other regions. Third—exchange of library and documentation information. Why are we not exchanging information? I have visited many institutions in the country and I can say every institute has a rich library in their own special area of interest. These libraries have the resources sometimes we need. In the absence of cooperation, it is very difficult to get a book or a research report we want. Why can not we have a system of sharing and exchanging information or for that matter Databank created through research.

Fourth, infrastructure facilities; many of our institutions who are very proud that they have wonderful infrastructure facilities and some institutions may not have it, but why not we share some of these and develop a kind of relationship, friendship and all that kind of things. It is extraordinary if we take a step for that. Now, we have to hire and we have to pay at the market rate.

Fifth, research collaboration; there are many possibilities for research collaboration. But I am afraid, in terms of the institutions in the country, the research collaboration is in a full-fledged manner and they may need information or some fragment of an idea. That is there. But in terms of real research collaboration, I am afraid; there is no cooperation or support. Sixth, sharing of the research findings; we have no system of sharing the research findings before it get published. Therefore, we have to wait. For instance, we know that there is a research going on in a particular topic in any particular institution, but we have to wait till the copy is edited and published by a publisher. It has several procedures and may take much time. Therefore we need to ask why can not we have a forum in which we can share the research findings. How much it will help each other and to take it to forward step by step or we have to wait till an article appears in journal?

Seventh, joint publications; this is also possible if we have collaborative research projects. We can bring out edited volumes on many contemporary and relevant issues. For this, we do not have to wait till the research is over. Nowadays, several edited volumes are coming, but they are all in the name of one editor or two editors and moreover, institutional collaboration is missing and this is one area I think, we should consider. Eighth and the final area of collaboration which I think is resource share, both financial and human. There may be many others and you may be able to enlighten us. It is related to some of the points I mentioned earlier. Financial resource sharing could be impossible in the present context except through projects and programmes. But whatever it is, we have lot of resources, one way or the other and why can not we think of sharing these resources. Taking the present situation in India as it was mentioned earlier by the chairman also, I feel there is more scope for cooperation between social science research institutions in India and abroad, not just within India. We have a MoU with many institutions abroad.

All the cooperation among social science researchers within the last few years have become a veritable slogan, I quote "veritable slogan"; nothing much has happened, and I think for this state of affairs, we the social scientists have to take the responsibility. I mean who else will come and say cooperate! What have we thought about it, what about our ideas and ideas lead to action. Have we developed any idea for this and how shall we break this impasse? Can we make a league of social science research institutions in India? I do not think making a league is going to solve the problem. Sometimes, it may create more problems, and therefore, we have to apply our minds in the present context of the development of social science research institutions for how we can go forward in knowledge generation and sharing it on the same platform. Again, in conclusion, I want to quote Prof. Harold Moulton. He said, "cooperation in social science research between Institutions, if it is to be made effective, on the part of all those collaborate therein requires four basic prerequisites or qualities. First, increasing modesty; the scholars, the researchers, the institutions, the heads of institutions must have increasing modesty. Next, need of great tolerance and endless capacity to stand for wear and tear and what often seems to be fruitless discussion. And, finally, infinite patience with fellow workers. Today, we share these qualifications." Do we share these qualities? We are in big deficit to my mind in all these aspects. Thus, my friends, we are in this state of affairs.

Index

A

B

C

I

J

K

L

M

W

Y